Imagining Italians

SUNY SERIES IN ITALIAN/AMERICAN CULTURE
FRED L. GARDAPHE, EDITOR

Imagining Italians

The Clash of Romance and Race
in American Perceptions, 1880–1910

Joseph P. Cosco

State University of New York Press

Published by State University of New York Press, Albany

© 2003 State University of New York

All rights reserved

Printed in the United States of America

No part of this book may be used or reproduced in any manner whatsoever without written permission. No part of this book may be stored in a retrieval system or transmitted in any form or by any means including electronic, electrostatic, magnetic tape, mechanical, photocopying, recording, or otherwise without the prior permission in writing of the publisher.

For information, address State University of New York Press, 90 State Street, Suite 700, Albany, NY 12207

Production by Kelli Williams
Marketing by Patrick Durocher

Library of Congress Cataloging-in-Publication Data

Cosco, Joseph P.
   Imagining Italians : clash of romance and race in American perceptions, 1880–1910 / Joseph P. Cosco.
      p. cm. — (SUNY series in Italian/American culture)
   Includes bibliographical references (p.   ) and index.
   ISBN 0-7914-5761-3 (alk. paper) — ISBN 0-7914-5762-1 (pbk. : alk. paper)
   1. Italian Americans—Public opinion. 2. Immigrants—United States—Public opinion. 3. Italian Americans—Social conditions—19th century. 4. Italian Americans—Social conditions—20th century. 5. Immigrants—United States—Social conditions. 6. Public opinion—United States. 7. Italian Americans in literature. 8. United States—Ethnic relations. 9. Racism—United States—History—19th century. 10. Racism—United States—History—20th century. I. Title. II. Series.

E184.I8 C654 2003
305.85'1073'09034—dc21   2002042632

10 9 8 7 6 5 4 3 2 1

With deep respect and gratitude I dedicate this book to:

Giuseppe and Carmella Frustaci, the maternal grandparents I never knew, who ventured from Italy to the New World to find a better life

Carmella Cosco, my mother, who was sent back to Calabria as a child when her mother died, and later sacrificed her life in Italy to return to America as a wife and mother

Anthony Cosco, my father, for convincing my mother to make the long return journey across the ocean for the sake of their two sons

All the Italian immigrants who journeyed to a new homeland, made a life there, but never completely forgot their native land

Contents

List of Illustrations		ix
Introduction	Magnificently Miserable Italians and Their Wretched, Princely Italy	1
Chapter One	Jacob Riis: Immigrants Old and New, and the Making of Americans	21
Chapter Two	Edward Steiner: All Is (Not) Race?	61
Chapter Three	Henry James's Picturesque Peasants: Heroes of Romance or Modern Men?	87
Chapter Four	Henry James's "Flagrant Foreigners": Whose Country Is This Anyway?	113
Chapter Five	Mark Twain: Racism, Nativism, and the Twinning of Italianness	143
Conclusion	The Fight for Whiteness	171
Notes		179
Bibliography		207
Index		227

Illustrations

1.1	A Vegetable Stand in the Mulberry Bend	44
1.2	Feast of St. Rocco, Bandit's Roost, Mulberry Street	44
1.3	Bandit's Roost, 39^1/$_2$ Mulberry Street	46
1.4	In the Home of an Italian Rag-Picker, Jersey Street	48
1.5	Pietro Learning to Write, Jersey Street	51
1.6	The Mott Street Boys "Keep Off the Grass"	53

Acknowledgments

Many people had a role, big or small, in advancing this project. My deep thanks to all of them and in particular to these few:

For their inspiration and encouragement, my mentors in the American Studies program at the College of William and Mary, including Robert Gross, Richard Lowry, Kenneth Price, Robert Scholnick, and Ronald Hoffman. For reading the first draft of this work, seeing value in the subject, and offering constructive criticism, my dissertation committee, including Ben Slote of Allegheny College.

For their support during my revision of the manuscript, the Department of English and the College of Arts and Letters at Old Dominion University. For promptly locating much needed texts, the interlibrary loan staff at Old Dominion's Perry Library.

For her timely and invaluable assistance in researching the Jacob Riis photographs, Bonnie Yochelson, former curator of prints and photographs at the Museum of the City of New York.

For permission to reprint photographs from the Jacob Riis Collection, the Museum of the City of New York.

For cheerfully enduring my periods of preoccupation, my wife Kathleen and daughter Marisa.

Thanks to all.

Introduction

Magnificently Miserable Italians and Their Wretched, Princely Italy

There is glut in the market. People have their house full of Italian views, and their libraries full of Italian travels, and the boarding school misses are twaddling *nelle parole Tuscane*.

—American Whig Review, 1847

Yes, yes, hang the dagoes!

—New Orleans lynch mob, 1891

They are beaten men from beaten races; representing the worst failures in the struggle for existence.

—Francis A. Walker, president of MIT and former superintendent of U.S. Census, 1896

A gloomy mist hung over New Orleans on the night of October 15, 1890, as David C. Hennessy, the popular police superintendent, walked home after a late-night snack of half a dozen oysters and a teetotaling glass of milk at Dominic Virget's saloon. As Hennessy walked alone in the gloaming along Girod Street, just before he reached Basin Street, a gang of five men burst from an alley, opened fire with a barrage of shots, and then fled into the night, chased by volleys of Hennessy's return fire. Seriously wounded, with three slugs in the stomach and one in the chest, Hennessy would live for nine hours. Did he identify his attackers? The local *Times-Democrat* reported that the chief, when asked, "shook his head from side to side in a negative way." However, Hennessy's friend, Capt. William J. O'Connor, reportedly offered a more dramatic account: "Bending over the Chief I said to him: 'Who gave it to you, Dave?' He replied, 'Put you ear down here.' As I bent down again, he whispered the word 'Dagoes.'"[1]

Hennessy's shooting and subsequent death shocked newspaper readers in the United States and Europe. The popular police superintendent had become a celebrity nine years earlier when he helped arrest a notorious Italian murderer and kidnapper in New Orleans. Newspapers on two continents had celebrated Hennessy as a model of heroic American manhood and the foremost expert on the Sicilian "stiletto" and "vendetta" societies seen to be threatening the United States. In New Orleans, the outraged citizenry quickly concluded that Hennessy had been killed in the crossfire of an ongoing feud between two rival Italian businesses. Nineteen Italians were soon indicted, and nine of these men went on trial February 28, 1891. On March 13, amid reports and rumors of jury tampering and intimidation of witnesses, the jury found six defendants not guilty and failed to return verdicts for the other three suspects. Despite the six acquittals and three mistrials, Judge Joshua G. Baker ordered all nine defendants returned to the Parish Prison to await further charges.

The next day, between six and eight thousand citizens gathered around the statue of Henry Clay. William S. Parkerson, a confidante of Mayor Joseph A. Shakespeare, stood atop the tall pedestal and asked the crowd: "Will every man here follow me, and see the murder of D. C. Hennessy vindicated?" The crowd responded, "Yes, yes, hang the dagoes!" (Gambino 79). The vigilantes, many of them in frock coats and derby hats, surged toward the Parish Prison, rammed their way in, and hunted down, beat, and shot eleven of the Italian prisoners. Of the Italians killed, three had been acquitted the day before, three had seen their cases end in mistrial, and five had not yet gone to trial. The victims included two U.S. citizens, six men who had formally declared their intention to become citizens, and three Italian subjects. It was, and remains, the largest mass lynching in American history, according to figures compiled by the NAACP (Gambino ix).

The incident did not end there. In Europe, the Italian government immediately demanded punishment for the lynchers and indemnity for relatives of the victims. Unappeased by President Harrison, the Italian government recalled its ambassador, sparking an intense upsurge in anti-Italian sentiment. Some Americans feared war with Italy, while others openly desired it as a way to unite North and South for the first time since the Civil War. Not until the following April, when the United States paid an indemnity of about $25,000—or just under $2,500 for each victim's family—did normal relations resume between the two governments.[2]

The New Orleans lynching and its aftermath stand in dramatic counterpoint to what, prior to the late nineteenth century, had been a long, often warm relationship between the United States and Italy and their respective peoples. While there had always been certain negative attitudes toward Italians, the lynching crystallized anti-Italian sentiments and dramatized America's rapidly changing opinions of Italy and Italians. These changes were in great measure influenced by the masses of generally poor Italian immigrants who had begun arriving in the United States in the 1880s with other so-called "new immigrants" from southern, central, and eastern Europe. These new immigrants, so unlike earlier American settlers in race, religion, and national origin, touched off heated debates on the subjects of immigration and assimilation, debates that engaged with a host of other prevailing discourses related to manhood, the family, disease and hygiene, race, culture, national character, and civilization. Italian immigrants often found themselves at the very center of these debates and discourses, and are uniquely suited to illuminate these discourses that so dominated the American scene in the late nineteenth and early twentieth centuries. With that in mind, this book looks at American representations of Italy, Italians in Italy, and Italians in America as a way to examine American attitudes about America, American identity, and American national character around the turn of the century.

The Italian experience is important and instructive for a number of reasons. Perhaps most important were the sheer numbers and impoverished socioeconomic background of the Italians who were entering the United States. As John Higham has noted, "The Italians were often thought to be the most degraded of the European newcomers. They were swarthy, more than half of them were illiterate, and almost all were victims of a standard of living lower than that of any of the other prominent nationalities" emigrating to America.[3] These Italian immigrants tended to congregate in the urban centers of the Northeast and Mid-Atlantic regions; more than one-third would settle in New York City, the nation's cultural and communications center.[4] In New York and other urban centers, a host of reformers, journalists, writers, artists, thought leaders, and opinion-makers commented on and wrote about the highly visible Italians. Massachusetts legislator Henry Cabot Lodge, reformer/journalist Jacob Riis, well-known writers Henry James and William Dean Howells, and Ashcan artists such as William Glackens and George Luks, among others, took note of the Italian presence. Many observers focused on the densely populated Italian neighborhoods that contributed to New York's role as America's turn-of-the-century "shock city"—

the metropolis that epitomized developing trends in American society and life.[5] Turn-of-the-century New York can be seen as a borderlands, what Mary Louise Pratt in *Imperial Eyes* calls a "contact zone"—a social space where disparate cultures meet and clash in uneven terms of power. By the 1880s, the metropolis had become shorthand for everything threatening to American society, and by the 1890s much of the focus was on Italians and other new immigrants.

The Italians constituted America's largest immigrant group. Between 1880 and 1921, some 4.5 million Italians came to America, some to settle permanently, some as seasonal workers who would eventually return to Italy. Approximately 80 percent of them came from the poor, backward southern portion of Italy known as the *Mezzogiorno*—"the land that time forgot."[6] The Italians, most of them Roman Catholics, would come to occupy a curious position in America's immigration spectrum. They were clearly different in socioeconomic status, religion, and appearance from most of the earlier immigrant groups from the United Kingdom, Scandinavia, France, and the German Empire. They were both similar to and different from the mid-nineteenth-century Irish Catholic immigrants who represented the first real radical break in America's traditional immigration patterns. The Italian immigrants had the Irish's poverty and Roman Catholicism (although there were significant differences in their practice of the religion, as we will see). However, many Italian immigrants lacked the Irish's Anglo/Celtic looks and English language. Finally, unlike other "new immigrants" from Austria-Hungary, Poland, and Russia, the Italians were a curious mix of the familiar and unfamiliar. The Americans' first encounter with large numbers of Slavs and Jews was indeed a new experience with "alien" peoples from countries with which the United States had had no extensive contacts. In contrast, the Italians hailed from a land that had long occupied an important place in the American psyche. Many Americans were already quite familiar with Italy and, perhaps to a lesser extent, with Italians themselves.

By the late nineteenth century, when large numbers of Neapolitans, Calabrians, and Sicilians started landing in the United States, Americans already had myriad ideas, perceptions, attitudes, and feelings about Italy and Italians, some negative, many positive. Italy had achieved canonical status in America in much the same way that the "Orient" had in England and France. Americans saw Italy not simply as a place, a geographical region or country, but as an aesthetic, cultural, and moral construct. To paraphrase Edward Said, Italy was for Americans a complex idea that had a history and a tradition of thought, imagery, and vocabulary that had given it reality and presence in and for America. Americans had an inherited knowledge of Italians, their race, character, culture, history, traditions, society, and possibilities.[7] Some of that knowledge derived from firsthand experience; much of it, however, was based on "textual" representations in newspaper and magazine articles; paintings, engravings, photographs, and illustrations; imaginative literature; and historical/political/sociological/scientific reports.

A rich, yet tangled relationship had developed between America and Italy during the early and mid-nineteenth century. Americans had begun going to Italy in noticeable numbers not long after the American Revolution. And long before that, Italians had been coming to the Americas as explorers, adventurers, religious missionaries, artists, and intellectuals.[8] Emigrants from the Italian states came in small numbers during the early and mid-1700s, but Italian contacts with colonial America were more numerous than generally assumed.[9] These Italians generally came from northern Italy, and often were artists, artisans, tradesmen, teachers, and political refugees. The traffic between Italy and America went both ways in these early days. Even before the founding of the American republic, and long before there would be a unified Italian state, Americans had begun traveling to Italy, mostly as intrepid tourists and cultural pilgrims. These "discoverers," as Paul R. Baker calls them, ignited an American passion for Italy that would burn throughout the nineteenth century. By the early part of the nineteenth century, "a European tour and a visit to Italy had become a significant American cultural phenomenon."[10] These cultural pilgrims carried copies of Madame de Staël's *Corinne* (1807) and Byron's *Childe Harold's Pilgrimage* (1818). Their mantra came from Byron's Italian Fourth Canto: "Italia! Oh, Italia! thou who hast/The fatal gift of Beauty, which became/A funeral dower of present woes and past—/On thy sweet brow is sorrow ploughed by shame,/And annals graved in characters of fame."

Contacts between Italy and America intensified during the course of the nineteenth century, and the two countries established an extensive cultural exchange that was often complex, conflicting, and contradictory. More and more Italians started coming to the United States, including large numbers from southern Italy who followed the citrus trade to New Orleans, and political exiles, including Giuseppe Garibaldi, who fled Italy following failed nationalist efforts. By 1880, almost forty-five thousand Italians lived in the United States, certainly a presence, but one that was small enough to blend into the national landscape.[11] American contacts with Italy and with Italians in Italy were also fairly extensive by mid-century. By 1858, some two thousand Americans, many of them artists, intellectuals, and leisured dilettantes, were visiting Florence every year. By the 1890s, travelers had become tourists and the aristocratic Grand Tour had become a middle-class package tour. Rome was getting some thirty thousand American visitors annually.[12] During the course of the nineteenth century, nearly every major American artist and writer, and a host of lesser artists and intellectuals, traveled to, often lived in, and nearly always wrote about or made art of Italy and Italians.[13] Many went with romantic notions about classical Italy already encoded in their imaginations. Very often their idealized picture clashed with the reality of the country. Emerson's reaction may have been typical when he wrote with disgust about the fenced-in ruins teeming with "this vermin of ciceroni and padroni." As Ann Douglas writes, "Emerson, in other words, expected Italy to look like prints of Italian scenes so in vogue in America; he wanted it to arouse the emotions Byron's and Goethe's poetic tributes to Italy evoked; he expected not a country but a museum, not life but art."[14]

However, many Americans *did* see a storybook Italy to which they responded with Byronic raptures. Americans embraced and appropriated different aspects of Italian culture and customs both abroad and at home. If nineteenth-century Americans saw Europe "not so much a real place as a very commodious signifier," as William W. Stowe says,[15] then Italy was for many Americans a particularly rich and complex sign—a source of social and cultural capital, a land of romance and the picturesque, and a site/symbol of self-definition. Accounts of travel in Italy and views of Italian landscapes filled American homes.[16] By mid-century, Americans had a mania for Italian opera.[17] The young Henry James typified the Italomania, recalling, in his autobiography, the Italian landscapes that hung in his home and trips to Castle Garden to hear the Italian singer Adelina Patti. However, there was also reaction against this passion for things Italian. In 1847, the *American Whig Review* complained: "There is glut in the market. People have their house full of Italian views, and their libraries full of Italian travels, and the boarding school misses are twaddling *nelle parole Tuscane*."[18] And if many Americans loved Italian opera, others were more critical, expressing anti-Italian sentiments that would harden and become more extreme by century's end. For some, "The sale of exclusive private boxes at the Italian opera house came to signify the Old World pretensions and effete snobberies that so frequently angered playgoers and served as a catalyst for the numerous theater riots of the first half of the century."[19] In 1858, *The Atlantic* said that "the passionate music of Italy" was the music of "hand organs," which "electrifies our cooler blood, but . . . does not express our feelings nor in any way represent our character."[20] For many Americans, the interest in Italy focused on the country's glorious past, its cultural and social refinements, and the pastoral Italian landscape with its picturesque ruins and rustic peasants. Their Italy was the Italy of art and romance, an idealized, heroic Italy. For many Americans visiting Italy, "the whole country was like a stage, while the Italians seemed to them like actors playing parts in some poetic drama."[21] Most of the American travelers ignored Italian politics entirely, and many showed insensitivity to Italy's contemporary social problems or sharply criticized its modern institutions. James Fenimore Cooper, Nathaniel Hawthorne, Ralph Waldo Emerson, Henry James, and many other Americans "concurred in slighting the political, intellectual, and domestic habits of the Italian people, even while they praised and envied the Italian's love of art and capacity for leisure. They unanimously resented the encroachment of the present on the classical past."[22]

There were exceptions. Many Americans took an interest in Italian nationalism, from the failed Italian revolution of 1848-1849 to unification in the 1860s. American assistance may have been decisive in Garibaldi's victories, and a number of those who had fought with Garibaldi earlier had volunteered in the Union Army during America's Civil War.[23] Perceptive Americans could not help seeing parallels between the nearly contemporaneous American Civil War and Italian Risorgimento: Italians struggling to define themselves as a people and pursuing a unified republic, Americans struggling to redefine themselves and reunify their threatened republic.[24] Americans could also measure themselves and their democracy against the early failures of Italy's republican dreams and the limited successes of Italy's evolving constitutional monarchy. Furthermore, thinking Americans remembered that their early republic was itself partly inspired by the Roman republic of antiquity that was so much praised by America's Founding Fathers.[25] Still, we should not overstate the case. American sympathies were often vaguely directed.[26] With the establishment of Italy's constitutional monarchy in the 1860s, Americans would praise Italian unification, but express disappointment at the nation's failure to create a democratic republic. And many Americans who traveled to Italy "were struck by the contrast between prosperous America and the fallen magnificence and languor of the Italian scene, where all things visible were in disrepair, cracking, crumbling, peeling, rotting, and everything seemed to speak of an irrecoverable past."[27]

When not rhapsodizing about cultural, romantic, picturesque Italy, American travel accounts often fixated on recurring negative images: the dirt and disorder; the oppressive Roman Catholic religion and pervasive superstition; and the stereotypical characters of the mercenary *vetturini*, the bloodthirsty *banditti*, the loafing *lazzaroni*, and the abject beggars—characters who had been mined by Washington Irving earlier in the century.[28] American travelers, even the mid-nineteenth-century expatriate artists in Florence and Rome, had little true contact with the Italians, and their overall attitude was based on superficial, often negative stereotypes.[29] The Italian people were seen as dishonest, mendacious, immoral, lazy, dirty, degraded, sensual, theatrical, and childlike. Bayard Taylor, who wrote a popular mid-century travel book, *Views A-Foot or Europe Seen with Knapsack and Staff* (1846), typified a general attitude of loving Italy, but disparaging the Italians. Foreshadowing Henry James, Taylor rhapsodizes, "Sweet, sweet Italy! I can feel now how the soul may cling to thee, since thou canst gratify its insatiable thirst for the Beautiful." A few pages later, he says that the Italian race is "indolent and effeminate," with little conception of human moral dignity, which he blames for Italy's woes.[30] Dissenting accounts (those of Howells and Margaret Fuller come to mind) spoke of the Italians' industriousness, courtesy, sociability, and temperance, as well as their bravery, democratic tendencies, and potential to be free and great. Paradoxical representations abounded. For example, Italians were often seen as being both intellectually deficient *and* remarkably witty. Overall, the Italian lower classes took the brunt of the criticism. The dirt and dishonesty, the begging, and the degradation of women into beasts of burden were often interpreted as deficiencies in Italian character, a vague attitude that would harden into racial nativism in late nineteenth- and early twentieth-century America. By observing, and usually disparaging, contemporary Italian national character, Americans could analyze and promote their own national character. Ultimately, many Americans maintained "a curious two-sided attitude that condemns, yet hesitates to condemn, praises and yet cannot help but disparage at the same time."[31] These contradictory perceptions persisted throughout most of the 1800s. "Italy was variously seen as friend of America, land of Garibaldi, party of popular liberty and freedom, birthplace of Dante, *la mère des arts*, Italy the brave, gallant, intelligent. Yet the image of Italian people as being fickle, immoral, and decadent persisted."[32] Americans found their artistic and political soul ancestors in the Italians of historic, heroic Italy; however, contemporary Italians were either sentimental subjects for picturesque art or exotic "Others" who both attracted and repelled.

The social and representational equations between Americans and Italy/Italians start to change around 1880, when large numbers of these sometimes picturesque, sometimes "Other" Italians turned up in America, challenged America's self-identity, and forever changed America's social fabric. This influx of Italians came at a time when America's obsession with Italy and Italians had reached a fever pitch. As Richard Brodhead has put it, "Never before or since has American writing been so absorbed with the Italian as it is during the Gilded Age." In large measure this fascination still expressed an American desire for high culture and gentility, what Brodhead calls the "aesthetic touristic" approach to Italy, and resulted in a flood of travelogues, guidebooks, antiquarian studies, historical novels, and poems that peaked at the turn of the century. America's golden age of travel writing lasted from 1880 to 1914, and for many Americans the richest treasure of all was Italy. However, this "aesthetic-touristic" attitude toward Italy abroad was being challenged by the image of the Italian as "alien-intruder" at home, and even as Italomania peaked, Italophilia was quickly turning into Italophobia.[33]

The southern Italian immigrants would come to be seen as doubly alien, not only different from the earlier immigrant groups, but also different from the mostly northern Italians who had come before them. The northern

Italian immigrants tended to be lighter-skinned and less poor. They were represented by political refugees, artists, language and music teachers, opera singers, and fencing masters. In contrast, immigrants from Italy's *Mezzogiorno* were generally darker skinned, and, if not the poorest of the poor, many were illiterate peasants, tenant farmers, field workers, and shepherds from rural districts and small villages. They had begun leaving Italy in large numbers when they realized that life in unified Italy was for them no better, and to some extent worse, than it had been under the oppressive Bourbon rule. The Risorgimento had been a creation of the wealthier, more enlightened, more privileged North. Women, clerics, and the vast majority of the population, including the peasants and the poor, were notably absent among the nationalists, and only 2 percent of the Italian people voted in the plebiscite that created the Italian state.[34] Although Italian unification had created a new nation, it had failed miserably in forging a unified people. There had been little progress at incorporating the South—Italy's "other half"—into the modern Italian state. The new national government quickly imposed new taxes and military conscription on the South. Pressure from Sicilian landowners forced Garibaldi to abandon sweeping promises of land reform that had been instrumental in winning support from the peasants. Most scholars agree that the South was palpably worse off after unification.[35] As a result, southerners transferred their hatred of the Bourbons to the new rulers in Turin, in some cases resisting the northern government, in many more cases turning to emigration. The push factors that led to massive emigration were many and varied, including agricultural problems, industrial backwardness, loss of trade, exploitation by the upper classes, delayed and imperfect national integration, and the racial attitudes of the inept northern-dominated national government.[36] Most galling was the North's tendency to attribute the "southern problem" to the inferiority of the southern Italians. As David A. J. Richards points out, "It is one thing to treat persons, acknowledged to be persons, unjustly; it is quite another to treat them unjustly and then to rationalize such treatment on the basis of dehumanizing stereotypes of racial difference that unjustly deny their very humanity."[37] The northern Italian moderates envisioned a new nation based on freedom, order, reason, legality, and civilization. "When the situation in the South failed to fit in with that grid of concepts, it became defined as Other, as the theater of serfdom, anarchy, irrationality, violence, and barbarism."[38]

Northern Italians tended to see and represent southern Italians as an inferior people, apathetic, fatalistic, backward, uncivilized, more African/Arabic than Italian. On the eve of unification in 1860, an envoy of Cavour in the South reported back: "What barbarism! Some Italy! This is Africa: the Bedouin are the flower of civilized virtues compared to these peasants."[39] With the rise of the radical cooperative *Fasci Siciliani* movement among sulfur miners and sharecroppers in Sicily in the early 1890s, southern Italians were also depicted as lawless. Under the Bourbons, Italian lawlessness had had links to political heroism. But now, the northern government characterized southern political activism as strictly criminal activity, exaggerated it, and attributed it to the mafia. This image of the mafia then went to justify the government's repressive policies in the South.[40] "Italy's new bourgeois leaders had stigmatized a majority of the new nation's citizens as racially inferior, rebellious criminals; these stereotypes would long adhere to Italy's workers of the world."[41] From the 1870s to the 1890s, these differences between northern Italians and southern Italians were not only essentialized, but racialized as well. "Precisely as the Southern Question took its turn toward a racialized essentialism, Italy, the nation, began to encourage the exodus of millions of its southern inhabitants."[42] The characterization of southern Italians as racial Other coalesced with the 1898 publication of *L'Italia barbara contemporanea* (*Contemporary Barbarian Italy*), the *locus classicus* of racist prejudice against the South, by social anthropologist Alfredo Niceforo, himself a southerner. "*L'Italia barbara contemporanea* is almost an inventory of the stereotypes of the South in the late nineteenth century: the *mafia* and the *camorra*; the lottery, brigandage and feudalism; illiteracy, superstition and magic; cannibalism and corruption; Southerners as 'woman-people', yet whose society is based on an 'Arabic' oppression of women; Southerners as pathologically individualistic, yet indistinguishable in their teeming masses; dirt and diseases as characteristic of the *Mezzogiorno* together with rustic beauty," John Dickie writes. "The barbarous, the primitive, the violent, the irrational, the feminine, the African. These an (sic) other values, negatively connoted, were repeatedly located in the *Mezzogiorno* as foils to definitions of Italy."[43]

By the late nineteenth century, scientific racialism/racism had become a powerful discourse in Western thought. Race theory did not emerge full-blown, but had its seeds in two influential works: the one-thousand-page *Essay on the Inequality of the Human Races* (1853–1855), by the French historian and social philosopher Arthur Comte de Gobineau, sometimes called the "father of racism," and an American book, *Types of Mankind* (1854), by ethnologists J. C. Nott and George Gliddon. Both books not only set up hierarchies of races by color, but also further subdivided the "white" race into the dominant Teutonic and Anglo-Saxon strains on top and many of the southern European groups at the bottom.[44] By the late nineteenth century, race had become a powerful, sometimes dominant discourse, stimulated by presumed empiricism, nationalism, and imperialism.[45] Thinkers were "scientifically" dividing the human species into countless races arranged hierarchically according to inherited, fixed, and inalterable physical characteristics and moral, intellectual, and cultural capacities. New "sciences" such as ethnology, anthropology, craniometry, anthropometry, and phrenology were employed to explain racial differences. Although Darwin called into question the idea of fixed racial types, thinkers found a way to link ethnology and Darwinian precepts into a race-based social Darwinism.[46] Thus, the work of Darwin, Herbert Spencer, and the eugenicist Francis Galton helped lend a "scientific" validity to the division of races into advanced and backward, superior and inferior, us and them. In America, intellectuals and ordinary citizens obsessed about the races, their differences, and, increasingly, their rankings. Samuel George Morton, the so-called father of American anthropology, developed arguments for polygenesis, the scientific theory that claimed separate racial origins for different peoples, and posited the existence of "natural repugnance" between human species.[47]

It is not surprising that Americans themselves would adopt the northern Italians' negative attitudes, apply them initially to Italian immigrants in general, and later direct them specifically to southern Italian immigrants. From the very beginning of the large influx of southern Italians into Boston in the 1880s, Brahmins differentiated between Italians, North and South, noting that the "Germanic blood" and "artistic achievements" of the northern Italians distinguished them from the ignorant peasants of southern Italy.[48] "Anti-foreign sentiment filtered through a specific ethnic stereotype when Italians were involved; for in American eyes they bore the mark of Cain. They suggested the stiletto, the Maffia, the deed of impassioned violence."[49] This discourse of differentiation became institutionalized in American policy, which was influenced by the Italian intellectuals' thinking on the racial differences between northern and southern Italians, particularly the alleged criminal propensity of the latter. Beginning in 1899, the United States recorded and analyzed northern and southern Italians separately in its immigration statistics.[50] If the nineteenth century had seen the construction of a romantic, heroic, cultured Italy—the trope that had run through the cultural pilgrimage of the Grand Tour, Margaret Fuller's "sad but glorious days" of the Italian revolution of the late 1840s, and the idyll of graceful *dolce far niente* life—the century would conclude with images of poor, ignorant, dark-skinned Italians pouring into New York and other parts of the country. These images produced a hardening of the more diffuse anti-Italian attitudes that had circulated earlier in the century.[51]

It was the misfortune of the Italians and the other new immigrants to seek their promised land in a country then experiencing an "age of anxiety," when many native-born Americans were nervous and insecure about a host of perceived threats to the nation's economic, social, cultural, and racial health.[52] American debates over immigration and assimilation would occur in a charged atmosphere of economic upheaval and recessions, tense race, class, and labor relations, and dizzying social change associated with the late nineteenth century's rapid advances in industrialization, urbanization, and communication. By the late 1880s, there was a palpable separation between workers and capitalists. "And more and more, as the industrial working class took on a distinctly 'foreign cast' with heavy immigration from Catholic and Slavic nations, the wealthy came to seem a homogenous group: white, Anglo-Saxon, Protestant, and Republican."[53] The period was marked by the Haymarket riots of 1886 and the great Pullman strike of 1894, the end of the Indian wars with the 1890 massacre at Wounded Knee, the *Plessy v. Ferguson* "separate but equal" Supreme Court ruling of 1896, and America's imperialist expansion into the Caribbean, Latin America, and the Pacific, among other events. Social reform movements and the flood of utopian writings reflected and fed the country's unsettled state and psyche.

Americans of this period were preoccupied with ideas of nationhood *and* manhood, and were sensitive to potential threats to those still ill-defined and increasingly unstable concepts. Closely linked to nationhood and manhood was race, which, although acquiring a patina of "scientific" validity, was still a much contested concept. Gail Bederman and others have shown that Americans obsessed over connections between manhood and racial dominance. Debates about child rearing, lynching, and the white man's imperialistic burdens revealed a middle class trying "to explain male supremacy in terms of white racial dominance and, conversely, to explain white supremacy in terms of white racial dominance." A countervailing discourse feared that excessive civilization threatened young American men and America itself with weakness and neurasthenic breakdown.[54] As a cure, Theodore Roosevelt and others urged, among other things, the "strenuous life." (It was Roosevelt who referred to the lynching of the New Orleans Italians as "a rather good thing" and boasted that he had said so publicly in the presence of "various dago diplomats.")[55] There were also fears that American Anglo-Saxon blood was being weakened through pollution and disease, and that the race itself was committing suicide. These concerns about national and racial health in turn were extensions of worries about public health, cleanliness, and disease, which arose from the new "germ theory of disease" developed by Louis Pasteur and Robert Koch in the 1870s. Thus, Italians and other new immigrants found themselves plunged into a maelstrom of discourses, and all too often these immigrants wore the guise of potential or actual threat. At the center of American concerns were race and racial differences, and the racial sciences being used to explain those concepts. These racial sciences were *racializing* sciences that responded to political imperatives such as slavery, expansionism, and immigration. Ideas of race were absolutely essential in the American reaction toward the new immigrants. Among all the reasons for prejudice against the immigrants, race was by far the most powerful source of objection to them by the late nineteenth century.[56]

During this period, countless articles in the popular press, many of them dealing with Italians, attest to the country's soul-searching over the "new immigrants." *Harper's, The Atlantic, The Forum, The North American Review, The Century*, and other influential periodicals offered titles such as "Italian Life in New York," "The Italians of New York," "Italian Immigrants and Their Enslavement," "Immigration from Italy," "Homicide and the Italians," and "The Black Hand Myth." Commentators, social critics, and thought leaders asked: Were the Italians and other "new immigrant" groups polluting the American stock? Were they capable of being assimilated? And, just what did becoming an "American" entail? One overriding question emerged: Was it advisable for the country to maintain open immigration? Beginning in the 1880s, immigration was increasingly being discussed "in terms of uncontrollable natural disasters, weakened bodies, illnesses, and quasimilitary invasions, for example, tide, stream, wave, flow, flood, torrent, tidal wave, fevers, hemorrhages, and the like."[57] The Immigration Restriction League, founded by Boston patricians in 1894, targeted the new immigrants on the basis of perceived "racial" differences between them and earlier American settlers. One of its founding members, Prescott Farnsworth Hall, drew a distinction between the "free, energetic, progressive" British/German/Scandinavian stock and the "downtrodden, atavistic, and stagnant" Slav, Latin, and Asiatic races.[58] As early as 1891, Henry Cabot Lodge, the blue-blood Massachusetts congressman, made distinctions between the common stock of older immigrants and the "new and wholly different elements" being introduced into America. In an article for *The North American Review*, Lodge distinguished between northern and southern Italians, depicting the northerners as a finer population.[59] Also in 1891, economist Francis A. Walker, president of the Massachusetts Institute of Technology and former superintendent of the federal census, blamed the "vast hordes of foreign immigrants" for a reduction of America's native stock. These new immigrants, Walker said, were formed by race wars and hard nature, and least adaptable to American "political institutions and social life." Among these immigrants incapable of adapting, Walker lists Huns, Poles, Bohemians, Russian Jews, and "*South* Italians" (my italics).[60]

Edward W. Bemis, a progressive economist, was the first intellectual to propose immigration restrictions based on a perceived racial shift in immigration patterns. In 1887, he called for a literacy test as a way to help native-born American wage earners by reducing the influx of the new immigrants and the low standards of living they insisted on maintaining in the New World.[61] In May 1891, Lodge used the lynching of the eleven Italians in New Orleans as a pretext to call for immigration restriction based on the ability to read and write a language. In his piece "Lynch Law and Unrestricted Immigration" for *The North American Review*, Lodge blamed America's open gates for the lynching. "[N]ot only are we doing nothing to protect the quality of our citizenship or the wages of our workingmen from an unrestricted flood of immigration, but we are permitting persons so ignorant and criminal to come among us that organizations like the Mafia are sure to rise in our midst," Lodge wrote. "The time has come for an intelligent restriction."[62] By 1896, Francis Walker could characterize the immigrants from Hungary, Austria, Russia, and "southern Italy" as "beaten men from beaten races" with no aptitude for self-government, unlike those races "who are descended from the tribes that met under the oak-trees of old Germany to make laws and choose chieftains."[63] In January 1904, Lodge argued in *The Century* that a literacy test would exclude large numbers of Italians and other new immigrants, while not seriously impeding more desirable immigration from northern and western Europe. Tracing the history of American settlement, Lodge spoke of the beneficial "normal" amalgamation of the primary stock of English-speaking races with Germans, Scandinavians, and French-Canadians. Having included those groups in America's native family, Lodge turns to Italian immigration. He says that although Italians had never amalgamated with the English-speaking people, he concedes that at least "they are people of the Western civilization like our own, that there is among the northern Italians an infusion of Germanic blood, and that they present in themselves no very alarming feature."[64] But, if Lodge is conceding a place in Western civilization to the Italians, it is for the northern Italians only, those he would refer to as the "Teutonic Italians."[65] Lodge, then a member of the Senate Committee on Immigration (a designation prominently attached to his byline for the article), says nothing about the southern Italians whom he had disparaged as inferior to their northern brethren in an article more than a decade earlier.

Behind these concerns about immigration, immigration restriction, and national identity lay nativist fears that mixed in fascinating ways with the Jim Crow racism of the period. During the late nineteenth century, blacks and immigrants were both victims of discrimination and violence. "Niggers" *and* "dagoes" were being lynched. This was most dramatically illustrated in the 1891 lynching of the eleven Italians in New Orleans, which was greeted with both condemnation and approbation from the American press. After 1870, Italians were the only presumptive whites to be lynched in significant numbers. In addition to New Orleans and other Louisiana localities, Italians were lynched in Colorado, Illinois, Mississippi, North Carolina, and Florida. Between 1874 and 1915, approximately thirty Italians were lynched.[66] Being targets of nativist violence was not the only link between Italians and blacks during this period; there was conflation in other ways. In his article "European Peasants as Immigrants," Nathaniel Shaler drew parallels between America's failure to assimilate its African population and the likelihood that the new immigrants would fail just as miserably. The European peasant was a peasant by nature and had little chance of escaping that condition. "He is in essentially the same state as the Southern negro," Shaler concludes.[67] Among the European peasants, the Italian serfs were most likely to be linked with American blacks. Italians were sometimes depicted as slaves with at least two masters in the New World: the American boss on the job and the Italian boss—the *padrone*—who played the intermediary and managed many of the immigrant's material affairs.

In recent years much has been written about the *padrone*, a complex, Medusa-like figure who appeared in many guises both in American labor history and in the daily lives of the immigrants. The *padrone* organized immigrant work gangs, contracted for employment, and sometimes operated the immigrants' "company store" in mining camps, construction sites, and plantations across the country. In the cities, he operated multipurpose "banks," some legitimate and others not, that also exchanged money, sold steamer tickets, forwarded remittances to Italy, provided notary and legal services, and dealt in jewelry and other commodities. Much like the old general store, these Italian banks served as a focal point for the immigrant community, a place to conduct business and to socialize. Unlike the impersonal and efficient American bank, "The Italian Bank had a more familial atmosphere, where ethnic bonds predominated and business was conducted in a more casual manner."[68] These are some of the roles the *padrone* filled. Who or what he was is more difficult to ascertain. As historian Robert F. Harney says, "The only workable definition of the padrone is ascriptive. The Padrone was a man whom other people called padrone."[69] While the vast majority of *padroni* provided work, services, and security for immigrants,[70] some were unscrupulous masters. It was the latter who received most of the attention. Accounts portrayed the *padrone* as "an ahistoric personification of greed and primitive cruelty," and in the eyes of many nativist Americans, virtually every middle-class immigrant was tainted with the suspicion of being a *padrone*. If the *padroni* were seen as rapacious masters, then the workers were stereotyped as "*padrone* slaves" who had no aptitude for American freedom.[71] Italians themselves promoted this image of Italian workers as helpless, childlike "slaves." Baron Fava, Italian ambassador to the United States, blamed the *padrone* system on southern Italian gullibility, saying that "so long as a large part of our Italian immigration comes from the southern provinces, represented mainly by the agricultural or rural classes, PROVERBIAL FOR THEIR SIMPLICITY, there will always be those . . . who are ready to take advantage of them."[72] S. Merlino, an Italian who researched the working conditions of Italian laborers in America, discovered that in some cases, the slave stereotype was close to the truth. Writing in *The Forum* magazine, he cited instances in which "Italian laborers have suffered actual slavery, and in trying to escape have been fired upon by the guards and murdered, as happened not long ago in the

Adirondacks."[73] In the South, there were several documented cases of Italian cotton workers who were forbidden to leave and arrested and returned in chains if caught leaving. However, the image of Italian workers as fools, puppets, or slaves was far from completely accurate. In a number of cases, Italian workers successfully resisted *padrone* abuses.[74]

Italians and blacks were also linked in other ways. Because Italians took jobs that only blacks would work, and because Italians showed little aversion to dealing with Negroes, they consequently were classed with Negroes socially and economically. In the American South, for example, Italians were the only whites to work in the fields and mills of the region's cotton and sugar plantations. Italians were sometimes seen as "black," and, if not "black," then "not white." At least a few southern schools barred Italians in an attempt to maintain the color line. In Louisiana, the Sicilians were often called *"black* dagoes," and payroll lists and other records lumped them into a separate category as neither white nor black.[75] At the 1898 Louisiana state constitutional convention, during debates over the disenfranchisement of blacks and other groups, some delegates conceded that the Italian's skin "happens to be white," but others held that "according to the spirit of our meaning when we speak of 'white man's government,' [the Italians] are as black as the blackest negro in existence."[76] The Italian's dark complexion, his willingness to associate with blacks in the workplace and to some extent in social settings, and his very "in-betweenness" made him a double threat in America, one that "might endanger not only the purity of the white race but also its solidarity."[77]

The Italians were not the only immigrant group caught in this "not-quite-white in-betweenness." Irish immigrants of the mid-nineteenth century and other new immigrant groups of the late nineteenth century, including Jews and Greeks, to one degree or another had to "become white" and join the "American race" in order to become American. Before the appearance of Italian *"padrone* slaves" and "guineas" (a term for African slaves being applied to Italians), there had been references to "Irish slaves" and "Irish niggers."[78] However, the Italians and other new immigrant groups accelerated the fragmentation of the monolithic "white" race that began with the Irish. The period of mass European immigration witnessed the fracturing of "whiteness" into a fluid, contested hierarchy of plural and "scientifically" determined white races. The "contest over whiteness—its definition, its internal hierarchies, its proper boundaries, and its rightful claimants"—raged as it had never done before. Whiteness was contingent on a number of factors, including occupation, residence, and the presence of other immigrant or nonwhite groups. Ultimately, however, *becoming* Caucasian was crucial to the politicocultural saga of immigration: For the Italians and other immigrants groups, acceptance and assimilation became a *"racial* odyssey."[79]

One objective of this book is to explore the Italian *"racial* odyssey" as a way of examining America's own racial odyssey. Ultimately, American debates over the new immigrants, particularly the Italians, and their potential and prospects for assimilation and Americanization were debates about America itself. In constructing the Italian and other so-called new immigrants, Americans were struggling to construct for themselves a modern national identity at the dawn of a new century. It is within this cultural and historical context that I will explore how American representations of Italians and Italian Americans engaged, reflected, and helped shape the United States's developing concepts of immigration, ethnicity, race, and national identity during the period from 1880 to 1910. As we have seen, it was during this period that America's romance with Italy clashed with the threatening reality of Italian immigrant "hordes" now pouring into the country. The "romantic" and the "real" each had a certain power and status as reality in the discourse. In a broad sense, I will look at Americans in Italy and the romance they constructed, and engage that with Italians in America and the reality they imposed on that construction.

My approach does not pretend to be comprehensive, but rather will involve close readings and analyses of various events, utterances, images, and texts. The Italians were represented and constructed in scientific treatises, government reports, political oratory, journalistic accounts, literature, the visual arts, caricature, and myriad other venues of popular culture. This book examines both so-called truthful texts and avowedly imaginative ones, including travel essays and narratives, journalistic reports, fiction, and, to a lesser extent, photographs and illustrations. For the vast majority of Americans, Italy and Italians were textual constructs. As Said says, a text offers "no such thing as a delivered presence, but a *re-presence*, or a representation," which relies on "institutions, traditions, conventions, agreed-upon codes of understanding for their effects." This applies as much to a Henry James short story and travel essay as it does to a Jacob Riis report or an illustration by William Rogers. These various texts, working together and with others, "acquire mass, density, and referential power among themselves and thereafter in the culture at large."[80] However, it is important to keep in mind that these texts were enmeshed in, responded to, and commented on specific historic realities.

The travel accounts are important because American travelers used the experience of Europe (in particular Italy, I would say) to help them think about questions of race and gender, and about ways of relating to their country, to their compatriots, and to the wider world. In addition, these travel accounts were immensely popular and therefore played an important role in shaping American attitudes. The raw material of travel also produced numerous short stories, tales, and novels by artists such as Nathaniel

Hawthorne, William Dean Howells, Henry James, Edith Wharton, Constance Fenimore Woolson, and other lesser writers. As Christopher Mulvey says, "The significance of this link between novel and travel book was not that the fictionalisation of nations and people was taking place because the men and women writing the descriptions were novelists and short-story writers. Rather it was that mythopoesis came into place as soon as the nations and national characters were described."[81] It will also be worthwhile to examine the literary representations of Italians in the light of corresponding images of Italians/Italian Americans found in journalistic accounts and commentary that began to appear with regularity in the late nineteenth century. These mixed media—newspapers and magazines, short stories and novels, "fact" and "fiction"—all contributed to the national discourses. By mixing these media, we may see how supposedly fictional accounts of Italians conflicted with or complemented supposedly factual depictions, and how that dynamic may have related to more generally held opinions and attitudes toward Italians and Italian Americans. That question is part of a larger question concerning the origin and dissemination of racist and nativist ideologies in the late nineteenth and early twentieth centuries, and the role that language and different "texts" play in challenging or reproducing those ideologies.

My primary focus is on a handful of writers and reporters whose "texts" are particularly rich and charged with the questions that interest me. I will use close textual readings as a way to examine the dialectic between the individual text or author and "the complex collective formation to which his work is a contribution." I am motivated by the belief that society and culture can only be understood and studied together.[82]

Chapters 1 and 2 look at the reporting and photography of the immigrant journalist/photographer Jacob A. Riis against the reporting of the immigrant journalist/academic Edward Alfred Steiner. These two writers serve as a good point of entry into the journalism of the period. Riis's attitudes can be traced over time, as he transforms himself from a struggling police reporter to published author and national reformer. His own autobiographical narrative of that progression, *The Making of an American* (1901), sheds light on his attitudes toward assimilation and American identity. Steiner's own autobiographies, *Against the Current: Simple Chapters from a Complex Life* (1910) and *From Alien to Citizen: The Story of My Life in America* (1914), make an excellent companion piece to Riis's autobiography. With Riis and Steiner, we have two immigrants writing about and representing other immigrants. It is a interesting pairing because Riis, the educated Danish craftsman, was a representative of the old migration to the United States, while Steiner, a Jew from Hungary, was very much a part of the new immigration. Both Riis and Steiner were reformers—Riis a secular preacher, Steiner an ordained minister—who spoke of Christian brotherhood, but were still imbued with the race thinking and race differentiation of their day.

Chapters 3 and 4 try to take a fresh perspective on Henry James. Numerous books and articles have made James virtually synonymous with Italy, but the critical literature is not as extensive on James's representations of the Italians themselves. James is a particularly rich source because there is so much to choose from, both in fiction and nonfiction, much of it written over an extended period of time. My study of James is directed primarily at *The American Scene*, the fascinating report on his homecoming visit to America in 1904–1905, but I also deal extensively with his travel essays and fiction. With James, we encounter many Italians in Italy, an Italian prince who marries an American heiress in England, a poor Italian peasant who finds a modeling job in London, and thousands of Italian immigrants in New York, New Jersey, and Massachusetts. While James had an unequaled passion for Italy, his feelings and attitudes toward the country and in particular its people were often conflicted. I will attempt to trace James's evolving representations of Italians, paying particular attention to shifts in those depictions when the picturesque Italian peasant on the Campagna becomes a rag-picker in the streets of New York.

The dualities of Mark Twain are at the center of Chapter 5. Twain traveled through Italy in 1867 on the *Quaker City* cruise that became the basis for *The Innocents Abroad* (1869). However, Twain is not generally acknowledged as having had much to say about Italians, immigration, and nativism. And yet two Italian immigrants—twins no less—play what has usually been mistakenly dismissed as a tangential role in one of Twain's most curious works, the hybrid *Pudd'nhead Wilson and Those Extraordinary Twins* (1894 first American edition). The novel and attached sketch clearly, if not consciously, engaged with the nativist discourse of the decade, the very discourse that made possible the lynching of the eleven Italians in New Orleans at about the same time that Twain was writing *Pudd'nhead Wilson*. True to his own dual nature, Twain's treatment of the Italian twins points to various dualities in America's perceptions of and attitudes toward Italians.

James and Twain knew each other and had mutual friends, most prominently William Dean Howells. Steiner apparently was familiar with Riis's work. However, these writers came from different class or ethnic backgrounds and had different social and literary agendas. Furthermore, their emotional and practical connections with immigrants and immigration varied greatly. However, all engaged with the immigrant issue, consciously or unconsciously, directly or indirectly, sometimes with purpose, sometimes not. In their depictions of Italians and Italian Americans, these writers engage with existing discourses, sometimes carve out new positions within these discourses, and occasionally point to discursive developments of the decades to come. As diverse as these four men were, they are connected by a complex relationship with the concept of America as home. Two are American immigrants and two are native-born Americans who spent much of their lives in Europe.

Jacob Riis and Edward Steiner leave their native homes for good, looking for and ultimately finding new homes in America. They finally come to know where home is. Henry James's identity was in great measure shaped by the question of home. Was home America or England? Did his homecoming resolve the issue, or did he die not knowing where home really was? The intensely American Twain spent many years away from home, but seems never to have forgotten that America was home, even if at times it did not seem like much of one. The final twist here is that many Americans, like James, found a cultural and spiritual home in Italy, while many, many more Italians came to American either to find a new home, or the economic wherewithal to return ultimately home to Italy.

Chapter 1

Jacob Riis: Immigrants Old and New, and the Making of Americans

The Italian comes in at the bottom, and in the generation that came over the sea he stays there.

—Jacob Riis, *How the Other Half Lives*, 1890

It was their home. They were children of the dump, literally. All of them except one were Italian.

—Jacob Riis, *How the Other Half Lives*, 1890

He was a poor little maimed boy with a sober face, and it wrings my heart now, the recollection of the look he gave me when I plumped out: "Pietro, do you ever laugh?" "I did wonst," he said.

—Jacob Riis, *The Peril and the Preservation of the Home*, 1903

In his chapter "The Italian in New York" in *How the Other Half Lives*, the journalist and pioneering photographer Jacob A. Riis begins by discussing the transformation of the Italian immigrant as he makes his way from the Old World to the New. Riis notes that Italians form a "picturesque, if not very tidy, element" in New York City's burgeoning population. By 1890, when *How the Other Half Lives* was published, the stream of Italian immigration was indeed threatening to become a flood, and that flood most threatened New York City. The Italian, Riis says, "claims so large a share of public attention, partly because he keeps coming at such a tremendous rate, but chiefly because he elects to stay in New York." Once ensconced in the tenements of New York's Lower East Side, the Italian "promptly reproduces conditions of destitution and disorder which, set in the frame-work of Mediterranean exuberance, are the delight of the artist, but in a matter-of-fact American community become its danger and reproach."[1] The Italian is equally picturesque, equally romantic, in both an Old World Campagnan field and a New World Manhattan alley. Any change in the Italian during transplantation is not so much with the Italian himself, but rather with his relationship to his environment and how Americans perceive that relationship. In Italy, in "the frame-work of Mediterranean exuberance," in its "natural" environment, the Italian's "destitution and disorder" can be naturalized, aestheticized, framed within the artist's canvas or the travel writer's prose sketches. Thus contained, destitution and disorder are a fit subject for artistic delight, as they had been for the countless American writers, artists, and amateur sketchers who had traveled to Italy in the nineteenth century. Having never been to Italy, Riis knew of this delight only secondhand, through America's entrenched vision of picturesque Italy and the images of poor, chaotic Italy that had been circulating in America for at least a century.

Riis was more directly acquainted with Italians in New York, where transplanted into the context of American "matter-of-fact" practicality and reality, these same destitute and disorderly Italians become something less benign. Their very picturesqueness, while still quaint, exotic, and seductive, becomes both a menace and a rebuke to American character and American progress. Here in America, the Italian is still a subject for the illustrators and sentimental travel writers who venture into New York's Lower East Side to produce colorful sketches and articles for magazines such as *Harper's New Monthly Magazine* and *The Cosmopolitan*. However, the Italian now is also a subject for the documentary photographer and the journalist and, perhaps more important, a "problem" for the social scientist and the reformer, all roles that Riis played at one time or another. In Italy, the Italian is the stuff of cultural romance; in New York, although still picturesque in his dirt and disorder, the Italian is a threatening, provocative, and seductive reality.

Riis's dichotomy is a neat one in that it schematizes commonly held contradictory attitudes toward the Italian at the turn of the century. For many Americans, Italy still was the land of art, history, culture, and romance. This continuing fascination resulted in a flood of travelogues, guidebooks, antiquarian studies, historical novels, and poems that peaked around the turn of the century, making the Gilded Age a golden age of travel writing, with Italy the crown jewel.[2] However, this golden age of travel writing coincided exactly with the period of greatest Italian immigration to the United States. And for many of those same Americans, Italy was becoming the distrusted source of the hundreds of thousands of picturesque, but dirty and menacing, Italian peasants pouring into a New York City ill equipped to handle, absorb, or assimilate them. By the mid-1890s, even someone as sympathetic to the Italians as William Dean Howells could begin seeing the immigrants as alien intruders. He wonders by what "malign chance" the Italians have metamorphosed from the "friendly folk" they are "at home" in Italy to the "surly race they mostly show themselves here: shrewd for their advancement in material things, which seem the only good things to the Americanized aliens of all races, and fierce for their full share of the political pottage."[3]

Riis's own reaction to and interpretation of the Italian's attractive yet threatening reality are curiously contradictory, and in their contradictions are representative of large segments of American society during the decades surrounding the turn of the century. In his writings about Italian and other immigrant groups, Riis melds stereotypes and sympathy, and reveals himself as a far more complex commentator than the classic progressive reformer he has been made out to be. A closer look exposes a journalist/reformer with deeply divided attitudes toward the new immigrants and their prospects for assimilation. Riis's written and photographic representations of the immigrants are of particular interest for a number of reasons. Riis himself was an immigrant who later in life wrote a very popular autobiography tellingly titled *The Making of an American*. Riis's commentary on the new immigrants becomes even more interesting when read alongside and against the work of another immigrant journalist, Edward A. Steiner, whose *On the Trail of the Immigrant* appeared sixteen years after *How the Other Half Lives*. Broadly speaking, Riis, a Scandinavian Protestant, and Steiner, a Hungarian Jew, represent the old and the new immigration to America, a distinction that was deeply etched into the American consciousness. The experiences of these two journalists and their writings on the new immigrants, when examined together, offer sometimes contradictory, sometimes complementary commentaries on the nature of the Italian (and other new) immigrants, the prospects for their assimilation, and what it meant to be and become an American around the turn of the century.

As an immigrant, Jacob August Riis was both typical and atypical. He was born in 1849 in the ancient town of Ribe in southwest Denmark, into "a homogenous, family-centered, industrious Lutheran society, with only mild manifestations of class divisions."[4] Riis's father taught Latin and Greek at a centuries-old preparatory academy and occasionally did part-time editorial work for the local newspaper. The father envisioned a literary career for Riis, but the young man, hearing of golden opportunities in America, left Denmark in 1870. Riis himself would say that it was James Fenimore Cooper's novels that "first set my eyes toward the west."[5] But Riis found little of Cooper's imagined America when he landed in New York. The city was half provincial capital and half world capital, a city on the brink of an incredible demographic transformation that would swell its population and give it a distinctly foreign look. According to *The Making of an American*, the greenhorn Riis lived on the edge of poverty, tramping in and around New York, and at one point ending up in a police lodging house. He did odd jobs and pursued odd schemes, becoming in succession a roustabout, laborer, salesman, and reporter for small newspapers. Through it all, he maintained his stubborn pride and unwavering optimism, relying on values that had been formed in Denmark, including religious faith, respect for education, and reverence for the family.[6] Two things happened in 1887 that would dramatically alter his fortunes. He landed a job as a probationary reporter for the New York *Tribune*, and he read a four-line dispatch from Germany announcing the discovery of flashlight photography. Riis hooked up with photographers Henry G. Piffard and Richard Hoe Lawrence, two distinguished amateurs interested in flash, and began making nighttime raiding parties into the tenement districts, essentially taking photos by proxy. On January 25, 1888, armed with one hundred slides of photos taken in New York's slums, Riis delivered a lecture, "The Other Half—How It Lives and Dies in New York," before the Society of Amateur Photographers. The lantern-slide lecture was intended to highlight the work of Piffard and Lawrence, but Riis, using the "sunshine and shadow" conventions of the day, took the talk to another level, giving his audience a titillating tour of the city's seamier side.[7] In short order, the lecture became a newspaper story ("Flashes from the Slums"), a magazine article, and finally the book that launched Riis's career as a influential journalist, lecturer, and reformer.[8] By the time of his death in 1914, Riis had delivered numerous latern-slide lectures across the country and written hundreds of newspaper stories, dozens of magazine articles, and fifteen books.

Riis tells his classic rags-to-respect story in his unorthodox *The Making of an American* (1901), which is by turns guileless and shrewd, idealistic and realistic, egotistical and disarmingly candid. In it, Riis takes most pride in his Americanness and in his work as "a reporter of facts" who loved his fellow man.[9] The book enjoyed great popular success, selling out two editions in three weeks.[10] Riis saw himself (and was seen) as the quintessential self-made immigrant whose life was a morality tale of complete assimilation and unabashed nationalism verging on jingoism.[11] Prominent reformer, confidante of Theodore Roosevelt, and national treasure, Riis was seen to embody the American Spirit.[12]

Obviously, Riis's tale is much different from the stories of the immigrants who would serve as the foundation for not only Riis's assimilation, but also his fame and prominence. Riis's middle-class northern European roots (and looks), rudimentary knowledge of English, and occupational skills gave him valuable advantages over the mostly lower-class southern and eastern European immigrant groups who constituted the vast majority of New York's "other half." Riis's native beliefs and values had more in common with native-born Americans than with the ethnic groups that constituted the so-called new immigration.[13] Consequently, Riis's relationship with the later immigrants is a curious one. At least one critic has argued that Riis rarely acknowledges the distinct advantage he had over the new immigrants and consequently exhibited toward them "a racism which from the outset closely coincided with the nativist ideology" of the day.[14] However, it is not as simple as that. Riis comes at the new immigrants from a number of different perspectives and for that reason serves as a particularly rich source on questions of American identity and national character, assimilation, and attitudes toward the Other at the turn of the century. "He invariably asked what the character of the American city was and what the future of an American society would be. His questions implicated almost every nativist fear about the transfiguration of the American city by the immigrant and the impoverished."[15]

By the time Riis began depicting the poor and the immigrants—these two groups were by now nearly synonymous—the slum dweller and the foreigner were already a topic of strong interest for police reporters, photographers, novelists, true-crime writers, muckrakers, and social reformers. There already existed an established tradition of urban literature in which magazines featured poor but picturesque urban peasants.[16] The same year that *How the Other Half Lives* was published, *Harper's Weekly* undertook a series of illustrated articles on "The 'Foreign Element' in New York City." William Rogers, the leading exponent of the picturesqueness of poverty, provided illustrations that depicted the immigrants as hard working, proud, and self-sufficient, if somewhat downtrodden. Rogers's illustrations provided a sympathetic, humanizing counterpoint to articles that sometimes carried a more negative tone. The piece on Italian immigrants describes two distinct classes of Italians: the fairer complected northerners who are enterprising and "full of energy" in the French mode, and the "swarthy" southern Italians who are "by no means slow to anger, and who repel an insult with a thrust of the stiletto." These Neapolitans and Sicilians are "inclined to the philosophy which finds its highest expression in loafing and lying at one's ease." Unlike their northern cousins, the poorest (read southern) Italians are vocational failures "simply because they are too ignorant to rise from the social slough of despond in which they find themselves." While praising the poor Italians' honesty and hard work, the article offers this faint and damning praise: "The poorer class of Italians are ignorant, but they are not *all* lazy or bad. They are keenly grateful for any kindness that is shown them, and most of them are not mentally vigorous enough to be evil." These comments are indicative of certain attitudes toward the Italians at this time, many of which are echoed by Riis. By italicizing the word "all," the article implies that *most* Italian immigrants *are* lazy and bad. And although most Italians are bad, they are not smart enough to be evil, a curious distinction.[17]

In addition to magazine articles, a number of books testify to the hungry market for glimpses of the city's "other half." By the 1880s, the press and popular literature had established the literary convention of an urban landscape so fragmented, so alien, as to turn quarters of the city into "another country."[18] Although Riis would claim that his title, *How the Other Half Lives*, was original, pure inspiration on his part, "'the other half' was not least among a battery of well-worn tropes evoking 'nether' regions that presented an 'excursionist' with scenes so alien, forbidding, or disgusting that they required the mediation of journalists or artists."[19] Increasingly, throughout the second half of the nineteenth century, the city was being seen as a symbol of menace, mystery, darkness, and shadows, a place in need of light and reason, a text to be deciphered, comprehended, and demystified. "American letters, often drawing upon biblical images of the fallen city or upon the hope of a New Jerusalem, made it possible and popular to see the city as divided. One half was dark, resistant to Christian virtue and not amenable to social control and order; the other half dwelt in light and was propertied, stable, virtuous, and domestic."[20] Afraid of losing touch with and control over the "other half," the privileged half sought ways to ward off the dangers. The urgency of the situation was evident at the Christian Conference that Riis attended in New York in early December 1888. Riis says the goal was "to discuss how to lay hold of these teeming masses in the tenements with Christian influences."[21] However, speakers "discussed how the 'foreign' element was responsible for vice and crime, how the non-Anglo-Saxon was resistant to assimilation, how a rising Catholic populace contested the hegemony of American Protestant mores."[22]

Charles Loring Brace's *The Dangerous Classes of New York* (1872) best typifies the charity writing that would to some degree influence Riis's work. It focused on the miserable living conditions in the slums (overcrowding, filth, extremes of heat and cold, lack of air and sunlight) and the ills of the urban poor (crime, beggary, disease, disorder, dissolution of family life). At the same time Brace proposed redeeming Protestant virtues (cleanliness, industry, order, temperance) as the solution to these social problems. Riis takes up the same subjects and employs many of the same tropes found in Brace. Like Brace, Riis combines anecdote and statistic, generalizes about ethnic and racial groups, compares immigrant types, and invokes the immigrant homelands as a contrast to the New York slums. While influenced by Brace and the religious groups that sponsored his lantern-slide lectures, Riis is usually seen as part of a newer reform movement that had begun to challenge traditional moral descriptions and analyses that attributed poverty to individual vice.[23] This new reform movement was more apt to offer an environmental explanation for poverty and vice. Riis attributed his reform impulses to his professional contacts with the genteel, progressive members of the New York Board of Health. "Part of the growing group of middle-class technicians who would manage the legislative fiats of the coming Progressive Era, they had a faith in science, reason, progress, and the cultural superiority of Anglo-Saxon institutions," James B. Lane writes. "Energetic, moralistic, sentimental, nationalistic, and above all optimistic, Riis was confident that the rational and scientific control of the environment would set the conditions for a world of harmony by allowing the spirit of goodness that was in all men to flower."[24] This standard view of Riis sees him as an enlightened moral and social crusader, but one who did not always rise above the racial and ethnic stereotyping of his day. "Riis justifiably could be chided for his occasional exaggerated characterization of some groups in the polyglot populations of New York," writes Alexander Alland Sr., who, like Riis, was an immigrant and a photographer interested in social reform.[25] In fact, racial stereotypes permeate Riis's descriptions in *How the Other Half Lives*: The Chinaman is stealthy and scrupulously neat, the Jew obsessively thrifty, the Negro sensual and superstitious.

Riis devotes separate chapters of *How the Other Half Lives* to five "racial" groups: Italians, Chinese, Jews, Bohemians, and blacks. By segregating these groups and their racial/national idiosyncrasies into discrete chapters, Riis not only perpetuated the stereotypes but also gave assurances that "the other half" was perfectly atomized, and therefore perhaps less menacing. "The general subject was not only more easily apprehended according to ready categories but also more easily contained given the evident internal divisions."[26] If these various racial/national groups were subsumed in "the other half," it was a half that Riis divides into discrete parts. He may speak of New York's "queer conglomerate mass of heterogeneous elements"(19), but he depicts the individual groups as homogenous. Riis consistently deals with each group in the singular—referring to the Italian, the Chinaman, and so on—thereby implying a certain sameness to members of each racial/national group. Riis's use of the singular case allows him to essentialize each group into a type; in essence, it serves as a shorthand for stereotyping the various groups, who can then be compared and contrasted to each other. We will see examples of this by turning to Riis's specific representations of "the Italian."

Not surprisingly, the Italians are the first group Riis treats in detail in *How the Other Half Lives*. Riis is both attracted to and repelled by the colorful, chaotic Italian and his colorful, chaotic neighborhoods. In one short passage about an Italian quarter of the Mulberry Bend, Riis conflates the Italian's colorful picturesqueness and his chaotic violent streak, making the

Italian the target of both the tourist and the police. Riis points out the Italian's red bandanna and yellow handkerchiefs, his "infinitely" sweet tongue, and all the "ristorantes" of the innumerable Pasquales. "[H]alf of the people in 'the Bend' are christened Pasquale, or get the name in some other way," Riis writes, before oddly segueing from Pasquale the restaurant owner to Pasquale the murderer. "When the police do not know the name of an escaped murderer, they guess at Pasquale and send the name out on alarm; in nine cases out of ten it fits" (52). Riis's contradictory responses to the Italian continue throughout *How the Other Half Lives*. Riis's Italian is colorful, destitute, disorderly, and dirty—and he does not seem to mind his degraded condition. With regard to cleanliness, the Italian is seen as immensely inferior to the Negro but on a par with the Polish Jew, with whom he constitutes "the lowest of the whites" (116). Riis here echoes the theme of the dirty, disordered Italian so vividly captured by Brace in *The Dangerous Classes*. Brace describes the Italian tenements as a "a bedlam of sounds, and a combination of odors from garlic, monkeys and the most dirty human persons," concluding, "They were, without exception, the dirtiest population I had met with."[27]

The Italian gravitates naturally to slums, according to Riis, and where he does not find a slum, he creates one, "if allowed to follow his natural bent, which is to come in at the bottom, and, at least in the first generation, to remain there" (43). The "Italian hordes" are pushing out from the Bend "in ever increasing numbers, seeking, according to their wont, the lowest level" (32). Rather than improve the Negro neighborhoods, the infiltration of the Italian in some ways only exacerbates the situation. Where the Negro, the Italian, and the tramp from the Bend meet on Thompson Street, what results is "the aptly-named black-and-tan saloon," the "border-land where the white and the black races meet in common debauch." Without elaborating, Riis concludes: "Than this commingling of the utterly depraved of both sexes, white and black, on such ground, there can be no greater abomination" (119). The depiction of the Italian as a slum-maker is intriguing in that it runs counter to Riis's environmental explanation for poverty and vice. Here, Riis seems to be saying that you can take the Italian out of the slum but you cannot take the slum out of the Italian. In a later chapter, "What Has Been Done," Riis qualifies his assessment. Pointing to a new model tenement in the Bend, Riis says of the Italian: "With his fatal contentment in the filthiest surroundings, he gives undoubted evidence of having in him the instinct of cleanliness that, properly cultivated, would work his rescue in a very little while" (218).

For all his faults, Riis's Italian is a docile, attractive tenant who makes less trouble than the "contentious Irishman" or the "order-loving German." The Italian is "content to live in a pig-sty and submits to robbery at the hands of the rent-collector without a murmur." He is an uncomplaining victim of the *padrone* system, trusting in his unscrupulous countryman "with the instinct of utter helplessness." He is a slow learner, unable to write his native language, knows no English, and lacks any instinct or desire to learn. "The man is so ignorant that, as one of the sharpers who prey upon him put it once, it 'would be downright sinful not to take him in.' His ignorance and unconquerable suspicion of strangers dig the pit into which he falls." Of course, all these attributes—fatalism, submission, helplessness—run counter to the American virtues of self-reliance, energy, and initiative that Riis valued so much and tried to emulate. Also un-American is the Italian's failure with the English language. "Unlike the German, who begins learning English the day he lands as a matter of duty, or the Polish Jew, who takes it up as soon as he is able as an investment, the Italian learns slowly, if at all" (43). Encoded in this comparison are important racial/national distinctions that go beyond the ability or willingness to learn. Riis's comparison sets up a hierarchy of learning. The Italian is at the bottom; he lacks both the ability and the desire to learn English. The Polish Jew learns quickly because he sees the English language as a utilitarian business investment. Learning English will help him make more money, a worthy American pursuit, even if Riis's grasping Jew takes it to extremes. The German, who is most like Riis and most like the Anglo-Saxon American, not only has the most aptitude for the English language, but also the best, most American motivation. Riis implies that if the Polish Jew learns for commercial reasons, the German learns for civic reasons, out of a dutiful desire to make himself a better citizen of his new homeland. In this hierarchy, the Italian is far inferior to the northern European Teuton, but also below his fellow "new immigrant" Polish Jew.

Despite his shortcomings, Riis's docile and ignorant Italian "manages to turn the very dirt of the streets into a hoard of gold." In Italy, the Italian might turn beggary into "a fine art," but in New York he represents a much smaller percentage of the street beggars than does the native-born American, Irishman, or German, Riis says, citing statistics. On this score, the tenement "has no power to corrupt the Italian, who comes here in almost every instance to work" (194). In general, the Italian finds his gold in recycling the bones, rags, and tin cans of New York's ash-barrel. "Whenever the back of the sanitary police is turned, he will make his home in the filthy burrows where he works by day, sleeping and eating his meals under the dump, on the edge of slimy depths and amid surroundings full of unutterable horror." However, even this example of individual Italian initiative is tainted. Once an "independent 'dealer,'" the Italian rag-picker is now a simple laborer in a work gang controlled by the corrupt, rapacious *padrone* (44).

A "born gambler," the Italian is at his worst on the Sabbath, "when he settles down to a game of cards and lets loose all his bad passions," Riis writes. "His soul is in the game from the moment the cards are on the table, and very frequently his knife is in it too before the game is ended" (44). This is a curious characterization in that it equates bad passions with the Italian soul, both of which are directed toward gambling on the very day that should be devoted to matters of the spirit. These bad passions are given vent with a knife that the Italian keeps concealed on his body. Just as the Negro has his "razor in his boot-leg" and the Chinaman his "knife in his sleeve," so too the Italian has his "stiletto in the bosom" (119). Riis's Italian is not only violent, but also underhanded in the manner of the Negro and the Chinaman. Riis himself apparently had no argument with *unconcealed* weapons. Landing in New York, he had spent exactly half his capital on a "navy revolver of the largest size," strapped it on, and strode up Broadway, thinking he was "following the fashion of the country." When a police officer suggested the revolver was better left at home, Riis was relieved to be free of the heavy weapon.[28] Riis need not have worried about being attacked by an Italian, for the Italian's violence is directed at his own kind. Justice, too, is the Italian's alone, Riis says. The Italian crime victim will not cooperate with the police, but instead "wards off all inquiries with a wicked 'I fix him myself,' and there the matter rests until he either dies or recovers." If the victim recovers, the police will get news of another stabbing, a dead or dying man "fixed, and the account squared" (47). Only the Chinese, Riis says, are more adept at putting up obstacles to police investigations (82).

"With all his conspicuous faults," Riis concludes, "the swarthy Italian immigrant has his redeeming traits. He is as honest as he is hot-headed." He may have been a brigand in Italy, but generally "the ex-brigand toils peacefully with pickaxe and shovel on American ground." He might murder a countryman over a card game, but his worst offense is keeping the stale-beer dives that contribute to dissolution and vice. In short, the Italian is "gay, light-hearted and, if his fur is not stroked the wrong way, inoffensive as a child." The Italian women, meanwhile, "are faithful wives and devoted mothers" whose costumes "lend a tinge of color to the otherwise dull monotony of the slums they inhabit" (47). However, the Italian family ignores America's siren song of upward mobility and falls far short in the domestic sphere that was so important to Riis. Riis's "Teuton" is clearly the most likely to resist the tenements' leveling tendency by making a strong home. In contrast, Riis writes, "The Italian and the poor Jew rise only by compulsion" (22). Clearly, Riis appears to have little hope for the Italian as he is represented in the text of *How the Other Half Lives*. The Italian's faults and shortcomings are many, and his so-called virtues—his docility, manageability, lightheartedness, and tendency to keep his violence strictly intramural—are not the type of values that could contribute to American national character and American progress. The Italian's industry and his very ability to turn dirt into gold are made to seem pointless because they are not translated into the American dream of social mobility. The Italian cannot or will not rise above the slum tide because of his natural tendency to seek and cling to the lowest level. For Riis, only the Italian woman has untainted, unqualified virtues, and these, not surprisingly, are the decidedly middle-class American ideals of domestic devotion and faithfulness. However, nearly as important are the Italian woman's "vivid and picturesque costumes," the (local) color she adds to an otherwise drab scene.

As is evident, Riis covers a lot of ground in *How the Other Half Lives*, depicting an Italian type that was becoming more and more represented to Americans at the turn of the century. Riis both condemns and praises the *Italian* (more of the former than the latter), but how well does he understand *Italians*? To a great extent, Riis the reporter completely fails to see—or at least write about—the diversity of the Italian immigrants. Wanting to see only poverty, dirt, chaos, and oppression, he fails to note the varied responses of Italian immigrants to the rich variety of their immigrant experiences. The text of *How the Other Half Lives* may capture the lived reality of a segment of Italian immigrants, but there is little indication that Riis truly questioned that reality, much less imagined alternative realities for New York's Italians. Of course, scholars disagree about the nature of Italian immigration on many levels. However, scholarship clearly shows that Riis presented a terribly distorted picture. It is not my purpose here to address every distortion point by point. A few examples should suffice.

Riis would have his readers believe that Italians in New York were little more than illiterate peasants who worked at nothing but menial labor for short-term economic gain, giving little thought to the more long-term goal of assimilation and social mobility. As Michael La Sorte says, "The oversimplified portrait of the Italians fixed at the bottom, the Germans and Jews in the middle, and the native born at the top of the job prestige hierarchy needs to be refined."[29] Although many of the southern Italian immigrants were in fact illiterate peasants, among them were fishermen, artisans, and petty merchants. According to Donna Gabaccia, during the 1880s very few Sicilian peasants migrated to New York. Instead, 80 percent of the earliest Sicilian migrants to the city were artisans, of whom shoemakers, barbers, and woodworkers formed the largest groups. Others included butchers, metalworkers, seamstresses and tailors, and pasta makers. And although Italians did work as unskilled laborers and rag-pickers in New York in the 1880s, they also performed slightly more specialized tasks and were involved in selling fruit, macaroni, plaster figurines, candy, and artificial flowers.[30]

Riis's image of the Italian immigrant as a natural, contented slum dweller also needs qualification. Riis correctly identified tenement overcrowding as a problem caused by high rent, slack work, and low wages. However, as a material determinist like many early reformers, he may have exaggerated overcrowding to better show how the "tenement housing evil" destroyed America's "home ideal." Although reformers like Riis made a connection between poor housing and social pathology, the Italian tenement dwellers were not entirely socially disorganized, but instead "created neighborhoods and communities in ways that they—not middle-class reformers—deemed appropriate." Many of the unskilled urban workers did tend to congregate in crowded tenement neighborhoods. The large numbers of Sicilians on Elizabeth Street would have considered the tenement apartments small, but the density and the absence of light, windows, running water, and toilets would have been less shocking to them than to the reformers.[31] Although nuclear families predominated, families often crammed boarders into their apartments, creating less expensive domestic arrangements known as "partner households" or "malleable households." These emerged as a way to accommodate arriving young immigrants, generate income from the boarders, and satisfy the Italians' preference to be with kin and countrymen from the same village or province. The Italians clustered together for a number of reasons, and consequently were seen as clannish. Lacking mobility, urban Italians often lived, worked, shopped, and socialized in the same tenement neighborhood. "The street served as playground, market, information center, and as the entrance to stores, cafes, and other institutions."[32] Italian tenement dwellers may not have liked their dingy apartments, but the evidence is that they enjoyed the social life of their neighborhoods, while appreciating that the rents, although high, were lower than elsewhere in the city. Concerned with jobs and making ends meet, they had little reason to fret over any unachieved housing ideals, at least for the present. A sizable number of women, both mothers and daughters, were often called on to produce income either in a factory or by doing homework (making or washing clothes, and fabricating candy, tobacco products, and artificial flowers).[33] This left little time and energy for housekeeping, as Gabaccia shows. "Like wives in Sicily, immigrant wives worked hard to keep their floors clean, but they remained oblivious to other chores that American social workers believed essential. The scrubbed wood or oil-clothed Italian tenement house floor might stand in odd contrast to the unpainted and smoke-begrimed wall."[34]

The Italian's clannishness and his image of willing victim/slave of the Italian boss, or *padrone*, is both misunderstood and overblown by Riis. The Italian's perceived insularity is usually attributed to *campanilismo*, an attitude of fear and distrust of outsiders symbolized by anyone living beyond the sound of the village church bell or *campanile*. *Campanilismo*, an attitude bred by centuries of foreign domination, was one reason southern Italians in particular sought security in family- or village-based networks. In New York, the immigrants maintained these tight social and economic networks, but these alone were not protection enough in the large, fragmented, and chaotic city. As a consequence, these Italians looked beyond their immediate circles and expanded their networks to include people from other villages and regions of Italy.[35] Sometimes these Italians put their trust in a more powerful countryman to help manage their materials affairs. They looked to the *padrone*, as this figure is called, for employment, banking services, and a variety of other needs. Most of these so-called *padroni* provided legitimate, much needed services to newly arrived immigrants, but as might be expected there were abuses by some unscrupulous *padroni*.[36] For Riis and other reformers, however, the *padrone* was "an ahistoric personification of greed and primitive cruelty," and virtually every middle-class immigrant was tainted with the suspicion of being a *padrone*.[37] Riis's depiction of a rapacious *padrone* taking advantage of docile, gullible immigrants was even supported by Baron Fava, Italian ambassador to the United States, who blamed the *padrone* system on the proverbial simplicity of the southern Italian peasant.[38] However, reducing New York's Italian immigrant population to corrupt *padroni* and oppressed workers is to ignore that very often this symbiotic relationship worked to the benefit of all. Just as Riis exaggerated tenement overcrowding, so too did he exaggerate and distort the *padrone*–worker relationship for purposes related to his reform work. The mythical *padrone* offered an easy target, while the worker served as a victim in desperate need of saving.

For now, I will not inquire into Riis's characterization of the Italian as a money-grubbing slow learner who has no interest in education or social mobility. As we will see, Riis qualifies in his later writings some of the attitudes expressed in *How the Other Half Lives*. Additionally, I will take a closer look at these negative images in my chapter on the immigrant journalist Edward Steiner, who more than a decade later reprised some of the same stereotypes found in Riis's work.

Two years after *How the Other Half Lives*, Riis again took up the subject of the Italian. Riis was investigating a murder at an East River dump when he found a crew of Italian men and boys living there. After visiting other dumps and finding similar living conditions, Riis wrote a newspaper piece in March 1892, "Real Wharf Rats, Human Rodents that Live on Garbage under the Wharves," in which he portrayed Italian children surviving on the offal of society. These children are scarcely human, not simply animal-like but real (wharf) rats.[39] That year Riis also wrote a series of articles for *Scribner's* that were collected in *The Children of the Poor* (1892). Here again, the Italian is content at the bottom, trapped in the "worst old world rookeries" by their smarter countrymen."[40] However, where *How the Other Half Lives* speaks generally of the Italian, *The Children of the Poor* specifically indicts the southern Italian, a distinction that began to appear in the 1880s and would have increasing currency throughout the succeeding decades. And now the image is not so much of the Italian as naturally content with degradation and squalor, but of the Italian as the natural and willing victim of his own countrymen (a clear reference to the *pardoni*). Riis says he has noticed a degradation in the quality of the children. "Perhaps the exodus from Italy has worked farther south," he writes, "where there seems to be an unusual supply of mud" (10–13). The bulk of Italian immigration was in fact coming from the poorer, less literate South, and Americans were increasingly making sharper distinctions between northern and southern Italians, as Henry Cabot Lodge had done in a piece for *The North American Review* in January 1891. Lodge depicted northern and central Italians as generally industrious, trustworthy, strong, capable, and moral. The same qualities did not apply to the illiterate southern Italian emigrants who, Lodge said, came from a land of endemic brigandage.[41]

Despite the worsening degradation of the Italian immigrant children, Riis struggles to find cause for hope. Italian schoolchildren—that alarming "black-eyed brigade of 'guinnies,' as they were contemptuously dubbed"— were now finding a favored place in the schools because of their "sunny temper." These Italian students were in fact teaching the teachers that even crowded schoolrooms could marvelously expand to embrace the slum children. As a result, "every lesson of cleanliness, of order, and of English taught at the school is reflected into some wretched home, and rehearsed there as far as the limited opportunities will allow" (18–19). Riis here offers a holy trinity of Americanization: cleanliness, order, and the English language. Wash up, impose some order in your life, and learn English if you want to become an American, Riis seems to be saying. Education means not only learning the English language, but also the Anglo-Saxon Protestant virtues of cleanliness and order.

However, Riis's chapter, "The Italian Slum Children," ends not with sunny-tempered Italian schoolchildren learning to become Americans, but with Italian children as scavengers and future dagger-carriers perhaps incapable of assimilation. The young Italian wood-gatherers are like "crows scenting carrion." Their "odd old-mannish or old-womanish appearance, due more to their grotesque rags than to anything in the children themselves," betrays their Italian race (21). Yet, the sunny child of Italy is not easily discouraged by poverty or hard knocks. "His nick-name he pockets with a grin that has in it no thought of the dagger and the revenge that come to solace his after years," Riis writes, condemning the Italian child to a future as a typically violent, vengeful Italian (21). The chapter ends with Riis finding a group of youngsters picking bones and sorting rags along New York's waterfront at a time when they should have been at school. The boys tell Riis that they slept at their work site. "It was their home. They were children of the dump, literally. All of them except one were Italian" (27–28). Absent here are both the home and the school, perhaps the two most important institutions for Americanization, according to Riis. Absent too is the cleanliness and order that Riis valued so highly.

In November 1896, we encounter an altogether different Italian boy in a sketch that Riis wrote for *The Atlantic Monthly* and later included in his collection, *Out of Mulberry Street: Stories of Tenement Life in New York* (1898). All these stories depict sympathetic if stereotypical characters, but it is "Paolo's Awakening" that best combines Riis's powers of description with his moralistic optimism.[42] The story concerns an eight-year-old boy whose father drowns on his way to a *padrone*-controlled job at an island dump. Paolo now lives with his mother and uncle in a dark basement tenement, and spends most of his days helping his mother do piecework at home. For pleasure, Paolo rummages for scraps, chases rats at the city dump, and builds castles and other things from abandoned clay, mortar, or sand. A teacher notices Paolo's artistry and persuades his mother to enroll him in school. "Paolo's slavery was at an end," Riis writes. Rich and powerful patrons find better jobs for his mother and uncle, and the family moves into a better tenement. Paolo wins a medal for a bust of his gentle, patient peasant mother, and his teacher praises his faithful work and "the loyal manhood that ever is the soul and badge of true genius." Paolo's award includes a travel stipend that will allow him and his mother to return to "the sunlight of his native land." Would Paolo return to Italy to pursue his art studies in the manner of countless other nineteenth-century American artists? Or were he and his mother returning for good, as successful birds of passage? Riis does not say. The question quickly becomes moot because Paolo's dreams are short-lived: He is killed in a train crash on his way home from graduation. Riis, however, turns the tragedy into triumph: "Brighter skies than those of sunny Italy dawned upon him in the gloom and terror of the great crash," Riis writes. "Paolo was at home, waiting for his mother."[43]

The story, while obviously marked by sentimental moralizing, is interesting. Most telling is that although Paolo is cut down just as he seems to be entering into the American dream, Riis's (and the boy's) vision of heaven is favorably compared to the romantic sunny skies of Italy, not to the sunny skies of Paolo's emerging assimilation and Americanization. Also suggestive is the fact that the vehicle for Paolo's success (and assimilation and Americanization?) is art, specifically sculpture, which had long been associated with Italy. Not for Paolo some more masculine American pursuit, such as business. Better that Paolo is an inspired artist and not some bootblack picking himself up by his bootstraps. And yet Riis's tale hints at an alternative ideal of manhood based not on success in the competitive arena of business, but on loyalty to mother and family, which the teacher equates with "true genius." If there was anything Riis consistently liked about the

Italians, it was the mothers and their familial feelings. Riis seems to be saying that Italians may have the right stuff in the domestic sphere, but doubts remain about their aptitude for the public spheres of business and citizenship.

Finally, Riis offers an extended treatment of the Italian when he revisits the tenement districts in *The Battle with the Slum* (1902), published twelve years after *How the Other Half Lives*. Riis was now at the height of his powers. In 1901, his friend Theodore Roosevelt was elected the president; reform had broken Tammany's hold on New York; and Riis published his highly popular *The Making of an American*.[44] "During this time his religious faith, his adulation for Roosevelt, his optimism, and his nationalism became more dominant features of his personality," and his response to the Spanish-American War was to become an unabashed jingoist, biographer James B. Lane writes.[45] With *The Battle with the Slum*, Riis was ready to become a national evangelist for reform. But first he would reassess what had been accomplished in the slums of New York City. Riis saw "only cause for hope" that "the day of the boss and of the slum" was ending, the gap between rich and poor no longer widening, and Americans "certainly coming closer together."[46] He invests his hope not in the professional social scientist whose "infallible system" reduced people to "mere items" and classified and subclassified them until they were "as dried up as his theories" (431). Riis turned instead to the "world-old formula of human sympathy, of human touch" (439). As the title of the book's penultimate chapter says, Riis would "Reform by Human Touch," which was an extension of the bridge "built of human hearts" that he invoked at the end of *How the Other Half Lives*.

Riis's depiction of the Italian in *The Battle with the Slum* does appear to be somewhat more sympathetic than that of *How the Other Half Lives*. But still the Italian is portrayed as a problem to be addressed, an immigrant who sorely tested America's ability to embrace him, a crude lump of clay that needed shaping in the American mold. Riis's most extended treatment of the Italian comes in the chapter "Pietro and the Jew," a curious title that links a stereotypically named Italian to a nameless, generic Jew with no direct narrative thread. Arguing that the problem of the tenement is "to make homes for the people" (175), in essence equating home/family and nation, Riis turns his attention to the tenement tenants. Piling up statistics from a government "slum inquiry," Riis begins by sounding much like the arid, systematic social scientist of whom he says "that man I will fight till I die" (431). The Italians surveyed in the inquiry were from the south of Italy, "avowedly the worst of the Italian immigration," Riis says, later adding, "Of last year's intake 116,070 came from southern Italy, where they wash less, and also plot less against the peace of mankind, than they do in the north" (177).

Riis's reprise of the dirty, docile southern Italian in *The Battle with the Slum* ran directly counter to events in Sicily, where workers battled for social justice from 1888 to 1894, when the movement was brutally suppressed by the northern-run national government. At its peak, the *Fasci Siciliani* was a popular cooperative movement with a membership of about 350,000 Sicilian farmers and sulfur mine workers, most of whom naively believed the *Fasci* would bring about independence of Sicily and, ultimately, social justice to all workers. The failure of the movement was blamed on the machinations of northern Socialist leaders, friction between Socialist groups, the backwardness of the Sicilian workers, and the strength of the bourgeoisie. Many of the most militant *Fasci* fled the repression by joining the great wave of migration to America.[47] However, Riis makes no mention of the *Fasci Siciliani*. Instead, he quotes a news report about a peasant in Italy who received less than half a bushel of grain after having his crop threshed. There follows one of Riis's patented anecdotes about an Italian immigrant family being detained in New York because the father was too old to be allowed into the country. "Two young women and a boy of sixteen rose to their feet at once," Riis recalls. "'Are we not young enough to work for him?' they said. The boy showed his strong arms" (180–181). These anecdotes are certainly designed to elicit sympathy, and the latter one may illustrate Italian initiative and dignity. However, Riis's Italians remain objects of pity, with no hint that, in Sicily, some of these same immigrants may have been actively involved in a struggle for political rights and social and economic justice. It is interesting that of all the news reports coming out of Italy over the last few years, including reports about the Sicilian *Fasci* disturbing the "peace of mankind," Riis highlights the unfortunate peasant farmer who is squeezed at the mill. In his efforts to make the Italian immigrants tragic, if sympathetic victims in desperate need of America's political, social, and economic opportunities, Riis erases complementary (and more complimentary?) images of Italians actively struggling to secure those same opportunities at home. These latter images simply did not fit into Riis's depiction of Italians as docile victims in need of a champion such as Riis himself.

Clearly Riis saw himself as the champion of these victimized Italians. Having played on the sympathies of his jury of readers, Riis assumes the role of defense attorney for the Italians, whom he collectively dubs "Pietro." Riis concedes that the Italian immigrant is dirty, ignorant, and clannish, and that he promotes child labor, gambles and uses a knife (mostly on his own people), and buys fraudulent naturalization papers. However, there are mitigating circumstances, Riis says, now beginning to show some understanding of the social, economic, and political factors that had influenced the Italian immigration and helped shape the Italian immigrants themselves. Italian immigrant children more than likely attend school, Riis notes, and there are signs that the Italian is shelving the old vendetta in favor of American law and justice. If the Italian acted like a starved wolf and dealt in fraudulent citizenship papers, was it not because he fled oppression in Italy to make a new life in America? "He came here for a chance to live. Of politics, social ethics, he knows nothing. Government in his old home existed only for his oppression" (181–187). Riis places his greatest hope in the public school, where the immigrant children speak English, salute the American flag, and give their "heads and hearts to our country" (204). While holding out hope that the second generation of the new immigrants can be assimilated through the public school, Riis rules out the possibility that the first-generation immigrant will ever become an American the way that he did. And, despite the public school's miracle of transformation, problems persist with America's open-door policy. He cites as an example "a nest of Italian thugs who lived by blackmailing their countrymen" in the Mulberry Street area. All are notorious Neapolitan criminals "who had been charged with every conceivable crime, from burglary to kidnapping and 'maiming,' and some not to be conceived of by the American mind." When Riis recalls that, he wants to "shut the door quick" (204–205). Of course, Riis here is making reference to the image of a mysterious, bloodthirsty Black Hand Society that was becoming etched in the public imagination. Italians themselves had helped propagate that stereotype during the period following Italian unification, when northern Italians firmly fixed images of brigandage, the mafia and camorra, and corruption to southern Italians.[48] The true extent and nature of Italian crime in America are difficult to gauge. In their search for security, some Italian immigrants turned to those in their networks who resorted to the kind of thuggery, extortionism, and criminality that critics claimed were the province of the mafia and the camorra, as Donna Gabaccia writes. "From the migrants' perspective, there was no criminal conspiracy or Black Hand behind protection rackets—just a desire for order and security and a handful of isolated toughs willing to sell their services promising order in a multi-ethnic city."[49]

The Italian appears again in *The Battle with the Slum* in a nostalgic chapter, "The Passing of Cat Alley," in which the sentimental Riis mourns the disappearance of one of the hellhole alleys that he had fought to abolish. He remembers Cat Alley as "properly cosmopolitan," with every element but the native-born American. "The substratum was Irish, of volcanic proportions." Other layers included the German, Frenchman, Jew, and Italian, "or, as the alley would have put it, Dutch, Sabe, Sheeny, and Dago." To the "Dago" the alley "did not take kindly," Riis says. The Italian was seen as an outcast among outcasts whose overcrowding threatened to turn Cat Alley into another Mulberry Street (314). Riis concludes the chapter with an anecdote from the last days of Cat Alley. As the clearing of the alley proceeds, Riis watches a troop of Irish children scream with delight on a makeshift seesaw. "A ragged little girl from the despised 'Dago' colony watched them from the corner with hungry eyes." The largest of the Irish girls saw the

Italian and made room for her on the ride, explaining to the others that the girl's mother was stabbed the day before. "And the little Dago rode, and was made happy" (339–340). Besides expressing Riis's romantic optimism and his abiding sentimental faith in children and women, the anecdote serves to balance and comment on an earlier incident in which an Italian family had been evicted from Cat Alley for overcrowding, for creating one of those "partner" or "malleable" households to which Italians sometimes resorted. Here we have inclusion replacing exclusion, a bridge built on human hearts, reform by human touch. But what is being included is an alien "with hungry eyes" from "the despised 'Dago' colony," a girl who is seen as at least one step below the Irish girls. The Italian girl is invited to play not for who she is, but rather for what she represents. She is an object of pity, someone whose mother was stabbed the day before. And stabbed by whom? Riis does not say. Perhaps that detail is extraneous to his simple parable of charity, human kindness, even sisterhood. However, the few details we are given, when placed in the context of Riis's writings, point to a probable culprit: either her husband, a relative, or some other Italian. Riis's clues add up: The victim was an Italian, the Italian's favorite weapon—presumably a knife—was used, and Italians often attack their own in fits of passion. This anecdote is one that cuts two ways, as interesting for what it says as for what it implies. In its apparent plea for human brotherhood (or, in this case, sisterhood), for reform through human touch, it humanizes and privileges one slum group, the Irish (who not long ago occupied the Italians' lowly position), while objectifying the Italian girl as victim of—most likely—her own kind.

As we know, Riis's written descriptions of the Italians and other immigrant groups are not his last words on the subject. There are the photographs that appeared either as illustrations or halftone prints in newspapers and magazines. Additionally, Riis used photographic images in the lantern-slide lectures that he delivered to church and charitable groups and other middle-class audiences. It will be worthwhile to look at these images before trying to draw some conclusions concerning Riis's treatment of the Italian immigrants.

Today Riis is best known for his photographs, a still powerful collection that represents the only full photographic record of the so-called new immigration. During his life, however, he was best known as a writer and lecturer, and that was how he saw himself. When he died in 1914, his family gave his personally annotated papers to the Library of Congress. Yet Riis had not bothered to save his collection of photographs since it had little meaning for him apart from its role in his books and lectures.[50] In fact, Riis used all these modes of communication—written text, visual image, oral address—very effectively for diverse rhetorical strategies. For example, *How the Other Half Lives*, which began as a public lecture, had something for everyone, as the New York *Evening Sun* pointed out: statistics for the social scientists, suggestions for the charitable worker, and stories, anecdotes, photographs, and freehand sketches for those seeking primarily entertainment. The paper's reviewer inventoried the contents of the book "as if he were strolling through that archetypal nineteenth-century site of consumption, the department store."[51] *How the Other Half Lives* was the first American book to include snapshots of the slums. The publisher, Scribner's, decided to use the newly developed halftone process, which allowed the direct transfer of photographs to the metal printing plate. This new method was cheaper than hiring artists and engravers to transform the photographs into illustrations, as had been done for Riis's newspaper and magazine pieces. However, Scribner's also "might have wished to capture, rather than mask, the unique, disconcerting graphic qualities of the photographs."[52] In some measure it was the small grainy photos that helped make the book an instant success, as at least one reviewer noted. One reviewer spoke of the "horror" of the photographs, while another simply saw them as an aesthetic feature that made the book a collector's delight. Only the reviewer for the *Critic* made any serious attempt to deal with the images. This reviewer said of the photos: "There is a lack of broad and penetrating vision, a singularly warped sense of justice at times, and a roughness of vision amounting almost to brutality. The 'Heathen Chinee' and the Russian Jew fleeing from persecution in his own land finds no mercy in Mr. Riis's creed."[53] This surprisingly harsh reviewer is on target, but only half right. The photographs generally associated with Riis do lack a unifying theme and style. They are alternately rough and soft, brutal and sentimental, merciless and sympathetic. One thing we can say for sure: The photographs offered radically new ways to represent reality, altering and enlarging the public's idea of what is worth looking at and what it had a right to observe, making of the photographs "a grammar and, even more importantly, an ethics of seeing."[54]

Any study of Riis's photography is risky because Riis the photographer is even more problematic than Riis the writer. To begin with, the photographs present a number of textual challenges for the critic. Riis's collection of photographs essentially disappeared from the public consciousness after his death, not to be rediscovered until the 1940s. The rescuers were photographer and Riis biographer Alexander Alland, who like Riis was an immigrant interested in social reform, and Grace Mayer, then curator of prints for the Museum of the City of New York. They convinced the Riis family to donate to the museum 415 four-by-five-inch glass plate negatives, 326 lantern slides (positives on glass), and 191 vintage prints found in the attic of the Riis family's Long Island home. Alland took fifty of the best negatives and transformed them into quality prints by using modern photographic techniques such as enlarging, cropping, burning, and dodging. These prints were shown at the Museum of the City of New York in 1947, captured the attention of the photography world, and kindled interest in Riis. Alland offered to sell to the museum a complete set of 415 prints, but the museum could not afford it, and the prints were later sold to the New-York Historical Society. In the 1950s, the staff photographer for the Museum of the City of New York, John Harvey Heffren, made a set of copy negatives and copy prints from the original negatives. Both Alland and Heffren cropped and enhanced the negatives, in the process creating problems for researchers and scholars, as Bonnie Yochelson has pointed out. In some cases, the cropping eliminated photographers' signatures, wreaking havoc with attribution. Additionally, the Alland and Heffren prints are much different from Riis's yellowed contact prints on cardboard, as well as from the printed engravings and halftones made from them. Furthermore, the documentation for some of the photographs is still at best sketchy. In 1990, the Museum of the City of New York began replacing the Heffren prints with ones more faithful to the original negatives. "The 'new Riis' will look like a turn-of-the-century photographer, not a modern photo-journalist, and the arbitrary croppings of the past will be eliminated," according to Yochelson, the former curator of prints and photographs who supervised the project, which was completed in 1995.[55]

Riis himself began taking photographs in early 1888, and in the three years leading up to *How the Other Half Lives*, he supplemented his stock of collected photos with some of his own work. In *How the Other Half Lives*, Riis used the photographs of others to generally illustrate preconceived types/ideas such as "the newsboy" or "the sweatshop." However, while researching *The Children of the Poor*, he took some of his own photos while collecting anecdotes and gathering impressions, and more fully integrated those images into his second book. Many of the twenty-four new photographs in *The Children of the Poor* are of people Riis interviewed. Yet, with a couple of exceptions, Riis seems not to have picked up a camera after 1895, relying instead on municipal agencies and private charitable organizations for additional photos to use in articles and lantern-slide lectures. Yochelson argues that Riis exploited the photograph's power as evidence, but did not try to master the craft or to compose pictures with the camera, as did other pioneers such as Louis Hine and Dorothea Lange. "Riis's photographs are neither bits of unmediated reality nor aesthetic constructions," Yochelson writes. "They are the unintended legacy of a man who called himself a photographer 'after a fashion.' "[56]

Was this photographer "after a fashion" the pioneering documentarian that some modern critics have made him, or was he little more than an amateur hit-and-run shooter, as a revisionist essay by Sally Stein argues?[57] Riis does represent himself as a bumbling picture-taker, but this may be a sly attempt to present the photos as unrehearsed raw reality.[58] Riis clearly had some understanding of photography's powers, and sensed that, as a rhetorical tool, the camera might be mightier than the pen in his crusade. He was alert to the gloomy expressiveness he had achieved by underexposing his first pictures at Potter's Field.[59] Peter Hales argues that Riis manipulated and distorted the medium to shock and terrify his middle-class Victorian audience into a complete and active commitment to social justice and economic reform. Exaggerating the effects of flash, Riis's photographs made everything dirtier, more crowded, more chaotic; using "jagged-edge" framing, Riis packed the photo with people, objects, and visual details that threaten to burst from the frame and overwhelm the viewer.[60]

But it is obvious that Riis's photographs, like his lectures and writings, offered an element of armchair tourism/voyeurism to the audiences. Riis himself told an interviewer in 1888, "The beauty of looking into these places without actually being present there is that the excursionist is spared the vulgar sounds and odious scents and repulsive exhibitions attendant upon such a personal examination."[61] But, if Riis himself went slumming, he often did it in the company of health department officials or policemen. And so some critics see a subcurrent of surveillance and control in the Riis photographs, questioning whether they are any different from the type of photographic surveillance employed by Riis's good friends in the New York police department. Sally Stein argues too dogmatically that Riis's intrusive camera made it "a criminal offense to live in poverty," and that Riis rarely used photographs in which the subject was composed enough to return the photographer's glance.[62] In another twist, Keith Gandal argues that Riis challenges middle-class Protestant control with his pursuit of the exotic picturesque. As one of the first connoisseurs of urban filth, Riis is willing to overlook the dirt and congestion of the Italian streets for the sake of entertainment. "What is good for traditional morals and Americanization—cleanliness and privacy—is bad for sight-seeing. And what is bad for Protestant virtue—filth and crowds—is good for viewing pleasure."[63] In other words, Riis and other so-called Americans were attracted to the colorful, exotic Italians for the very qualities that were anti-Protestant, anti-Anglo-Saxon, and, by extension, anti-American. The Italians were the stuff of great spectacle, but that disqualified them for assimilation into American society.

In their zeal to categorize Riis the photographer, critics have overlooked the fact that the photographs reveal elements of the sympathetic social reformer, the urban tourist/voyeur, and the master of surveillance, all of whom are both attracted to and repelled by what is on the other side of the lens. As Susan Sontag says, photographs redefine reality "as an item for exhibition, as a record for scrutiny, as a target for surveillance."[64] The Riis photographs serve all those purposes. This heterogeneity of the Riis photographs is a reason for the "lack of broad and penetrating vision" cited in the *Critic*'s review of *How the Other Half Lives*. Some of the photographs associated with Riis are sympathetic portraits, while others are little more than police mug shots. Some of the human subjects are caught off-guard and frozen at a distance, but others are fully cognizant of the photographer and even appear to welcome him. Some of the photographs exaggerate the crowding and chaos, with subjects that threaten to burst through the "jagged-edge" and overwhelm the viewer; other photos are more spare and ordered, and draw the viewer into the frame.[65] Furthermore, these images appeared in a variety of formats and contexts, and sometimes carried different titles and captions. Ultimately, each photograph is unstable, resistant to efforts to secure meaning, and has "the plurality of meanings that every photograph carries." But if photographs cannot themselves explain anything, as Sontag says, they remain an "inexhaustible invitation to deduction, speculation, and fantasy."[66]

It is in that spirit that I want to look at some "Italian" photographs associated with Riis. Many of the Riis photographs touch on subjects and themes that Riis links to Italians, including the Mulberry Bend neighborhood, stale-beer dives, illegal lodging houses, and rag-pickers. Consequently, my examination of Riis's photographic images of Italians is far from exhaustive, but instead seeks to focus on a limited number of images that can provide some insights.

"A Vegetable Stand in the Mulberry Bend," the first image I want to touch on, apparently was taken by a photographer at the *Evening Sun* identified only as Collins, and never published.[67] It is interesting for several reasons. Unlike some of the dirty, dilapidated, and crowded street scenes in the Riis photos, this image of a modest, but relatively neat vegetable stand on a sunny day has a sense of order and cleanliness despite the prominent trash barrel on the sidewalk. The sidewalk vegetable stand is in front of a row of buildings, including a small post office and two Italian banks, which seem to speak of stability and permanence. Judging from the attractive signs, the banks do not appear to be a couple of those fly-by-night *padrone*-run "banks" described by Riis in *How the Other Half Lives*, the ones that "hang out their shingle as tempting bait" to the unwary greenhorn (52, 43). Just as all of Riis's Italian bankers are unscrupulous, so too are most of Riis's Italian immigrants typically rag-pickers and operators of stale-beer dives. Only in passing does *How the Other Half Lives* mention that the Italian scavenger "is fast graduating into exclusive control of the corner fruit-stands" (20), which is borne out by this photograph. "Vegetable Stand" also seems to counter Riis's revolting descriptions of Italian markets with their "frowsy weeds," "stale tomatoes," "oranges not above suspicion," "slimy, odd-looking" fish, "awkward sausages," and "decaying vegetables" (50). Ultimately, "Vegetable Stand" seems a typically touristic photograph that highlights the picturesque qualities of Italian immigrant life in New York City, while also sending a message

44   IMAGINING ITALIANS

Figure 1.1 *A Vegetable Stand in the Mulberry Bend*
Museum of the City of New York
The Jacob A. Riis Collection #265
90.13.1.270

Figure 1.2 *Feast of St. Rocco, Bandit's Roost, Mulberry Street*
Photograph, 1895.
Museum of the City of New York
The Jacob A. Riis Collection, #266

of workaday order. It is curious that Riis apparently never published this image with one of his articles, but apparently it did not fit into his rhetorical design.

If "A Vegetable Stand in the Mulberry Bend," absent its Italian signs, could be a photograph of any working-class district of New York, "Feast of St. Rocco, Bandit's Roost, Mulberry Street" clearly treats an Italian subject and draws us further into the world of the immigrant. Also taken by the photographer Collins, this image was published with Riis's article "Goodbye to the Bend," which appeared in the *Evening Sun* on May 25, 1895. The photograph funnels the viewer down a stone-paved alley to a makeshift shrine bathed in a shaft of sunlight in the background. The interior of the altar, which has what appears to be a depiction of Christ the King, is recessed in partial shadow, with a hint of mystery. Lining the alley, arranged to provide clear sight lines to the altar and even allow a passage through, are groups of people, most of them in shadow. A young boy stands in the foreground, looking toward the camera. All the people in the photograph seem to be fairly well dressed.

Compositionally, "Feast of St. Rocco" recalls "Bandit's Roost, 39½ Mulberry Street," which was used in the same *Evening Sun* article, and is one of the most famous Riis photographs. "Bandit's Roost," the work of Richard Hoe Lawrence or Henry G. Piffard working under the direction of Riis, was made with a two-lensed stereoscopic camera that produced a pair of images on one double-width negative. Unlike "Feast of St. Rocco," which draws the viewer in, inviting one to walk down the alley to the shrine, the better-known version of "Bandit's Roost," with its hint of menace, has the effect of either keeping the viewer out, or of tempting an imaginative approach with its fascinating promise of danger. In this version, two imposing men dominate the foreground, appearing to stand sentinel over the alley, which was notorious for its stale-beer dives and rough crowds. One man has a wary look in his eyes; the other holds what appears to be a beveled stick or double-barreled pipe. The second version of the photograph includes a group of women and children in the foreground to the left. Although somewhat blurred, this group softens the better-known photo's sense of menace. Riis used both versions in print and in lectures, and also had a hand-colored lantern-slide that gave the image a cheerful and picturesque feel.[68] "Feast of St. Rocco" and "Bandit's Roost" complement and contradict each other. The latter offers a motley array of characters that are both picturesque and menacing, attractive when colorful, but defensively staking their territory. "Feast of St. Rocco" features a decently dressed and fairly well-scrubbed homogenous group gathering for a saint's day, a bit of local color that Riis wrote about for *The Century* magazine.

In that *Century* article, "Feast Days in Little Italy" (August 1899), Riis praises the Italians' picturesque religious festivals because they symbolized hope, family, and a unified community—even if that community was fragmented by fierce ties to one's native village and the patron saint of that

Figure 1.3 *Bandit's Roost, 39½ Mulberry Street,* circa 1988.
Museum of the City of New York
The Jacob A. Riis Collection, #101

village. "To the Italian who came over the sea the saint remains the rallying-point in his civic and domestic life to the end of his days," Riis writes. "[T]he saint means home and kindred, neighborly friendship in a strange land, and the old communal ties, which, if anything, are tightened by distance and homesickness."[69] What Riis (and others) often criticized as Italian clannishness here is more sympathetically characterized as community. And now, Riis is alert to the positive communal element in the southern Italian's *campanilismo*. The immigrants might show extreme loyalty to their *paese* and a phobic distrust of outsiders, but there were reasons for this, and Riis, unlike many other commentators, was beginning to realize that. Riis underscores the festival's positive influence with an anecdote about his visit to the festival with Theodore Roosevelt, then president of the New York police board. An Italian immigrant tells Roosevelt that San Rocco is "just-a lik'-a your St. Patrick here," and Roosevelt nodded. "He understood" (493). Riis is also attracted to the feast days for the initiative they show. The immigrants used sheets, draperies, tinsel, and "their strange artistic genius" to transform the ugly tenements and streets (491, 493). Riis recalls that one of his few pleasing memories of the Bend was seeing Bandit's Roost lighted in honor of St. Rocco. "It made a very brave show, and, oddest of it all, not a displeasing one.... Perhaps it was the discovery of something in the ambitions of the Bend that was not hopelessly of the gutter that did it" (495). However, fealty to village and patron saint—*campanilismo*—also has its negative side, the bloodshed between rival villages. For this reason, Riis says, police detectives do not haphazardly search for "the man with the knife," but instead discover the man's village and then determine which village is that one's "pet enemy" (494). What Riis does not realize is that the Italian immigrants were beginning to overcome the most extreme form of *campanilismo*, and that the *festa* was one sign of this change. As Italian immigrants met and socialized with immigrants from other towns and regions, they began to form broader networks and started to think of themselves as Italians rather than as members of a particular family, town, or region. "The *festas* in the United States gradually transformed from events that expressed a village or particular identity into expressions of southern Italian national ethnicity."[70]

At the very least, the photograph of "Feast of St. Rocco" and the article about "Feast-Days in Little Italy" may be signs that some Protestant Americans were overcoming their fear and hatred of Catholicism. Much like the earlier Irish Catholic immigrants, the Italians were distrusted by native-born American Protestants who saw Catholics as superstitious idol-worshippers subservient to the awesome power of the Pope in Rome. Italian immigrants also suffered discrimination at the hands of established Irish-American Catholics. The Irish saw the Italians as sensual and violent, sinfully anticlerical, unsupportive of the parish, indifferent to official liturgy and doctrine, infected with pagan and folk beliefs, and concerned only with the superficial and showy aspects of the religion. Some Irish-dominated churches sat Italians in the back with blacks, while others completely rejected the Italians and denounced them as "dagoes." The *festa* was a favorite target of Irish Catholics.[71] However, "Feast of St. Rocco" and its accompanying article bring southern Italian Catholicism into the open air and partially out of the shadows. Here Riis depicts religion as not only a force for good, but religion as culture, religion as the source of a colorful communal event that can serve as entertainment for both the Italians themselves and the native-born American spectators.

"In the Home of an Italian Rag-Picker, Jersey Street" is another interesting image when looked at in the context of Riis's writings. Riis apparently took this photo in 1889, and it appeared as an illustration in *How the Other Half Lives*. The photo takes the viewer inside a tenement, where a woman sits cradling a swaddled baby. The overall effect of this photograph is much different from the cramped, ill-lighted, chaotic interiors often associated with Riis. However, appearances are deceiving. When Riis took this photograph in a windowless room, he could barely see his subject. What might be mistaken as natural light actually came from flash powder placed in a frying pan and lighted with a match at the time of exposure.[72] It is unclear what Riis had in mind for this image. Was it designed to capture the picturesque essence of Italian women, Riis's "faithful wives and devoted mothers" whose

Figure 1.4 *"In the Home of an Italian Rag-Picker, Jersey Street"*
Photograph, ca. 1890.
Museum of the City of New York
The Jacob A. Riis Collection #157
90.13.4.160

"vivid and picturesque costumes lend a tinge of color to the otherwise dull monotony of the slums they inhabit"? (*The Other Half*, 47). If so, Riis could have found colorful Italian women more easily at a *festa*. It is more likely that Riis here is trying to say something about the Italian home and the woman's role there. Although this particular room may have no windows, it lacks the clutter and disorder of many Riis interiors. Here most of the clutter is behind the woman, contained and ordered against the wall. Are the grimy sacks behind her filled with rags? We might presume so, but it is interesting that in the home of a rag-picker family not one rag is clearly visible. And if the room is not clean, for how could it be with its ingrained grime, it is still relatively tidy. The handy dust pan and the nearby scrap of litter indicate a never-ending battle against dirt, but it is a battle against which the Italian woman seems to be holding her own.

As we saw in *How the Other Half Lives*, Riis's attitudes toward Italian women were generally more positive than those he had toward the men. "In the Home of an Italian Rag-Picker" appears to follow that line. The dark-skinned woman, wearing a coarse soiled apron, appears to look older than her presumed years. Her eyes gaze upward, away from the camera. What is in her look? Fatigue, resignation, the vaunted Italian fatalism? Piety, devotion, dullness? Viewers will read what they want into the woman's look. Some critics see the photo as a secular "Madonna and Child" along the lines of the famous Renaissance versions. There is certainly some of that in the pose and in the tilt of the mother's face. Consequently the woman becomes a figure of great sympathy, even if it is a sentimental sympathy that pities without truly attempting to understand the reality behind the woman's need for pity. The photo's rhetorical work does not end there. The caption that was printed with the image in Riis's book, "In the Home of an Italian Rag-Picker, Jersey Street," focuses attention beyond the mother-and-child iconography to the idea of home. The woman might be the wife of a rag-picker, the quintessential Italian occupation for Riis, but her tenement is a home. Although work has invaded this home (something the middle-class Riis deplored), at least it has not taken over, but instead is contained. It might be argued that there are no visible signs of domesticity in the room beyond the woman and child and the straw hat hanging on the wall (a sign of the missing husband off collecting rags?). That, I think, is the point: It is the woman, her love and sacrifice for her child, and the order she has imposed on her space that make a tenement apartment a home and serve as a counterweight to the obvious poverty. The woman is one of the "faithful wives and devoted mothers" that Riis praises. It is this woman, and women like her, who will make the home a site of domestic order and a force for civilization. We are reminded that rather than exclude the Chinaman, Riis would force him to come with his wife to avoid his being "a homeless stranger among us" (*The Other Half*, 83). Riis here is making "the increasingly common suggestion that a family would lead to a *home*, an investment—literally and figuratively—in the nation, which would motivate the alien's Americanization."[73]

Ultimately, "In the Home of an Italian Rag-Picker" seems to express an undercurrent of optimism that was often a part of Riis's outlook. A bit of daylight is shining into the rag-picker's hovel, brought there by Riis's flash powder. There is a door in the picture, but it is in shadow and only leads to another tenement room. The real escape is up the ladder—the ladder of social mobility—on the other side of the room, the photograph seems to imply. It is only by rising above the slum that escape is truly possible. Will the Italian climb that ladder? Although the woman gazes upward, she is not looking at the ladder. In fact, she may be looking heavenward, thinking of escape into the afterlife, or even imagining a return trip to Italy. Much of the family's fate will depend on the husband, the rag-picker himself who is missing from the photo. The woman's devotion and domesticity have made her more than a rag-picker's wife. Now the man, through industry and social mobility, must make of himself something more than a rag-picker content with picking rags. This family's future remains unclear in light of Riis's remark that the Italian, unlike the German, rises only by compulsion. One thing is clear: To become an American is to leave the slum-like ghetto behind and to cultivate American middle-class virtues of domesticity, self-reliance, industry, initiative, and progress. For Riis, "the vitality of our Republic" depended on the preservation of the home: "[U]pon the home rests our moral character; our civic and political liberties are grounded there; virtue, manhood, citizenship grow there. We forget it to our peril," Riis writes. "For American citizenship in the long run, will be, *must be*, what the American home is."[74]

The Jersey Street rag-picker's home, which was photographed in 1889, stands in stark contrast to "An Italian Home Under a Dump," photographed by Riis three years later. That image appeared as a line engraving in the *Evening Sun* article "Real Wharf Rats" and later was republished in *The Children of the Poor*. This "home" at a dump on Rivington Street is no home in Riis's idealization of that institution. Here there is no woman, just a man bundled in rather tattered clothes inside a cramped, cluttered, and filthy makeshift shelter.[75] The man appears to be a willing subject posing for the photographer, not one of the startled victims of a Riis raiding party. However, the photograph underscores Riis's image of Italian immigrants as rag-pickers and "real wharf rats," people with little hope of assimilation and Americanization.

Riis pursues the home theme with two photographs he made of a young boy named Pietro working at a writing lesson in his Jersey Street apartment. In one version Pietro is sitting with his father; in the other the boy is with what appear to be his mother and little sister. I am interested in

Figure 1.5 *Pietro Learning to Write, Jersey Street,* ca. 1890.
Museum of the City of New York
The Jacob A. Riis Collection, #160
90.13.3.24

the first image, "Pietro Learning to Write, Jersey Street," which appeared as an illustration in *The Children of the Poor* with the caption, "Pietro Learning to Make an Englis' Letter." In one sense this photograph can be seen as a companion piece to "In the Home of an Italian Rag-Picker, Jersey Street," completing and extending Riis's image of the nuclear Italian family. The illustration that appears in the 1892 edition of *The Children of the Poor* alters the original image a great deal. The setting is no longer "the wretched room . . . in one of the vile old barracks" that Riis describes in the book. Instead Pietro and his father are sitting in front of a large window with a view of grass and trees. The rather idealized illustration is in line with Riis's accompanying narrative, which, despite the sadness of the boy's case, has an undercurrent of optimism. Yes, Pietro was crippled right after he found a steady job as a bootblack in a saloon. Running across Broadway, "full of joyous anticipation of his new dignity in an independent job," he did not see the streetcar until it was too late. Pietro's shoe-shining career prematurely ended, the boy is now "bending all his energies," Riis says, "toward learning to make the 'Englis' letter' with a degree of proficiency that would justify the hope of his doing something somewhere at sometime to make up for what he had lost." But, Riis concludes: "It was a far-off possibility yet" (31–33). The possibility is that young Pietro is learning to use the language of America as a necessary first step toward escaping the poverty of tenement life and assimilating into American society. However, if we turn to Riis's original photograph, it is clear that Pietro is having a hard time of it. The hands that hold the pencil and rest on a notebook are now more clearly deformed. The crumbled papers at his feet might signify false starts and missteps. He is not actually writing, but instead sits at the edge of his chair, tensed, hunched over his notebook. His set, downturned mouth and scrunched-up chin speak of hard work, a difficult task.

Will Pietro learn to write English? Is Pietro capable of becoming an American? These are the questions that the photograph poses. And what of the father? Although he appears fatigued, his posture and the notebook under his hand would indicate that he is not simply taking his rest at the table after a hard day of picking rags or digging ditches. His look is detached and dull, with little sign that he is engaging with his son. If the son is learning to write English, then his father most likely has nothing to teach him since it is unlikely that the father speaks much English, or much less writes in that foreign language. The father may even be incapable of writing his native tongue. In fact, Riis recounts that Pietro also was "taking nightly writing-lessons in his mother-tongue from one of the perambulating school-masters who circulate in the Italian colony, peddling education cheap in lots to suit" (33). There is the possibility that the father is actively learning to write English, but would he have the time, energy, or inclination, given Riis's contention that the Italian "learns slowly, if at all"? Riis's anecdote makes no mention of the father other than to say he is a laborer and heads a family of six on "an unsteady maximum income of $9 a week, the rent taking always the earnings of one week in four" (31). The photograph seems to be saying that young Pietro alone may rise out of poverty to become an American, and that he will do it through schooling. Pietro's father, rooted in Old World customs, habits, and backwardness, will never complete the entire journey that his son may make.

However, Riis himself undercuts this guardedly optimistic reading with a brief reference to the photo, now labeled "Pietro and His Father," in *The Peril and the Preservation of the Home*. Here, Riis obscures the meaning of the photograph by ostensibly shedding light on it. Riis says that "not even the slum can wipe out in me the memory of little Pietro, who sat writing and writing with his maimed hand, trying to learn the letters of the alphabet and how to put them together in words, so that he might be the link of communication between his people and the old home in Italy." Now, the focus is not on Pietro learning to write English as a means of becoming an American, but instead on the boy learning to write Italian to help preserve the family's ties to Italy. "Pietro and his father may be ignorant, may be Italians," Riis writes, "but they are here by our permission, dead set on becoming American citizens, and tremendously impressed with the privileges of citizenship." What Riis does not say—but perhaps implies—is that while Pietro and his father may be impressed with the privileges of citizenship that come with "permission" to be in America, they are not nearly as impressed with citizenship's responsibilities. Otherwise Pietro would be learning to write English. Still, Riis concludes his anecdote with a plea for sympathy for Pietro, just as he had done in *The Children of the Poor*. "He was a poor little maimed boy with a sober face, and it wrings my heart now, the recollection of the look he gave me when I plumped out: 'Pietro, do you ever laugh?' 'I did wonst,' he said."[76]

Two other photos can be seen as extensions of the Pietro images. The first, "The Mott Street Boys 'Keep Off the Grass'" (sometimes called "Boys from the Italian Quarter with a 'Keep Off the Grass' Sign"), was most likely taken by Riis, but apparently not published in any text. However, it connects to an anecdote in *How the Other Half Lives*. Riis leads up to his little tale by

Figure 1.6 *The Mott Street Boys "Keep Off the Grass,"* ca. 1890.
Museum of the City of New York
The Jacob A. Riis Collection, #125
90.13.1.128

arguing that the slum, with no true home or home life, turns children into "rough young savages" who have no decent place to play. Then he recalls an incident in an Italian neighborhood. "I came upon a couple of youngsters in a Mulberry Street yard a while ago that were chalking on the fence their first lesson in 'writin'.' And this is what they wrote: 'Keeb of te Grass.' They had it by heart, for there was not, I verily believe, a green sod within a quarter of a mile" (139–140). The photograph shows two small look-alike boys that have the appearance of men–children, with faces both cherubic and old. They are in a dirt field in front of a wooden wall. One boy leans casually, almost swaggeringly, against a ladder, holding what appears to be the same sort of beveled double-barreled stick or pipe held by the rough, bearded man in "Bandit's Roost." The other boy holds a wooden stave between his legs. Both boys have rather blank facial expressions, with their eyes shadowed. Clearly visible on the wall are large block letters, presumably half of a message reading, "PLEASE KEEP OFF THE GRASS." Who wrote that sign? Obviously not the boys. The lettering is too accomplished and it appears to be in paint, not chalk. On the evidence of Riis's anecdote, we know the boys are not great spellers. Granted that this is identified as their first lesson in "writin'," but, contrary to what Riis says, they did not have the message—at least the spelling—"by heart." Indeed, the message is right there on the wall, in large capital letters, apparently spelled correctly. Without Riis's anecdote, we would not even know that the boys are spellers, good or bad. They do not hold any chalk, and their own writing—if in fact they are the writers mentioned in the anecdote—is nowhere to be seen. Rather than being photographed in the act of writing in which they were caught by Riis, the boys are posing, looking idle and slightly rough, holding sticks rather than chalk. While Pietro is learning to write at his Jersey Street home, these two Mulberry Street boys are getting their first "writin'" lesson out in the slum by supposedly copying a sign that may essentially tell their future: "Keep off the grass." Stay in your place. Keep to the margins. The two boys do not appear to be of school age, although they could well be. Will these boys learn to write as Pietro is learning? And will that education, and some grass to play on, put them on a level with the children of the better half? Or will both boys grow up to become the two tough-looking characters in the foreground of "Bandit's Roost"? These questions are raised, but never resolved by the photograph and the accompanying text, which both complement and contradict each other.

If Riis's Italian boys raise more questions than they answer, the three young girls in another photograph represent a less equivocal expression of Riis's faith that education would assimilate and Americanize the immigrant children. "First Board of Election in the Beach Street Industrial School," which appeared in *The Children of the Poor*, relates to an Americanization ritual in the New York public schools. Immigrant students were offered the chance to vote for or against a morning salute to the American flag, and instructed to discuss the issue with their parents. Each school then chose a "board of election" to supervise the vote and report the results to the principal. Riis witnessed the election at the Beach Street Industrial School, where nearly all the students were Italian. The student body chose three representatives for the board, one Italian, one Irish, and one African American. The latter two girls "did not seem in the least abashed by the fact that they were nearly the only representatives of their people in the school." Although the board exhibited a certain dignity, there was also humor in the exercise, Riis recalls. "It was clear that the negress was most impressed with the solemnity of the occasion, and the Irish girl with its practical possibilities. The Italian's disposition to grin and frolic, even in her new and solemn character, betrayed the ease with which she would, were it real politics, become the game of her Celtic colleague." After an overwhelming vote in favor of saluting the flag, the girls sang a sweet rendition of the popular Neapolitan ballad "Santa Lucia" (204–208). Riis's photo is a multicultural portrait of the three board members, freshly scrubbed and posed outside what is presumably the school. Despite Riis's verbal depiction of the Italian girl as rather frivolous, and aside from the pessimistic allusion to the Italian serving as the Irishman's political "game," the anecdote and photograph form one of Riis's most optimistic images. Of course, the subject is children and females, two groups for whom Riis reserved much of his sympathy and hope.

What, finally, are we to make of these varied images of Italians in Riis's writings and photographs? As we have seen, Riis the reporter leaves something to be desired. On occasion his depictions of the Italian immigrants and the lives they lived in America are roughly accurate, in accordance with the subsequent scholarship. Too often, however, Riis either distorts or fails to see the complexity of the Italian immigrants' lived reality. And too often many of Riis's representations do not rise above the level of stereotype, images that may have an element of the truth but are primarily a simplistic shorthand for reducing complex groups and beings to a few, often negative characteristics. However, what is interesting about Riis's writings about Italians is not so much what they tell us about the immigrants themselves, but rather the insight they may give into Riis the reformer, and the powerful segment of American society that he represented. How did Riis the liberal progressive see the Italians and their lives as immigrants, what does that say about their ability to become assimilated Americans, and what does that in turn tell us about American attitudes toward immigration, race, and American national identity as those ideas were being explored and contested around the turn of the century?

It is clear that Riis is attracted to the Italians, but it is just as clear that as a progressive social reformer he had some deeply divided attitudes toward them. Like so many other Americans, particularly those who went to Italy in the nineteenth century, he is drawn to the Italian's picturesque color and "otherness." Mass immigration now had made that colorful "otherness" readily available in the nearby tenements. Old World picturesque poverty and other exotica no longer required a trip to Europe but could be found only a few blocks away. Even as industrialization, centralization, and homogenization seemed to be destroying America's distinctive regional color, foreign local color was appearing in the American cities in the form of immigrant neighborhoods and immigrant life. The downside to the immigrant tenements was that, for all the reconceptualization and confinement provided by photography, the touristic approach, and Riis's generalizations and anecdotes, the foreigners were spilling out of their aesthetic frames, stretching the slums, and threatening the very fiber of American society. Or so it seemed. The immigrants were too numerous to remain a simple spectacle, which has a beginning and an end, and implies some control. The rising tide of immigration seemed endless, a movement that had taken on a life of its own. The middle classes could, like Riis, show these immigrants sympathy or suspicion, intimacy or estrangement, acceptance or rejection. They could turn the immigrants into pictures and tourist attractions. They could divide, schematize, tabulate, index, characterize, and otherwise record the immigrants. Ultimately, however, Riis and other Americans had to deal with the Italian immigrants and their perceived differences on more practical levels. At some point, the immigrants' perceived differences (including those that made Italians a fit subject for spectacle, tourism, and "otherness") would have to be rejected, condoned, or embraced by native-born Americans.

There is little doubt that Riis had a genuine sympathy for the Italians and other immigrants and saw them as part of a universal brotherhood despite all their perceived faults. Like many of his contemporaries Riis saw striking racial differences among the various groups, and yet he seemed to believe in a unified human race. It is interesting that Riis framed the text of *How the Other Half Lives* with verses from James Russell Lowell's poem, "A Parable." This parable, Riis says, furnished "the text from which I preached my sermon" and tells "in a few lines all I tried to tell on three hundred pages."[77] Lowell and Riis were both moral and political crusaders who for all their enlightened and humanistic ideas entertained deeply divided notions on racial matters.[78] Lowell's own attitudes toward Italy and Italians were representative of his social and artistic class, which saw Italy as both a sort of American soul mate and a seductive siren with her "fatal fascination." Lowell confesses he grew up with the idea that all Italians were either monks "who drink your health in poison" or bravos who profited by "digging your person all over with a stiletto." His attitudes toward contemporary Italians, formed during several trips to Italy, are a mixture of praise and condemnation similar to that of other American artists and writers.[79] Lowell's "A Parable," written prior to the Civil War, tells of Christ returning to Earth to find that the rich and powerful have built their churches, palaces, and judgment halls on the "living foundation" of the weak, oppressed, and poor. Riis uses four of the poem's five concluding stanzas to introduce *How the Other Half Lives*. In these verses, Christ condemns the oppression and points to a "haggard man" and a "motherless child" as the true images that the oppressors have made of Him. The coda for Riis's book is a question Christ asks of his rich and powerful hosts: "And think ye that building shall endure,/Which shelters the noble and crushes the poor?"

While "A Parable" can be read as an anti-slavery poem, its broader theme of oppression of the poor and weak is an appropriate text for Riis's sermon. The message can be seen to privilege American society at the expense of Old World corruption, while also serving as a warning to that very American society. In this reading, the thrones and altars built on "the bodies and souls of living men" could refer to the monarchies, aristocracies, and Catholic Church of southern and eastern Europe. The "low-browed, stunted, haggard" artisan and the "motherless girl" might be poor Italian or Jewish immigrants from whom middle- and upper-class Americans draw back their garment-hem for "fear of defilement." The poor and powerless are different because the wealthy and powerful have made them oppressed sheep rather than symbols of human brotherhood, of Christ's human flock. Christ—and presumably Riis—cast their lot with the poor. The poor may look and act different, but they too are made in the image of Christ and are part of the universal brotherhood, worthy of Christian love and compassion. Although Riis has a much more secular outlook than we will see in the ordained minister/journalist Edward Steiner, there is a strong undercurrent of the Protestant social gospel in him, and we see that here. Riis concludes *How the Other Half Lives* with talk of erasing the dangerous gap between the classes and races by building a bridge "founded upon justice and built of human hearts" (229). It is a theme that he states even more forcefully in *The Battle with the Slum*, in which he expounds on his ideal of "reform by human touch." Riis argues that the poor and oppressed must be elevated, but whether—and how—the poor, oppressed immigrants can or must be made Americans he leaves unclear in *How the Other Half Lives*. The new immigrants might be made in the image of Christ. They might ultimately be brothers with native-born Americans. And as members of the universal brotherhood, they can be objects of sympathy and pity. However, were "poor and oppressed" immigrants compatible with American society and American character? Here Riis seems to waver. For Riis, it is not entirely clear that membership in the human brotherhood qualifies someone for membership in America's citizenry.

Critics have traditionally seen Riis as wanting to turn immigrants into middle-class Americans following his own model. Because he had more in common with the better classes than with the "other half," Riis measured immigrant societies in part on how well they adopted American habits and values.[80] He criticized the clannishness of Italians and other immigrant groups as a detrimental cohesiveness that made Americanization incomplete. And he ultimately sought a "bleaching of style," an Americanization that "should whiten an informing, particularist past when it contrasted too strongly with the color of what he believed to be the national culture."[81] However, James B. Lane makes of Riis somewhat of a cultural pluralist, arguing that Riis praised diversity and Americanization equally. This Riis wanted the schools to teach about foreign heroes such as the Italian Garibaldi and Hungarian Kossuth. This Riis was a member of the Society for the Protection of Italian Immigrants, which provided legal aid, publicized employment opportunities, and furnished loans to the needy. This Riis "asked his audiences to accept hyphenated Americans as brothers and to work to create conditions that would cause them to be loyal citizens." But Lane elsewhere qualifies his argument nearly to the point of negation: Riis's zeal for Americanizing the immigrants "perhaps blind him into too great a desire for cultural homogeneity," and his "class and race snobbery" and condescension toward "this queer conglomerate mass" of aliens is never totally suppressed. "While not unsympathetic toward immigrants, *How the Other Half Lives* contained racial slurs which others could use to support nativist shibboleths and restrictionist legislation."[82] In fact, Riis supported some immigration restrictions, including the 1882 law barring paupers, criminals and the insane, and the 1885 legislation banning importation of contract labor, which was an attempt to destroy the power of the *padrone*. However, Riis opposed other measures, including Henry Cabot Lodge's attempt to impose literacy requirements in 1900 and 1902, which were clear efforts to keep out southern and eastern European immigrants.

Although Riis increasingly spoke of Americanization as an effort to neutralize the immigrants' undesirable folkways, competing allegiances, and radical politics, he himself maintained dual loyalties to Denmark and the United States after becoming an American citizen in 1885. The two national flags he is said to have kept symbolize this division. And yet *The Making of an American* comes to a dramatic climax when Riis, lying sick off the coast of Denmark during a visit to his native land, sees a ship flying the American flag. This "flag of freedom, blown out of the breeze till every star in it shone bright and clear," inspires in him an overwhelming realization that he was first and foremost a loyal American. It is then that this American—and other true Americans?—is truly made. "I knew then that it was my flag; that my children's home was mine, indeed; that I had become an

American in truth" (443). It is interesting that the first-generation Riis could become just as much an American as his children, unlike the first generation of Italians for whom he held out little hope. For Riis, becoming/being an American meant not only adopting Anglo-Saxon middle-class values and habits, but also becoming a citizen and professing loyalty to the American flag and the ideals it represented.

Ultimately, neither generalities nor labels can synthesize Riis's contradictory responses to the immigrant, for he expressed elements of the country's own varied reaction. In his treatment of the new immigrants, Riis alternately affirmed middle-class privilege, played on middle-class fears, and titillated middle-class desires. In Riis we see attraction and repulsion, praise for the good and condemnation for the bad, and both optimism and pessimism for the prospects of assimilation.

As Lewis Fried argues, Riis's "fascination with New York's immigrants and their often ambivalent response to Americanization became a way of defining his own acculturation and lent itself to American nativism."[83] Riis's engagement with the Italian and other immigrant poor was a way to define himself not only as an American, but also as a particular type of American, solidly middle class and upwardly mobile. "Riis was a reformer for many reasons: moral crusades assuaged his sense of outrage at injustice, meshed well with his vocation, and brought upward mobility and prestigious status and palatable by-products."[84] In many ways, Riis longed for status and recognition more than wealth. He was able to achieve that prestige by simultaneously engaging with and disengaging himself from the new immigrants. Curiously, Riis rarely credits fellow immigrants in his autobiography. Why? Did he purposely avoid friendships with other foreigners or was he still denying any associations that separated him from the native-born American population by linking him to the new foreigners? "Either way," as Sally Stein says, "it says a great deal about the price paid in the making of an American."[85] In his preface to *How the Other Half Lives*, Riis personally thanks the president of the New York City Board of Health, the city's registrar of vital statistics, the chief inspector of the police force, and his wife. There is no mention of the people he wrote about and photographed—those very people who willingly or unwillingly served as the living foundation for Riis's fame and upward mobility. Riis further solidifies his position in *The Battle with the Slum*, which has a dignified portrait of Theodore Roosevelt on the frontispiece and portraits of a who's who of progressive reformers sprinkled throughout the text. In writing and lecturing about and photographing the poor immigrant, Riis was able to enter the ranks of the privileged middle class, while at the same time providing that class with a combination of reassurance, titillation, and challenge. But having entered the ranks of middle-class America through a combination of pluck, initiative, virility, and domestic order, Riis defines his identity and what it means to be an American in opposition to his representations of the Italians and other new immigrant groups. Riis can sympathize with these immigrants, include them in the international brotherhood, and be attracted to their color and other pleasing/enticing qualities, but ultimately that is not enough for Riis to welcome the immigrants into the American civic, social, and cultural family. The immigrant's faults, whether inherited or produced by environment, as well as some of the immigrant's more attractive qualities, are barriers. However, Riis maintains a grudging optimism that, at the very least, the Italians and other European immigrant groups can in time overcome those barriers, become less different, more like him, more like his image of what an American is.

Chapter 2

EDWARD STEINER: ALL IS (NOT) RACE?

The Italian is very fertile in inventing excuses for the purpose of evading the law, and his ethical standard in that direction is extremely low.

—Edward Steiner, *On the Trail of the Immigrant*, 1906

The Italians were from the South of Italy and had lost the romance of their native land but not the fragrance of the garlic.

—Edward Steiner, *On the Trail of the Immigrant*, 1906

At about the same time that Jacob Riis was becoming an elder statesman in the urban reform movement and Henry James was probing the immigrants' coloring of the American scene, a lesser known academic/journalist was spending vacations trailing and documenting European migrants to and from the New World. Edward Steiner's research took him through Ellis Island, where James was chilled to the soul. Steiner reported some of his experiences in *The Outlook*, and then published his *On the Trail of the Immigrant* in 1906, one year before the first American edition of James's *The American Scene*. Steiner's book details the immigrant's story from his arrival in America ("At the Gate") through his immersion in New York's ethnic ghettos ("On the Day of Atonement") to his acculturation into American life ("In an Evening School, New York"). Steiner deals exclusively with the Slav, the Jew, the Italian, and, to a lesser extent, the Greek and the

Hungarian, all of whom he classifies under the rubrics the "new immigrant" and the "new American." Steiner examines these various immigrant groups both in their native lands and in America. The chapters on the Italians are specifically titled "The Italian at Home" and "The Italian in America," as if those designations represented two entirely different categories of being. Like James and Riis and many other Americans, Steiner sees the Italian in Italy as one thing, but that same Italian in America as something quite different. Steiner's conceptions of the Italian at home and abroad are a jumble of lingering romantic notions about Italy in conflict with prevailing racial discourses and less attractive ideas about Italian character, many of which echo Riis. The Italians of *On the Trail of the Immigrant* come across as a confusing, conflicted, contradictory lot, who reflect the confused, conflicted, contradictory—if deeply sympathetic—thinking of social liberals/progressives such as Edward Steiner and a section of the American population. Steiner, in his efforts to deconstruct the prevailing racial (and often racist) discourse, very often gets caught up in that very discourse of racial differences that Riis had only begun to explore. There is no doubt that Steiner was a committed proponent of the Social Gospel who wrote and worked tirelessly on behalf of the new immigrants, and yet we see him engaging in some of the same language of racial distinctions employed by those he sought to critique.

Whereas Riis dealt with immigrants as part of the larger problem of urban poverty, as members of an "other half" that also included blacks and some native-born whites, Steiner focuses on immigrants as immigrants. In his chapter, "The New American and the New Problem," Steiner makes clear what was less forcefully articulated by Riis: By the turn of the century immigrants from southern and eastern Europe were definitely being seen as a different order of being. And these new immigrants were thought to be testing American ideas about assimilation in ways different from previous immigrant groups, including the supposedly intractable Irish. "The miracle of assimilation wrought upon the older type of immigration, gives to many of us, at least the hope, that the Slavs, Jews, Italians, Hungarians and Greeks will blend into our life as easily as did the Germans, the Scandinavians and the Irish," Steiner writes, glossing over the difficult experience of the Irish and their efforts to make themselves "white" in the mid-1800s. "The new immigrant, or the new American, as I call him, is however in many respects, more of an alien than that older class which was related to the native stock by race, speech, or religious ties."[1]

This notion of the "new immigrant" was firmly entrenched in the American mind by the turn of the century, having developed during what John Higham calls "the Nationalist Nineties." During this decade, some Americans began targeting "the new immigration as a unique entity, constituting in its difference from other foreign groups the essence of the nation's peril." This idea that Slavs, Jews, and Italians constituted a collective type of "new immigration" dawned early in the 1890s and was linked to powerful traditional ideas about a loosely defined Anglo-Saxonism. "The old idea that America belongs to the Anglo-Saxon race would define the special danger of the new immigration if one assumed that northern Europeans were at least first cousins to the Anglo-Saxon."[2] That assumption was easily accomplished in the fluid, fermenting debates over racial differences and racial similarities that marked the period. Writers and thinkers in Britain and America had long speculated about the racial/cultural genealogy of the Anglo-Saxon race. For generations, race thinkers had traced Anglo-Saxon ancestry back to the forests of Germany and beyond to the Caucasus mountains of western Asia. The idea that Anglo-Saxons were a vigorous branch of the sturdy Germanic tree was already current in the seventeenth century, and was transplanted to the American colonies. "Both directly from Germany and by transmission through England, the Americans were inspired to link their Anglo-Saxon past to its more Teutonic or Aryan roots." In their genealogical gymnastics, some writers brought Normans, Nordics, and Celts into the Anglo-Saxon's extended family. But it was the Anglo-Saxons who were seen as "the elite of an elite" that traced its roots back through a common Germanic and Indo-European (Caucasian) heritage. These doctrines of Caucasian/Aryan/Anglo-Saxon superiority and special destiny were already flourishing at the time of the Mexican War. By 1850, American expansion was being seen less as a victory of democratic republicanism and more as evidence of the innate superiority of American Anglo-Saxons.[3] Toward the end of the century, Anglo-Saxon exclusion of the Negro, the Indian, the Mexican, and the Oriental would be extended to the new non-Anglo-Saxon/Germanic/Nordic immigrants. "When sentiments analogous to those already discharged against Negroes, Indians, and the Orientals spilled over into anti-European channels, a force of tremendous intensity entered the stream of American nativism."[4] As Roediger and others have shown, the fragmentation of the white race had begun earlier in the century, when the Irish immigrants were characterized as less-than-white or not quite white enough. Native-born Americans often described Irish immigrants as low-browed, bestial, simian, lazy, and sensual, the same terms applied to blacks.[5] This fragmentation of whiteness accelerated later in the century with the arrival of the so-called new immigrants. "This increasing fragmentation and hierarchical ordering of distinct white *races* (now in the plural) was theorized in the rarified discourses of science, but it was also reflected in literature, visual arts, caricature, political oratory, penny journalism, and myriad other venues of popular culture."[6]

If American race nativism had its roots in Britain, as Higham and Horsman have pointed out, there was also another strain of racialism/racism in Italy itself from which American nativists could draw. In fact, American race nativism, whether consciously or unconsciously, borrowed northern Italian stereotypes of southern Italians as ignorant, lawless, and primitive, and used them against Italian immigrants in general. Eventually, those stereotypes would be directed specifically at southern Italian immigrants. Around the turn of the century, the Italians often found themselves in a very ambiguous position between people of color (Negroes, Indians, and Orientals) and America's fully white European cousins (British, Germans, Scandinavians, and the now whitened Irish). If the southern Italians were considered European, then they constituted a branch so far removed from the Anglo family tree as to make the connection virtually meaningless. Often, the southern Italian would be seen as less than white, with something of the Oriental or black about him. Like the Irish before him, he would have to prove himself white. As Roediger says, "The sad drama of immigrants embracing whiteness while facing the threat of being victimized as nonwhite would have many sequels after the Irish experience."[7]

Just about the time that Steiner was researching and writing *On the Trail of the Immigrant*, a resurgent nativism had established itself. If it did not have the hysterical intensity of the 1890s, it was still rooted in the distinction between the old and the new immigration. "Among the score or more of nationalities funneling through Ellis Island, only Italians and Jews were commonly distinguishable in American eyes from the nameless masses who accompanied them, and the Italians and Jews continued to suffer the most resentment. The Italian still bore as vividly as ever the stigma of impassioned crime." Even during the ebbing of nativism at the beginning of the twentieth century, metropolitan newspapers "trumpeted the tale of Italian blood lust incessantly," and by 1909, "the image of a mysterious Black Hand Society, extending from Italy into every large American city, was fixed in the public imagination."[8] That image was not an original one, having been hung on southern Italians by their northern brethren in the period following Italian national unification in 1871. Alfredo Niceforo's *L'Italia barbara contemporanea* (*Contemporary Barbarian Italy*), published in Italy in 1898, had firmly linked images of the mafia and the camorra, brigandage, and corruption to southern Italians.[9] As will be seen, Edward Steiner's depictions of the Italians and other new immigrant groups clearly express some of the crosscurrents, hopes, and fears of the new century's first decade, at once contesting and reflecting the race nativism that had infiltrated American thought.

Like Jacob Riis, Edward Alfred Steiner was an immigrant who had many early misadventures in the United States before rather quickly assimilating into American life. Steiner tells his life story in three autobiographical works: *Against the Current: Simple Chapters from a Complex Life*, *From Alien to Citizen: The Story of My Life in America*, and *The Eternal Hunger*. Together these works serve as a corollary to Riis's *The Making of an American*. Unlike

Riis, who was born and raised in a rather racially homogenous and cohesive society in Ribe, Denmark, where the Lutheran Church was dominant, Steiner was born and raised a Jew in Szenica, Slovakia, in a racially diverse area of Austria-Hungary where Slovaks and Magyars, Jews, Protestants, and Catholics lived in sometimes uneasy coexistence. "I played with the children of three distinct races and loved those best who hated my people most," Steiner writes in *Against the Current*, the chronicle of his early life. However, his love was returned with hate, and a series of incidents forced the child into a new race consciousness. In a chapter titled "Dawn of Race Consciousness," he says that "the bond between me and my former playmates was broken; for I knew I was a Jew. The Gentile boys knew it, even the geese, I thought, must know it, for the ganders seemed to hiss at me: '*Schid, Schid.*'" Steiner counterbalances his childhood persecutions with images of America and American freedom. An old townsman returns from fighting for the Union in America's Civil War and tells young Edward of the great Lincoln, the Christian Abraham who was as good as the Jewish one, and, like Moses, led his people out of slavery. Hearing the veteran read and translate *Uncle Tom's Cabin*, Edward is so moved by the spirit of the book that he gathers his friends and preaches his "first revolutionary sermon." Later, the young boy discovers James Fenimore Cooper in a large illustrated German edition of the *Leatherstocking Tales* brought to the village by a family of Hungarians from America. Much like Riis, Steiner is transported by Cooper's romances. "That ozone from free airs stirred my whole system and seemed to purify me of all inborn fears and littleness," Steiner says, echoing Riis's own childhood response to Cooper.[10]

After earning a doctorate at the University of Heidelberg, Steiner made a pilgrimage, most of it on foot, across eastern Europe to Russia to visit his religious/philosophical hero, Leo Tolstoy, who affirmed for Steiner the oneness of people. Steiner would make at least six trips to visit Tolstoy over the years. Shortly after the first encounter with the Russian writer, Steiner left for the United States in 1886, in some measure to avoid military conscription. Both his father and older brother had been killed in Austro-Hungarian wars, and Steiner had grown up in a staunchly anti-militaristic family whose attitudes would remain with him the rest of his life.[11] Steiner arrived in American with but one personal asset, his linguistic ability and training in the philology of Slavik languages. Finding no work suitable to his training in New York, he landed a succession of short-lived jobs in garment factories, a baker's shop, a feather renovating establishment, and a sausage factory. Reading "the advice of a famous man, 'Go West, young man,'" he did just that. Working as a coal miner in Pennsylvania, he got caught up in a strike, was beaten, and thrown in jail. Like Riis, Steiner ended up a tramp. "For more than six months I was with thugs, tramps, thieves and vermin," he writes. "I was a criminal immigrant, a component element of the new immigration problem."[12] Unlike Riis, however, Steiner consistently identifies himself as an immigrant and attributes his early difficulties to being a "problem" immigrant. Although Riis's early years in America were also difficult, we rarely get the sense that he is a victim of discrimination based on his immigrant status.

Following a run of good luck, Steiner earned a divinity degree at Oberlin College in 1891, and that same year was ordained a Congregational minister. He had converted to Christianity soon after arriving in the United States, and clearly this religious conversion contributed to his efforts at assimilation and assuming an American identity. But there are also strong signs that Steiner was motivated by genuine religious feelings. As a young man, he was drawn to Christ's teachings on nonviolence, tolerance, and brotherly love, teachings that Steiner saw embodied in Tolstoy. Steiner says of his conversion: "In reality, I have found the church of the Puritans the best that my race has bequeathed me.... In its cry for righteousness and personal purity, in its emphasis upon a Christian democracy, in its demand for rational self-sacrifice to achieve great, social ends, it appeals to me and claims my allegiance."[13] During World War I, when Steiner was publicly attacked for his pacifism, he wrote to the Des Moines *Capital*, "I cannot so amend my patriotism that it will nullify my Christianity. My soul is still my own and my God's. My money and my body my country can claim."[14] All this seems to indicate that his religious conversion was more than a simple attempt at cultural assimilation. However, the full circumstances of this religious conversion are not clear.[15] Three years after his ordination, Steiner became a naturalized American citizen. He would later say that although his peripatetic life had made him an alien nowhere, he became "a loyal American" through his love of liberty and his faith in America's spirit of fair play.

While working as a minister, he experienced the power of Christian love to bind together in a "new blood kinship" people of different races, tongues, and nations. "There, for the first time, I came in touch with the 'Melting Pot,'" he writes in *From Alien to Citizen*. "It was not a chafing-dish, with an alcohol lamp under it, as many, forming their conception of it from Mr. Zangwell's rather mild drama, imagine it to be; it was a real, seething cauldron, with its age-old fires of hate threatening to consume its contents. Then came the torrent of love, with its mighty power, putting out the old fire by kindling a new one." In 1903, Steiner was named to the Chair of Applied Christianity at Grinnell College in Grinnell, Iowa, and remained there until his retirement as professor emeritus in 1941. His academic duties did not interfere with his efforts on behalf of the immigrants. Although he perhaps did not attain the stature of Jacob Riis, Steiner was an influential writer and public lecturer who would sit on the twenty-member American Immigration Commission appointed by President Woodrow Wilson. A prolific writer, he not only wrote extensively about immigrants/immigration in magazine articles and books, but also produced novels, short stories, and memoirs/autobiographies. Reflecting on his life in *From Alien to Citizen*, he praised the holy trinity that had thrilled his whole frame with an unearthly joy: "Thank God for the Christ, Thank God for America, Thank God for humanity."[16] However, those words came on the eve of World War I, before the crisis of faith and alienation that Steiner would suffer during the conflict and its aftermath. World War I and the subsequent Red Scare would sorely test Steiner's belief in America tolerance and brotherhood, but he would again find spiritual sustenance in the immigrants themselves.

As a minister, Steiner had begun spending vacations on the trail of the immigrants through steerage and Ellis Island to the mills and mines of America. He eventually made more than thirty trips abroad by boat, many of them in steerage, to study immigrant conditions and problems.[17] The result was a series of books on immigration, American national character, and Americanization, including *On the Trail of the Immigrant* (1906), *The Immigrant Tide* (1909), *Introducing the American Spirit* (1915), *Nationalizing America* (1916), *Old Trails and New Borders* (1921), and *The Making of a Great Race* (1929). It is toward *On the Trail of the Immigrant* that I will turn most of my attention, for it is here that Steiner's attitudes and ideas are best laid out.

In his *On the Trail of the Immigrant*, Steiner assumes the persona of an American and often comments on the arriving immigrants from the perspective of a native-born American. But Steiner catches himself late in the book, where he expresses shock and shame for forgetting that he himself is a "new immigrant" and "New American" among "those who make up the racial problem" of America. He realizes that his case is an example of and a model for the other immigrants. Although he looks upon America as his Fatherland, and is "completely and absorbingly an American," he realizes that he is no better than the millions of so-called new immigrants who are regarded as a menace. "I came here with the same blood as theirs and the same heritage of good or ill, bequeathed by my race; yet I feel myself completely one with all of which this country possesses, that is worth living for and dying for" (307–308).

Steiner's is an interesting, if somewhat convoluted, rhetorical strategy. He is an American because he says he is an American. He is not just any typical American, but "completely and absorbingly an American." However, his blood—his race—reminds him that he is also a Slav and a racial, if not a religious, Jew. If he is the same as the Slavs/Jews who have followed him to America, then they are the same as he: They, too, can become Americans. One is an American when one comes to consider America as the Fatherland, Steiner says. His choice of the term Fatherland is doubly interesting. One does not become an American by simply assuming American citizenship.

The political and civic transformation of citizenship certainly represents a very important step, as emphasized by the title of Steiner's autobiography, *From Alien to Citizen*. In becoming a citizen, one ceases to be an alien. However, one truly becomes an American by recognizing America as one's father and other Americans as one's brothers and sisters; one becomes an American by mixing one's blood with the American blood. This introduces a blood/family element into the idea of Americanization. By recognizing America as the Fatherland, Slavs and Latins and other immigrants become blood brothers with Anglo-Saxon and Germanic Americans. The idea of a Fatherland is itself a very Germanic idea, as Steiner the student of Germany would have known. Steiner's linking of America, the Fatherland, and Christian brotherhood is interesting in light of his numerous other comments about race and blood. It is not enough, Steiner seems to be saying, that the new immigrants become blood brothers with native-born Americans by declaring their allegiance to the American Fatherland. For their part, native-born Americans, in the spirit of Christian brotherhood, must not only show sympathy toward the new immigrants, as Riis would have them do, but also accept them as Americans, as members of the American family.

In *Against the Current*, shortly after visiting Tolstoy, Steiner ruminates about the presumed primacy of race. "'Alles ist Rasse' was the note which dominated the teaching of History in all its multitudinous divisions. I sometimes think that the opposite is true and that there is nothing in race; for I have experienced oneness with all sorts of people, both in the lower and higher spheres of life."[18] Steiner also seeks to critique contemporary race thinking when he says that *From Alien to Citizen* was "not written to increase prejudice, but rather to allay it; it is not a call to a new propaganda but to a new spirit."[19] This new spirit is the Christian Social Gospel spirit of universal brotherhood. Therefore, it is not simply blood, but also spirit, that connects people. In essence, Steiner wants to subvert divisive blood-based race prejudice with the unifying spirit of Christ's universal brotherhood. He hopes to use love to reconnect the blood ties that people such as Henry Cabot Lodge and other Anglo-Saxonists sought to sever. Steiner, like other dissident voices of the time, is arguing that we are all one race, the human race, created once and for all time by God. However, Steiner's depictions of the Italians and other immigrant groups is imbued with the race thinking of his day, which more often than not emphasized hierarchical differences among the world's peoples. Consequently, Steiner vacillates between the belief that race is nothing and that race is all.

Steiner is aware that becoming an American involves much more than changing one's clothes, learning some English, and erasing what he calls "external racial characteristics." He in fact prides himself on his ability to distinguish groups through their racial features. "Give me the immigrant on board of ship, and I will distinguish without hesitation the Bulgarian from the Servian, the Slovak from the Russian, and the Northern Italian from the Sicilian," he writes in *On the Trail of the Immigrant* (294). It is interesting that under Steiner's scheme, northern Italians and Sicilians constitute separate races, just as the Bulgarians, Serbians, Slovaks, and Russians do. Here, Steiner echoes a division made official by the U.S. Bureau of Immigration, which for statistical purposes was distinguishing between northern and southern Italians. But if Steiner makes much of external racial differences, he also tries to undercut their power. These racial characteristics may seem ineradicable, as if written by an "iron pen upon the rock." But in most cases they are like "chalk marks on a blackboard" and easily washed away, so much so that Steiner, despite his expertise "in detecting racial marks," is "often puzzled and mistaken." These outward racial marks, "things created by long ages of neglect, hunger, persecution and climate, are often lost within one generation," if not sooner (294). Steiner appears to be arguing that physical racial features are the product of the environment rather than of blood. In the American environment, therefore, the Jew begins looking less Jewish, the Bohemian less Bohemian. As a result, Steiner often has "the greatest difficulty" distinguishing between members of different races two or three years after the men have landed in America. "It is true that in the first generation, the old racial marks still lie in the foreground, and that even in the second generation, the blood will speak out here and there; but it will require a very sharp scrutiny to detect this, and in the most cases there will be no hint of the past." These "racial marks are most tenacious among certain Orientals where strange strains of blood have accentuated the difference," Steiner says. But, he adds, even the Oriental Armenians, "people bearing the mark of their race most strongly," had lost, at the end of ten years in America, "the peculiar sharpness of their features and were in that stage of transition where the American image was being imposed upon them" (295).

Steiner concedes that looking like an American does not necessarily mean becoming American; appearances do not necessarily translate into character. But Steiner does not totally discount the possibility. He says he wants to avoid the dogmatism of Prescott Farnsworth Hall of the Immigration Restriction League, who believed that America would inherit the immigrant's disagreeable racial characteristics. Steiner argues that such fears are "too early to foretell" and that "the whole question of racial characteristics is still an open one." But, Steiner asks, given "the undisputed fact" that outward racial marks disappear, "may we not also believe that with them go the peculiar racial qualities which mark and mar the life of the stranger?" Steiner offers as an example the case of the Polish peasant, who in the Old World "is known for his inability to distinguish between 'mine and thine,' and between truth and falsehood." In America, Steiner asserts, the Polish communities can be accused of neither thieving nor lying (296). However, if there are signs that the American environment can wash out the immigrant's defects, there are also questions about America's ability to replace those defects with American virtues and political ideals. Steiner here is more circumspect. "Whether we shall enrich this New American by our own ideals, whether we shall implant in him the broad culture of our own spiritual and intellectual heritage, is a real problem whose solving may puzzle even future generations" (300).

Another problem is the possibility that the new immigrants may bequeath to the American some of their own degenerate traits, may in effect contaminate American blood, as Hall and the Immigration Restriction League were warning. To this, Steiner argues that although Slav, Jewish, and Italian blood already flows in the veins of some Americans, "there is no perceptible physical or moral degeneration visible which can be traced to the foreigner" (304). Steiner quickly turns the tables, suggesting that the main problem may lie with the native-born American himself. Steiner specifically targets those idle, perverted, and "over-ripe" rich Americans who alone constitute the problem that should be feared. Steiner says: "The question which the American faces is not whether the foreigner can be assimilated, but who will do the assimilating" (306). Old and new immigrants alike are progressing, Steiner claims, leaving behind the physically, mentally, and spiritually bankrupt "sons of the shrewd and inventive Yankees" who "are keeping fast company, riding in fast automobiles, and drinking strong cocktails." Here Steiner is challenging what he implies is the less-than-pure, perhaps even corrupt, Anglo-Saxon branch of the American family tree. Steiner ends his chapter on "The New American and the New Problem" by concluding: "It does not follow that these New Americans do not present a racial problem; but the problem is largely one of assimilating power on our part. The real problem is: Whether the American is virile enough and not so much whether the foreign material is of the proper quality." Steiner argues that America's assimilating power "increases rather than decreases with the mixture of blood." The average New American may be "like wax, hard wax sometimes,—perhaps more like lead or steel; but he will be molded into our image and bear the marks of our characteristics whatever they may be" (307). Sounding very much like Hector St. John de Crèvecoeur in *Letters from an American Farmer*, Steiner describes the making of Americans as "planless, involuntary, even automatic, a natural result of this New World environment."[20] Included in this New World environment are the bracing ozone-rich air that stirs sluggish blood; the public school that "grinds all the grain into the same grist"; America's food, economic opportunity, and standard of living; and the most vital force of all, the English language (72–73). Although Steiner raises the possibility that the immigrants can add assimilating power to the native-born

American blood, he does not elaborate on the resulting American image and characteristics. He seems to be implying that the American people were evolving with the assimilation of the new immigrants, that Old World blood and culture would contribute to the emerging American character. At this point, at least, Steiner seems to believe in a more liberal melting pot ideal than Riis's more one-sided assimilationist model.

Steiner politely addresses *On the Trail of the Immigrant* to someone he calls "My Dear Lady of the First Cabin," an obviously privileged American woman most likely returning from a tour of Europe. His tone is mild and courtly, unlike Riis's blunt, sometimes in-your-face approach to preaching. Steiner presumably meets his "Dear Lady" on a ship carrying cabin-class Americans returning from Europe and immigrants in steerage emigrating to America. The "Dear Lady" is representative of a broad section of her gender and class, like Riis sympathetic to the poor immigrants but concerned about their effect on American society. Steiner gently reminds her: "You pitied them all; the frowsy headed, ill clothed women, the men who looked so hungry and so greedy, and above all you pitied, you said so,—do you remember?—you said you pitied your own country for having to receive such a conglomerate of human beings, so near to the level of beasts" (10). The lady's sympathy extends a long way: During the voyage she greets a group of Italians in their native language and they smile back on her "all the joy of their native land." Under Steiner's tutelage, she learns to distinguish not only Italians from Slavs, Jews, and Greeks, but also "the difference between a Sicilian and a Neapolitan, between a Piedmontese and a Calabrian" (12). It is clear, despite the woman's liberality of interest and sympathy, where her primary loyalties lie, for Steiner's are in the same place. "I know no fatherland," he writes, "but America; for after all, it matters less where one is born, than where one's ideals had their birth; and to me, America is not the land of almighty dollars, but the land of great ideals." If the "crude and unfinished" immigrant was a peril to those ideals, Steiner says, "I would be the first one to call out: 'Shut the gates,' and not the last one to exile myself for your country's good" (14). Steiner's argument is a simple one: I am an American because I believe in American ideals. But if the new immigrants are a problem, then I'm a problem. Exclude them and you will have to exile me, an American who cannot call "your" country mine. It is hard to imagine the Nordic Riis having to make such an argument.

Steiner's avowed purpose is to "win a little more sympathy" for the immigrant crammed in steerage from the American in first class. "I think that the peril lies more in the first cabin than in the steerage; more in the American colonies in Monte Carlo and Nice than in the Italian colonies in New York and Chicago," Steiner writes to his dear lady and others of her class. Here echoes his muted critique of the physically, mentally, and spiritually weakened "sons of the shrewd and inventive Yankees" who keep fast company, drive fast automobiles, and drink strong cocktails. By inference, it is they who can be revitalized by an infusion of more vital, if more primitive immigrant blood. "Not the least of the peril lies in the fact that there is too great a gulf between you and the steerage passenger," Steiner tells the lady, expressing the hope that his book "will mediate between the first cabin and steerage; between the hilltop and the lower town; between the fashionable West side and the Ghetto" (13–14). *On the Trail of the Immigrant* is also a more frontal attack on American race nativists such as two delegates to a recent immigration conference who referred to the immigrants as "yellow worms from Southern Europe" and "durrty furriners." No doubt, Steiner concludes, the two delegates "voiced the common prejudice which rests itself entirely upon its ignorance" (75).

Despite Steiner's sanguine attitudes about the immigrants, they continue to show some of the same old vices that Jacob Riis saw sixteen years earlier in *How the Other Half Lives*. If the immigrants in general were not the problem, individual groups such as the Italians continued to be problematic. Using the essentialized singular case employed by Riis, Steiner notes that the Italian "comes primarily from Southern Italy, from the crowded cities with their unspeakable vices; the smallest number of immigrants come from the villages where they have all the virtues of the tillers of the soil." The Italian is the "most volatile" and "perhaps the most clannish" of America's immigrants. As a group, the Italians "represent a problem recognized by their home government, which was the first to concern itself with it, to study it systematically, and to aid our government so far as possible in a rational solution" (28). Still the Italians come, filling the steerage of transatlantic steamers. Steiner condemns conditions in steerage and calls for its abolition by law, even while conceding: "It is true that the Italian and Polish peasant may not be accustomed to better things at home, and might not be happier in better surroundings nor know how to use them; but it is a bad introduction to our life to treat him like an animal when he is coming to us" (37). Steerage is not such a bad deal for the Italian and Pole, but it is unflattering to America's image and a bad first step in welcoming the immigrant. And yet the picturesque steerage, much like the ghetto tenements to which the immigrants were going, has a certain allure for the privileged passengers who can gaze on those below from their higher social and spatial planes. Voyeurism did not get much better than this for the privileged dear men and dear ladies of Steiner's America. Says Steiner: "This practice of looking down into the steerage holds all the pleasures of a slumming expedition with none of its hazards of contamination; for the barriers which keep the classes apart on a modern ocean liner are as rigid as in the most stratified society, and nowhere else are they more artificial or more obtrusive" (41). Steiner's shipboard slumming has an advantage over Riis's ghetto slumming because here the aliens are more tightly contained, with little threat that they will break through the aesthetic frame and invade the middle-class neighborhoods, as they do in New York's tenement districts. Steiner's steerage scene obviously brings to mind Alfred Stieglitz's well-known photograph "The Steerage," taken one year after publication of *On the Trail of the Immigrant*. The photograph was itself the product of a slumming expedition on the luxury liner *Kaiser Wilhelm II* bound for Europe. On the third day out Stieglitz, depressed about financial and family problems and oppressed by the *nouveaux riches* in first class, escaped to the end of the first-class deck. There, laid out below him, was the image that he would later call his best and most representative work. "I stood spellbound for a while," Stieglitz recalls. "I saw shapes related to one another—a picture of shapes, and underlying it, a new vision that held me: simple people; the feeling of ship, ocean, sky; a sense of release that I was away from the mob called 'rich.' "[21] Whatever the photograph means, in one sense this image of the steerage passengers was a means of psychological and spiritual escape for Stieglitz.

Steiner makes of the scene something rather different. His steerage has a more intimate connection with the rest of the ship, which in an extended metaphor becomes an Old World monarchy—a Russia, Austria, Poland, or Italy. The average steerage passengers are contented and resigned peasants, Steiner says. "The cabin passengers are the lords and ladies, the sailors and officers are the police and the army, while the captain is the king or czar" (41). The Italians are both peasants and court jesters, whose antics are enjoyed by tourist cabin passengers who presumably gaze down from above. The Italian peasants on board perform Punch and Judy shows, hurdy-gurdy music, and sleight-of-hand tricks that made them seem "still more uncanny than the Slavs." The hurdy-gurdy man announces the national anthem of the great American country to which they are traveling, and breaks into the ragtime notes of "Ta—ra—ra-boom—de-a" (52). Of course there is all the dirt, one of the reasons Steiner seeks to abolish steerage, but also one of the attractions of steerage as a slumming destination. All the steerage passengers are dirty, with "the Italians being easily in the lead," Steiner writes. These southern Italians "had lost the romance of their native land but not the fragrance of the garlic." They quarreled loudly, but were generally good neighbors during the sixteen-day trip. Despite the Italian immigrant's reticence with outsiders, Steiner says that the average American could easily discover something he had trouble believing—"that all Italians are not alike, that they do not look alike, and that they are not all Anarchists." But, if all Italians are not *all* anarchists, "many criminals come, especially from Italy," Steiner says (51). We see here the recurring theme first voiced by Riis and later taken up by James, that out of his native element, the Italian loses some of his attractive qualities, especially his romance, while retaining less attractive features, in this case his garlic smell. On the one hand Steiner individualizes and humanizes the Italians, while on the other he stereotypes and exoticizes them. Italians are not all alike, yet all smell of garlic and are easily the dirtiest immigrants. All Italians are not anarchists, but all quarrel and gesticulate wildly, and many are law-breakers.

For Steiner, it is not enough to divide Italians into northerners and southerners. Rather, Italians constitute a conglomeration of types that are touched, influenced, and formed by mixtures of other racial/national types. When the Slav touches the Italian, you see "a rough exterior, a slower gait, a harsher speech, more industry and less art." The Italian who has been "enthralled and governed" by Austro-Germans is "more governable, more sedate, more a statesman and less a revolutionist, 'a captain of industry' rather than a leader of brigands, more a businessman and less a dreamer." French tastes and habits "blended quickly and easily into the Italian character," which is like that of the French people, who had been the Italians' friends and enemies in turn, and often both at once. Arabians and Greeks brought to the south of Italy "thought and thoughtfulness," "culture and vices," and "rest and restlessness," contrasts that are accentuated in the Italian, who, although "small in stature, is great in passion and desires" (253).

Even as Steiner purports to show the rich variety of Italians by imagining a multiethnic, perhaps pluralist Italian culture, he perpetuates stereotypes and links physical and moral qualities, much in the manner of the period's less tolerant race nativists. Even as Steiner distinguishes between types of Italians, he essentializes conventional Italian types: the dreamer and art lover who is not much for business and industry; the brigand and the revolutionist who destroys order; the Italian who is less governable, less rational, and less self-controlled than his northern cousins; the excitable, passionate, grasping Italian. Steiner never explicitly defines the uniquely Italian character to which elements of Italy's neighbors/conquerors were added, but the stereotypes are implicit in the passage. It is also interesting to look at what these other nationalities/races have contributed to the mix. The northern European Austro-Germans who "enthralled and governed" the Italian gave him only the valuable traits of order, industry, and statesmanship, those very ideals dear to Anglo-Saxonist Americans. The French, those friends/enemies who can be seen as a bridge between Mediterranean/Latin Italy and Nordic/North Europe, add their own tastes and habits, but Steiner never specifies what those are, just as he does not detail the Italian character with which these French traits so quickly and easily blend. While the eastern European Slav brings unattractive physical characteristics (rough physical exterior, slow gait, harsh speech), he contributes the vital moral value of industry. This virtue allies the Slavs, the "Slavic" Italians, and the Slavic Steiner himself with the Austro-Germans, and, by extension, with the native-born Americans. Finally, it is the southern European Greek and the Asiatic Arabian, itself a strange pairing, who are truly a mixed blessing for the people of the south of Italy, where they had their influence. These two groups are the only ones who add moral defects to the Italian character, where they are accentuated by the Italians' innate passion and desires.

Having categorized the Italian into geographical/racial subdivisions, Steiner now proceeds to dichotomize him into polar opposites. The first image is of the Italian as the railroad builder—temperate, inventive, easily adjusted to any task. This image links the Italian to America's great railroad builders, both those unskilled laborers who wielded the pick and shovel and those captains of industry who directed the glorious enterprise. This Italian's traits are American traits, Yankee/Anglo-Saxon traits: temperance, inventiveness, and enterprise. This "Anglo-Saxon" Italian has a "lazier brother," the "pioneer of Italian migrations" who traveled to America "with a trained monkey and a hand-organ out of tune," and caused many Americans to believe that he was the typical Italian. However, this organ grinder and his Italian cousins, the beggars who besiege tourists in Naples and the "lazy Lazzaroni" stretched out on the ground, are but the exceptions, numerous as they seem (254–255). And, numerous as they were in the pages of nineteenth-century American travel writing, we might add. What is most interesting in this passage is that the dichotomy between the Italian railroad builder and the Italian organ grinder/beggar/lazy lounger is subtly transformed into one between the northern and the southern Italian. The begging or idling Italian had a long history in American accounts of Italy, from Washington Irving to Mark Twain and Henry James. Although the beggar and idler were sometimes ascribed to all of Italy, these types were most associated with Naples and the South. In contrast, it is the northern Italian, the Austro-Germanized Italian with his industry and order, who builds Italy's railroads.

As a rule, Steiner says, the Italian at home in Italy asks for but little in life. The Italians have the advantage of living in a country whose "inexplicable charm" makes its name "synonymous with beauty and art." Despite claims of knowing and loving Italy well, Steiner overlooks the probability that the Italians in steerage, the ones who foolishly mistake "Ta—ra—ra—boom—de-a" for the American national anthem, have very little connection to the romantic, heroic Italy of beauty and art. Still, Italy's charm makes its people gay. "Sombre as is the Slavic world, from which both Jew and Slav emigrate, so bright and joyous is all Italy the home of most of the Latins who come to us" (252). Satisfied as he is with his condition in Italy, the Italian "is equally unsatisfied with any restraint by authority; lawlessness has cut so deep into his life, that it may be said to be a natural condition." The Italian's lawlessness is not immanent in the Italian character, but springs from environmental and political causes, Steiner argues. "The root of it lies in the fact that for centuries the lawmakers were aliens and conquerors, the laws being made for the strong and not for the weak; to oppress and not to protect" (255). Consequently, brigandage and heroism often became "synonymous," while murder and theft were easily excused for the sake of expediency. Much of this spirit of brigandage still infects Italians, especially in the South, Steiner writes. "The consequence is that many of the criminals who come to our shores are Italians who are trying to escape punishment or who are entangled in the meshes of the Maffia or Camorra, and the officials are very glad to have their room rather than their company." Having earlier commended the Italian government for helping to control undesirable emigration to America, Steiner now says that "[e]vidences are not lacking that their way out is made easy, even if it cannot be proved that the government aids them to come" (255–256). As Steiner implies, if the Italian's lawlessness was a reaction to conquest and oppression, it was most active in the South under Bourbon rule. In fact, the phenomenon of southern Italian brigandage was a manifestation of the *contadini*'s oppression. "The formation of the bands of *briganti* was the result of a people who reacted, not with a political platform or with terrorist cunning, but ... with unplanned aggression against the threat to their way of life posed by outside forces."[22] This lawlessness continues in the form of the mafia and the camorra, Steiner says, but now it is not brigandage alloyed with heroic political resistance. Here, Steiner seems to ignore the continuing subjugation of southern Italians by the dominant northerners after unification. By highlighting southern Italian lawlessness without placing it in a deeper sociopolitical context, Steiner is essentially parroting the charges leveled by northern Italian leaders against unruly southerners throughout the second half of the nineteenth century and into the twentieth century. As John Dickie writes: "The barbarous, the primitive, the violent, the irrational, the feminine, the African. These and other values, negatively connoted, were repeatedly located in the *Mezzogiorno* as foils to definitions of Italy." The anti-brigandage campaign initiated in the 1860s represented the first traumatic encounter between the new Italian state and the South. And in the minds of the army officers and many northern Italians, the fight was "between civilization and barbarism, reason and violence, humanity and inhumanity, social order and crime," with bandits often depicted as animals.[23] These attitudes, in less virulent form, clearly seep into Steiner's writing.

And what of the Italian's other traits? Steiner concludes that on balance the Italian is not dishonest. However, he subverts this point by developing and qualifying it. The Italian compares well with the other European immigrants, "but in his ethics he is decidedly mixed, and his poetical temper does not always help him to tell the exact truth" (256). The Italian is not dishonest, but neither does he always tell the truth. The fault lies with one of his virtues, his passion for poetry. Oddly enough, these same lovers of poetry are highly illiterate and poorly educated, Steiner says quite rightly. By 1901, nearly half of all Italians were still illiterate, but within this overall figure were radical regional differences. For example, the northern Piedmont had an illiteracy rate of less than 20 percent, while Calabria's was nearly 80 percent in the South.[24] Despite the Italian's poor education, Steiner says, he "is a good business man and a good organizer, having a talent for the dollar which today makes him a new business force in Europe, and one to be reckoned with; especially if he improves his business morals, which are very poor" (258).

Steiner concludes his sketch of "The Italian at Home" by exposing the curse of the Catholic Church, the traditional target of Americans and one perhaps more suited to a Protestant Anglo-Saxon such as Mark Twain rather than the Jew-turned-Congregationalist Steiner. "The Italian is sick and sore because the Church which has so long been his physician, acknowledges no error, and even its humble Pope will not persuade it that it must radically change its treatment; this is not only for the sake of Italy but for the sake of America also," Steiner writes. The Italians' relationship to the clergy and the Catholic Church is a complicated one, and there is not room here to explore all its nuances. Historically, the Catholic Church had been allied with the exploitative landowning aristocracy and had shown little sympathy for the misery of the *contadini*, particularly in the South. For those reasons the southern Italian peasants had little sense of reverence for the institutional church. Although the Italian masses were profoundly religious, their religion had elements of paganism, and their beliefs and practices did not conform to the doctrines and the liturgy of the official church.[25] "In short, through the centuries, a chasm—spiritual, social, intellectual, economic—developed between the church, as represented by the local priest, and the working masses."[26] Anticlericalism was even more pronounced among the northern nationalists, liberals, and intellectuals who struggled to create an Italian state in the nineteenth century and saw the Catholic Church as perhaps the main enemy of liberty and progress. "Unlike the Irish or Poles whose Catholicism was an integral part of their national identity, it was difficult to be both an Italian patriot and a faithful Catholic," Rudolph Vecoli writes. "An aggressive anticlericalism became a powerful force in late nineteenth-century Italy as nationalist, liberal, and socialist views prevailed." These Italian anticlerical attitudes meshed well with longstanding Protestant American prejudice against the Catholic Church, which was seen as the cause of Italy's oppression and backwardness. However, these same anticlerical attitudes bitterly angered Catholic Irish Americans who traditionally were "more devout sons of the Mother Church."[27] For his part Steiner, the Protestantized Jew, allies himself with those Americans who saw the Italian Catholic Church as perhaps the main problem, both in Italy and in the

United States. Steiner says, "The most dangerous element which can come to us from any country, is that which comes smarting under real or fancied wrongs, committed by those who should have been its helpers and healers. Such an element Italy furnishes in a remarkably great degree, and I have no hesitation in saying that it is our most dangerous element" (261). Steiner here is saying that as victims Italians are a dangerous lot, but that the responsibility for the remedy lies at home, with the Church, and not with the Italian government or with America. In essence, he is asking Italy to make its masses less huddled, less yearning to breathe free, before it sends them off to America. Not stated explicitly, but perhaps implied, is the idea that less victimization of the Italians in Italy might also relieve the necessity of their coming to America in the first place.

Having surveyed the Italian in his homeland, Steiner follows up with his chapter "The Italian in America." He says that the "most dangerous element" now migrating to the United States in frightening numbers began benignly enough with the first Savoyard with his trained bears and the organ grinder with his monkey. Here Steiner forgets, and in effect erases, the Italian artists, artisans, professionals, and political exiles who came in small numbers during the early and mid-nineteenth century. It was the bear-trainer and organ grinder, and not Thomas Jefferson's philosopher friend Filipo Mazzei, who were at the "vanguard of a vast army of men who were to come; first with a pushcart, later with shovel and pickax." It is with the shovel and pickax—with his muscle, that is—that the Italian can lay claim to contributing to American life. "While the average Italian immigrant is not regarded by any of us as a public benefactor, it is a question just how far we could have stretched our railways and ditches without him; for he now furnishes the largest percentage of the kind of labour which we call unskilled, and he is found wherever a shovel of earth needs to be turned, or a bed of rock is to be blasted" (262). Steiner's railroad builders will reappear as Italian ditchers and diggers on the New Jersey shore in Henry James's *The American Scene*, published one year after Steiner's *On the Trail of the Immigrant*. However, where Steiner's railroad builders inspire praise, James's ditchers and diggers are aliens who conjure up such agonizing qualms in James's heart. If hardworking, Steiner's Italians-in-America have a "'helter-skelter, I don't care' sort of atmosphere about their squalor" (263) and are considered an asset by landlords and real estate businesses because they "can be crowded more than any other human being" (268). Often, the Italian immigrants are being packed in tenements by one of their own, one of the eight hundred Italians who own $15 million worth of housing, much of it tenements of the worst sort, in New York City. "The narrow quarters he rents are invariably sublet, and he imposes upon the newcomer conditions as hard as, or harder than, those under which he began life in the land of the free" (268–269). But the

Italians prefer to be among their own, "not so much from a feeling of clannishness, although that is not absent; but because among their own, they are safe from that ridicule which borders on cruelty, and with which the average American treats nearly every stranger not of his own complexion" (263).

Steiner's confused and confusing representations of the Italians perpetuate a couple stereotypes and qualify another. Steiner expresses sympathy, struggles to get behind appearances, but ends by criticizing both the Italian and the American. The Italian is made out to be naturally messy and unconcerned about his personal space, a subject on which Riis became less dogmatic over time. Steiner gives no reason for the Italian's natural messiness; it just exists. However, the Italian's clannishness can be explained. He isn't as clannish as reputed (or as painted by Riis and others); he simply prefers his own kind. His isolation and apparent clannishness are not essential character traits but a shield against the average American's ridicule—ridicule that is *almost* but not quite cruel. This ridicule is directed by the typical American toward *almost* everyone of different complexion, which implies that the average (native-born) American has a similar complexion, one that differs in some way from that of the Italian.

In focusing on Italian railroad builders—the unskilled laborers—Steiner rightfully chooses one of the most representative of the Italian immigrants, at least in the public consciousness. Most of the migrants worked at manual labor, laying and repairing railroad track, paving streets, digging tunnels, cutting cane and picking cotton, and building bridges, factories, tenements, department stores, and skyscrapers. However, as we have seen, there was a diversity in the Italian immigrants' occupational pursuits that Steiner and other commentators of the period erase or overlook. Italian immigrants throughout the country worked as self-sufficient truck farmers, fishermen, artisans, petty merchants, and professionals. They were produce vendors, shoe repairmen, waiters, barbers, tailors, stone masons, importers, bankers, doctors and pharmacists, and teachers.[28] In New York in 1900, for example, nearly a third of Italian males worked as unskilled laborers, while the remainder pursued semiskilled and skilled jobs such as those listed earlier.[29] Steiner, like Riis, correctly identifies tenement overcrowding as a problem, but, like the prominent housing reformer, Steiner may have exaggerated conditions to underscore the danger of the "tenement house evil" to "the home ideal" of America. Donna Gabaccia's study of the Elizabeth Street neighborhood in New York shows that in 1905 Italians did own a quarter of the properties, but only a quarter actually lived in or near the buildings they owned. Many of the unskilled urban workers did crowd into tenement neighborhoods, but much of the overcrowding was the result of relatively high rents and low wages.[30] To generate income, and for other reasons, families often crammed boarders into their apartments. The Italians may have clustered together as a shield against cruel ridicule, as Steiner asserts, but there were other reasons. Because they often lacked mobility, urban Italians tended to live, work, shop, and socialize in the same tenement neighborhood.[31] As we have seen, because many mothers and daughters had to work at paying jobs, they had little time or energy for housekeeping.[32] So, although Steiner's assessment of the Italian tenement-house immigrant is sympathetic, it only scratches the surface of his or her lived reality.

Steiner's admixture of sympathy, limited understanding, and subtle nativism continues throughout his representation of the Italian. Addressing the concerns of farmers who fear the Italian's incursion into rural America (an incursion that Riis and other social reformers promoted as a remedy for urban congestion), Steiner cites the case of the peaceful town of Bryan, Texas, composed of "what we usually call the least desirable element, the Sicilian." By 1905, this farming town had a majority population of three thousand Sicilians, many of them successfully growing corn and cotton for the marketplace on bottomlands near the Brazos River. Steiner says that for native-born American farmers the word "dago" has an element of dread—"it carries the sound of the dagger, and the dynamite bomb" (270). But the fear of Italian violence is overblown, Steiner implies, making his case with the model town of Bryan and some twisted and tortured logic of his own. He claims that Italian prison statistics are misleading because, despite the large numbers, there are far fewer Italian criminals in America than the numbers would seem to indicate. Besides, the Italian's crimes are Old World crimes. Although most Italians in prison "have used the stiletto and the pistol too freely," they are not real criminals motivated by gain, but another type of criminal motivated by jealousy or affairs of honor. "The worst thing about the Italians is that they have no sense of shame or remorse" (272–273).

The image of the Italian beggar is also overblown. Despite "the fact that Italy seems to be the land of beggars, the Italian immigrant is rarely a mendicant," Steiner writes, here directly citing statistics that appeared in Riis's *How the Other Half Lives*. However, the Italian is mercenary and unethical, Steiner says. Contradicting Riis on Italian child labor, Steiner claims that the Italian drives the Jew out of the clothing business through the use of his children's labor. The Italian has no educational ambitions for his children and is "a sinner above all others in the use of his children's labour." Furthermore, the Italian "is very fertile in inventing excuses for the purposes of evading the law, and his ethical standard in that direction is extremely low. This comes from his inherited hatred of all governmental restrictions" (271–272). The Italian "is not religious by nature," usually "has no understanding for the serious and ethical side of religion," and "is a heathen who still needs to have his spiritual nature discovered and stirred" (278). Having damned the Italian to the realm of the heathen, Steiner offers yet another qualification, but its faint praise is perhaps no less damning. "Nevertheless the Italian is no degenerate; he usually survives the wretched years of his infancy and then like all people who share his environment, grows up less rugged, perhaps more subtle, and hardened to some things which would prove a very serious handicap to those of us who know the value of pure air and of soap and water" (277).

Putting aside all the racial stereotypes, we might ask to what extent Steiner understood the Italians' material reality in the United States. Steiner rightfully singles out Bryan, Texas, as an ideal. Many of the Sicilians who settled in Bryan had initially worked cutting sugarcane in Louisiana. They began arriving in the Brazos County area of Texas in large numbers after 1880, lured by generous sharecropping terms offered by Texas agricultural leaders who faced labor shortages in their corn and cotton fields. Working as sharecroppers, a number of the Italians managed to save enough money to buy their own farms and businesses. In 1905, one year before Steiner published *On the Trail of the Immigrant*, the Italian ambassador visited Texas, where he was told that Bryan had three thousand Italians and wished it had ten times that number.[33] However, as a rule Italians did not do well in general farming or staple crops. And despite efforts by state governments and private agencies, including Italian chambers of commerce, most rural ventures came to little. The Italians were more successful operating truck gardens/farms near large urban centers in the East, Midwest, and California. When Steiner was writing *On the Trail of the Immigrant*, two of the most promising Italian rural colonies were at Vineland and Hammondtown, New Jersey, where former berry pickers had become landowners and now hired itinerant Italians. Northern Italians originally formed these colonies, but by 1908 they were giving way to Sicilians.[34]

Although Steiner argues that the fear of Italian violence is exaggerated, it is difficult to say what exactly he is getting at in his comments on Italian crime. Like Riis, he seems to imply that Italian crime in America was motivated by passion and honor and directed at other Italians. The true nature of Italian crime in America is difficult to gauge, but it was more than simple crimes of passion. Italian immigrants to some extent were governed by *campanilismo*, an attitude of distrust toward the outsider that sought security in a family- or *paese*-based social network. Yet these networks alone were not security enough in threatening cities such as New York, so migrants sought protection beyond their immediate circles. "In small ways, they recreated the thuggery, extortionism, and criminality their critics claimed to find in the Sicilian mafia and the Calabrian camorra," Donna Gabaccia writes. "From the migrants' perspective, there was no criminal conspiracy or Black Hand behind protection rackets—just a desire for order and security and a handful of isolated toughs willing to sell their services promising order in a multi-ethnic city."[35]

Like Riis, Steiner contests the image of the Italian beggar, but his "mercenary" Italian (and the more general image of the Italian as a grasping money-grubber) tarnishes another hidden story, that of countless Italian families successfully surviving in America. Baily cites studies that show that between half and three-quarters of Italian families earned less than the minimum necessary to support four to six people, while another 15 to 20 percent were in the marginal zone.[36] Early in the twentieth century, Italian male immigrants earned about $250–$350 a year, but a family of four to six required about $800 to live adequately. Still, according to one study, more than half of Italian families surveyed reported a budgetary surplus and savings.[37] Italians showed this ability to economize early on, as remittance data from 1884 to 1902 indicate that considerable sums were saved.[38] Of course, the Italian's penchant for saving came with a price. At least temporarily, the Italians were willing to seek the cheapest quarters, take on boarders, send children to work at an early age, and skimp on clothing, recreation, and entertainment, but not food. "Married women (and their youngest children) sometimes still went barefoot, made their own clothes, and remodeled cast-offs. Men claimed only very small pleasures for themselves—notably tobacco, coffee, or a beer at a nearby café. . . . Their desire to save—an otherwise highly valued 'Yankee' characteristic—kept them from becoming American consumers."[39]

It seems clear that the Italian focus on domestic economy did tend to have a detrimental effect on the education of Italian children. According to a U.S. Immigration Commission survey in 1908, Italian education patterns followed that of the general population, with fewer children attending school as they grew older. However, Italian school populations diminished at a faster rate. As Riis had correctly noted, young Italian males were not so much kept out of school to work, but instead made to work before and after school, doing piecework at home such as pasting flowers, finishing coats, picking nuts, or willowing feathers.[40] Italian daughters were kept at home because families thought that there they could better learn the skills necessary for work and homemaking, and because time in school diminished their ability to contribute to the family.[41] Italian attitudes toward formal education are too complex to fully explore here. Early on, Italians were stereotyped as poor students with very low aspirations for academic achievement and advanced schooling, a view that persisted in serious literature into the twentieth century. Part of the problem, however, lies with early test data. Educators judged Italians to have lower intelligence and consequently directed them toward manual occupations. Schools officials and teachers often did not understand the problems of the immigrants, and there was a serious shortage of Italian-American teachers.[42] "Cut off in such a way from the school life of their children, not having an appreciation of education because of lack of opportunity and peasant background in Italy, imbued with the tradition that the family was the transmitter of knowledge and that a person succeeded by hard work, the Italian parent saw no additional value in advanced schooling."[43] And yet in 1904, when social workers surveyed students from the poorest Italian neighborhoods in New York, more than three-quarters said they aspired to earning a higher living than their parents, and a number of the children aspired to a profession.[44]

However, many Italian immigrants aspired to little more than returning sooner or later to Italy, and others simply decided for one reason or another that they could not make it in the New World. And so the "trail of the immigrant" finally brings Steiner back to the steamship, now the *Kaiser Wilhelm II*, departing Hoboken, New Jersey, for the Old World. This was the same luxury liner on which Alfred Stieglitz shot "The Steerage" a few years later. Steiner says the steerage again is crammed to the limit with Jews, Slavs, Italians, and Germans who settle in their congested quarters "in a somewhat closer fellowship than on the westward journey; for now they have a common experience and a few sentences of a common language to bind them to one another" (334). However, the success or failure of their immigrant experiences separated these polyglot immigrants into two distinct classes: "those who go home because they have succeeded, and those who go home because they have failed." Even the successful ones have not yet graduated from steerage to cabin-class, but still belong to "that large class which goes back to the Fatherland for a season and then returns, to try again the road to fortune" (335). Steiner claims that more than a quarter of America's immigrants were "birds of passage," many of who were Italians. The class of relatively successful "birds of passage" is far from Americanized, Steiner claims, for they still recognize their old country as the Fatherland. However, the relatively successful returning emigrant "has lost much of the Old World spirit and is neither so docile nor so polite as it was when it first occupied these quarters," Steiner says, echoing Henry James's lament that Italian immigrants in the New World lost much of their charm and manners. This more assertive emigrant commands greater civility from the ship's crew because he "has grown to be something more of a man, has more self-assertion and more dollars; all of which has power to subdue the over-officious crew" (335). It is interesting here that Steiner measures manhood on the basis of American will power, individualism, and dollars, rather than on the spirit of Christian brotherhood or loyalty to mother and family, which Riis seems to have done in "Paolo's Awakening." Manhood was a contested terrain around the turn of the century, and here we can see three different manifestations of the concept.

Steiner does not categorize the returning Italian immigrants. Most likely he would have seen some Italian immigrants who were going home because they succeeded, some who were returning because they failed, and some who were "birds of passage" that had not yet made a final choice between Old World and New. It is estimated that Italians had the highest rate of return migration, which hovered around 50 percent from 1880 to 1910, but repatriation rates fluctuated widely from year to year with changes in the American economic picture.[45] The figures do not tell the whole story. Although many Italians went to America with no intention of staying and returned to Italy, many again returned to America and established permanent residence. Disputing the 50-percent return rate for the early 1900s, Patrick Gallo argues that by this time the number of returnees was dropping significantly, with an overwhelming number of Italians deciding to stay in America.[46]

Steiner observes that among the small numbers of returning immigrants capable of commanding a cabin, there were maybe half a dozen Italians "who had reached that degree of prosperity." These came from America's South, where they had been involved in the prospering cotton business, and now were "indulging" in a trip to Europe. Steiner gives no details of these Italians' involvement in the cotton business. Possibly they were successful cotton growers from Brazos County in Texas. These cabin-class Italians were "genteel, and quiet, and so well dressed and well groomed, that it came as a surprise to most of the passengers to find that they were Italians, and that they had risen from the 'Dago' class. On them America had performed the miracle of transformation, in spite of its sordid instincts and its materialistic atmosphere; a miracle which art-filled Italy could not perform, a task before which both sculptor and painter are powerless" (354). The change that Steiner sees in these successful Italians is a change in appearance and demeanor. Whether they have become Americans in Steiner's definition of the word, whether they recognize in America a new Fatherland, Steiner does not say. They are no longer dirty, poorly dressed, loud, and uncouth, but now solidly middle class in their well-scrubbed gentility, all of which would make Riis happy. And what has effected this miracle of transformation if not American capitalism and American money, despite the sordid instincts and materialism that characterized much of American money making. The very things that supposedly dismay Steiner—and those very forces that Henry James saw as a blight on American society and culture and a cancer on American character—effect the most visible changes in these few cabin-class Italians. American capitalism, not Italian culture, which is represented by the (powerless) arts of the sculptor or painter, is what makes these Italians look more American. What Americans had most valued in Italy, its art and music and poetry, were of little value in modern America. Art-filled Italy could not turn dirty, uncouth peasants into genteel folk; commercial America could and did. Artistic beauty and truth could not refine these lowly workers, but sordid American capitalism could. This surely would be food for thought for Henry James's "brooding analyst" in *The American Scene*.

Steiner's cabin-class Italians had taken on the trappings of Americans, but had they in fact been Americanized, and just what did that mean? Had they accepted America as their new Fatherland? And was that the real test? Steiner would continue to struggle with these ideas with the approach of World War I and the Red Scare. As a pacifist, he favored neutrality but was pained to hear immigrants attacked as the primary resisters of war. Only reluctantly did he endorse President Wilson's call for support, seeing the conflict as a defensive war. However, he denounced the mounting wave of anti-German hostility and, during the summer of 1917, he made frequent speeches calling on Americans not to hate the enemy or suspected enemy. And he explicitly denounced the vigilante activity of Iowa's self-proclaimed patriots. In return, a statewide campaign led by the Des Moines *Capital* "vilified his ancestry, branded him a 'slacker,' and questioned his patriotism." Under the headline "Dr. Steiner Must Amend His Patriotism," the newspaper said his lectures were dangerous because he was such a well-known and brilliant orator. Steiner had his supporters, among them former President Roosevelt. Although Roosevelt disagreed publicly with Steiner on political issues, he telegraphed Steiner in early 1918, saying, "From all I know of you and your writing I am sure you are entirely loyal." One year later, and now a member of President Wilson's American Immigration Commission, Steiner went to live among the immigrants in New York's Lower East Side to gather firsthand information. While in New York during the Red Scare, he attacked the postwar prejudice against blacks and ethnics. Audiences reacted with hostility, thereby challenging Steiner's remaining optimism about America. "I suddenly realized that the times, and not I, had changed," he writes of the experience in *Old Trails and New Borders* (1921). "I was made conscious of it every time I faced an American audience; something had come between us, and we were no longer in rapport."[47]

For solace, Steiner turned to his immigrant neighbors and to fiction writing. The novel *Sanctus Spiritus and Company* (1919) expresses his sense of grief and alienation, while making a heartfelt appeal for tolerance and understanding. It was the immigrants themselves who helped Steiner to begin to overcome his crisis of spirit. "His New York neighborhood of Italian, Bohemian, Polish, and Russian immigrants had restored some faith in the possible good-will and mutual cooperation of men and women from different backgrounds, and Steiner placed more emphasis on personal action with less confidence in the political structure of the United States."[48] The idealistic Steiner may have overestimated the reserves of good will and mutual cooperation between people from different backgrounds, as cases of inter-ethnic strife suggest. However, he wisely placed less confidence in the politicians and government, as the racist immigration quota laws of the 1920s make clear. Steiner's emphasis on personal action sounds like Riis's call for a "bridge founded upon justice and built of human hearts." For all their differences, Riis and Steiner both ask for sympathy and brotherhood as the basis for tolerance and justice for the immigrants. Both speak of loyalty as a prime requisite for Americanization. Steiner is more the cultural pluralist, at least holding out the possibility that immigrants could contribute enduring values, something more than bits and pieces of their culture, to the American character. But in speaking of national character and national characteristics, Steiner never fully disengages from the racialist discourse of differentiation and hierarchy prevalent during his day. Steiner wanted to believe that all was not race, but the reality of turn-of-the-century America (and Europe) was that all *was* race.

Chapter 3

Henry James's Picturesque Peasants: Heroes of Romance or Modern Men?

The fellow's a bankrupt orange-monger, but he's a treasure.

—Henry James, "The Real Thing," 1892

There is generally a rabble of infantile beggars at the door, pretty enough in their dusty rags, with their fine eyes and intense Italian smile, to make you forget your individual best to make these people, whom you like so much, unlearn their old vices.

—Henry James, *Italian Hours*, 1909

Young Italy, preoccupied with its economical and political future, must be heartily tired of being admired for its eyelashes and its pose.

—Henry James, *Italian Hours*, 1909

In 1904, Henry James returned to the United States from Europe, after a twenty-one-year absence, for an extended visit to his native land. The trip produced a series of seismic shocks for the sixty-one-year-old James. Big ugly factories, a society grasping for dollars and goods, and swarms of urban immigrants assaulted his senses. He encountered much in American society that was strikingly alien, in particular the Italian and Jewish immigrants he saw (and often sought out) in New York City and other places in the Northeast. James's reaction to the industrial growth, rampant materialism, and "new immigration" was a complex, subtly shaded one, as recorded in the highly idiosyncratic account of his homecoming, *The American Scene* (1907). At least one overriding theme stands out: Henry James as a stranger in a strange land, the prodigal son returned home to a country from which he has been dispossessed. In many cases, the dispossessors are the foreigners with whom James finds little possibility of communication. James often recoils from the American scene. He frets about the foreign element—what he calls the "alien"—and wonders what effect it will have on the country and on American national character. He speculates about America's ability to assimilate these new immigrants.

Many of the aliens that James encounters are Italians, immigrants from a land that James knew and loved so well. James had been acquainted with and written about Italians for decades, but these Italian immigrants were, for James, something quite different, something entirely alien, from the picturesque *contadino* of the Roman Campagna. James's encounters with Italians in America are unsettling for him, characterized by a lack of any communication with them. That these Italians should appear as alien as the much less familiar—or more truly alien—Jews, Russians, and Slavs, whom James had not known in their native lands, speaks volumes about James's complex relationship to Italian immigrants. James's encounters with Italians in America raise fundamental questions about his relationships to Italy, Italians, and Italian Americans, and how those relationships ultimately help to shape and illuminate James's relationships to America and Americans.

Prior to *The American Scene*, the subjects of Italy, Americans in Italy, and Italians in Italy played varying roles in a significant portion of James's fiction and travel sketches.[1] In his fiction James almost always places his Italians in an imagined Italy. However, on at least two occasions James creates an Italian character that has ventured forth from his native land, in each case ending up in James's own adopted home, England. The first Italian in England is Oronte, the young Italian model in James's curious tale, "The Real Thing" (1892). He is followed by James's most elaborated Italian character, Prince Amerigo of *The Golden Bowl*, published just a couple months after James arrived in the United States for his American scene tour.

The Italian in America, then, was an entirely new theme for James, one that, coming as it did late in life, can be read against his earlier depictions of things and people Italian. One significant question is whether James saw the Italian in America as fundamentally different from the Italian in Italy. Had the Italian immigrant lost his color, as James suggests in *The American Scene*, or had this Italian simply taken on another less colorful color in the New World? To some extent, the colors of romance, so evident in the travel essays of James's *Italian Hours* and some of his fictional works, have been replaced by the grimy black and white of reality in *The American Scene*. However, were the Italians themselves so much changed, or was James simply seeing them from a different position, against a different background, and in a different light? On one level, *The American Scene* turns the familiar, picturesque Italian into the alien foreigner. However, does James also make some tentative efforts to identify with these immigrants and to incorporate them into the American scene? Is James ultimately trying to imagine a new American culture and national character radically different from the essentially Anglo-Saxon society that he had known some two decades earlier? In attempting to address these questions it will be worthwhile to trace James's attitudes toward and images of Italy/Italians from a childhood saturated with romantic notions, through a young manhood and maturity filled with numerous trips to Italy, and into an old age in which he confronts large numbers of Italian immigrants who have invaded his native land, forcing him to reconsider and reevaluate his earlier ideas. As we will see, James's life and writings, in their broader contours, raise or reprise—and sometimes resist—many of America's prevailing ideas about and responses to Italy and Italians.

Of the countless American writers, artists, and intellectuals who traveled to, lived in, and professed undying love for Italy in the nineteenth century, perhaps none loved it with the passion of Henry James. His was a lifelong love affair marked by all the intense contradictions of being in love. In James's writing about Italy the word "passion" crops up in letters, travel essays, and fictional narratives.[2] His infatuation with Italy and things Italian began in childhood. He remembers his elders returning from the opera, "sounding those rich Italian names, Bosio and Badiali, Ronconi and Staffanone." Later, he accompanies those elders to Castle Garden in New York City to hear "that rarest of infant phenomena, Adelina Patti . . . the most prodigious of fairies, of glittering fables."[3] It was not only on the strains of music that Italy stole into James's consciousness. The lines, colors, and contours of art also made a deep and lasting impression. An ample landscape of Florence by Thomas Cole in his childhood home captured his fancy. There was also another large landscape in the house, this one "a so-called 'view of Tuscany'" by a French painter. When a friend of the family criticizes the painting for missing Tuscany's soft colors and "certain haze in the atmosphere," little Henry pipes in: "'Why, of course,' I can hear myself now blushingly but triumphantly intermingle," James recounts in his autobiographical *A Small Boy and Others*, "— 'the softness and the haze of our Florence there: isn't Florence in Tuscany?'"[4] Little Henry's first trip to Italy was still in the future, but already Italy was a geography, an idea, a reality for him. Florence was his Florence, something soft and hazy, something to be appropriated aesthetically. Although Italy at this stage was strictly an aesthetic experience mediated, as it was for many Americans, through music and art, it signified for the young James more than just a source of imported high culture. Here, for the sensitive and imaginative "small boy," were exoticism ("those rich Italian names"), sensuality (the "softness" of Florence), and romance ("the most prodigious of fairies, of glittering fables").

James first crossed the Alps into Italy in September 1869 as a mature young man of twenty-six and the author of fourteen published short stories. He would later say, in the short story "Benvolio" (1875), that "the world has nothing better to offer a man of sensibility than a first visit to Italy during those years of life when perception is at its keenest, when knowledge has arrived, and yet youth has not departed."[5] In Rome, James gushed about the Eternal City in a letter to his brother William: "At last—for the first time—I live." He staggered "reeling and moaning thro' the streets, in a fever of enjoyment," traversing the whole of Rome in four or five hours and gorging on the ruins and monuments. "The effect is something indescribable," he told William. "For the first time I know what the picturesque is."[6] Eight years later, after a visit to a now unified Italy struggling to modernize, James still felt the country's seductions, even if his response was not as immediate and unqualified as it was during his first visit. In a letter to longtime friend Grace Norton, he wrote, "Italy was still more her irresistible ineffable old self than ever. . . . In spite of the 'changes'—and they are very perceptible—the old enchantment of Rome, taking its own good time, steals over you and possesses you, till it becomes really almost a nuisance and an importunity."[7] Although older and presumably wiser, James still feels the enchantments of the stealthy seductress Italy and her threat of possession. The trope of possession will recur in *The American Scene*, but there it is Italian immigrants who threaten possession even while facing the risk of being possessed. In 1887, in another letter to Grace Norton, James again wrote of his continuing love affair with Italy despite his maturing years. "It was a great satisfaction to me to find that I am as fond of that dear country as I ever was—and that its infinite charm and interest are one of the things in life to be most relied upon. I was afraid that the dryness of age . . . had reduced my old *tendresse* to a mere memory. But no—it is really so much in my pocket, as it were, to feel that Italy is always there."[8] Italy finally ends as a symbol of constancy and endurance in a world of sometimes disconcerting change. No longer a young seductress, Italy is now an old dear (female) friend, still capable of occasional surprise, toward whom the mature forty-four-year-old James feels tender.

James would eventually make fourteen trips to Italy over a span of thirty-eight years. Like other Americans of his gender and class, he derived varied benefits from travel.[9] Among the most important for James was what William Stowe calls "acquisitive cognition," or the accumulation of cultural, aesthetic, and spiritual capital. James often referred to Italy itself as perpetual capital that he wants to let slumber in his mind.[10] For James, as for so many others who came before him, Italy represented history, art, culture, and romance. "If 'Europe' to James meant form and style and social variety, if it meant beauty, art, and a present suffused with the past, then Italy seemed to represent for him the quintessence of Europe," writes Alan Holder. "He thought Italy the most beautiful country in the world and his love for her is revealed in his travel sketches, a love, he said late in his career, he had never been fully able to express." James may have been most personally and deeply involved in the life and culture of France, England, and America, but his deepest spiritual and aesthetic affinity was with Italy.[11]

James began writing his Italian travel essays at about the same time that he was imagining the first fictional Italian characters for his early tales. These essays started appearing in leading American periodicals during the 1870s. A few were included in *Transatlantic Sketches* (1875), but it was not until 1909 that his nonfiction writings on Italy were collected in *Italian Hours*, to which James attached a postscript of four brief essays based on more recent impressions. In these Italian travel essays, we see James as a self-confessed "sentimental" pilgrim collecting impressions and moments for his "mental sketch-book."[12] For James, putting the impressions into prose means fitting them for a double frame, that of the essay or book itself, and that of a picture frame. "All Venice was both model and painter, and life was so pictorial that art couldn't help becoming so" (21–22). James talks of "the old Italian sketchability" in Genoa (105) and "the picture-making street life" of Rome (156). He speaks of passing "from one framed picture to another beside the open arches of [a] crumbling aqueduct" in the Roman Campagna (156). Like a child gathering more berries than he can possibly eat, James gathers "from the hurrying hours more impressions than a mind of modest capacity quite knows how to dispose of" (140). The impression is of a frenetic artist who has neither the time nor money to frame all the paintings and sketches that pile up and clutter his studio and attic.

James's "vacationistic prose" underlines the connection Richard H. Brodhead sees between the consumption of travel, the generation of social distinction, and the new prestige of art during the late nineteenth century.[13] William Stowe says: "James's traveler acts out of his privileged position, then, by maintaining an aesthetic detachment from and a proud nationalistic superiority to the social and political concerns of 'foreign' people."[14] There are, to be sure, Italians in some of James's Italian pictures, but often they are there simply as an aesthetic touch, a colorful detail in a picturesque scene that usually conforms to conventional ideas about Italy and Italians. Stowe argues that James reaffirms the superiority of his own class, nationality, and gender by naturalizing indigenous populations as part of the scenery, or by treating them as commodified, consumable "Others," much in the way tourists typically do. James reenacts "the archetypal tourist-imperialist moment, what Pratt calls 'the monarch-of-all-I-survey,' in which landscape and all it contains are presented to the traveler and represented to the reader to be enjoyed, interpreted (or, rather endowed with meaning), and mastered."[15] But if James is going to consume Italians and Italian culture, he will not do it in the gourmand manner of a vulgar tourist on a package tour. Not for James the *Quaker City* cruise, which Mark Twain turned into *The Innocents Abroad* and published in 1869, the same year James made his first solo trip to the Continent. James is too subtle a writer to be a tourist, a role he consciously avoids by turning his more finely tuned sensibility to the finer things of Italy. As Stowe says, James does often naturalize and romanticize the Italians through the picturesque perspective. However, James also critiques these tendencies of the sentimental traveler, either through irony or in more direct fashion. We will see this dialogue between the picturesque and the more cold-eyed approaches to Italy in James's early tales, where romanticizers are set against the more cynical Americans in Italy. That same dialogue appears in *Italian Hours*, with James alternately employing and critiquing the aestheticizing, romanticizing picturesque perspective. Put another way, James's habitual use of words such as "picturesque" and "appropriation" suggests a conflicted, conscious use of the picturesque to convert travel into cultural capital. However, James both embraces and critiques the tendency, making the travel pieces both acts of appropriation and subtle subversions/exposures of the act.[16] James is aware of the social price of picturesqueness. He knows that Italy's and the Italian's aesthetic appeal often goes hand in hand with decay, poverty, and degradation. However, more often than not, he focuses on the aesthetic appeal of what he sees and does not consider the conflict between aesthetics and politics as one to be resolved in principle.[17]

James's travel writings feature numerous images of picturesque poverty and misery. There is a tendency to see Italy through the rose-colored lenses of the literary and the romantic—that is, conventionally. But if James is drawn to the romantic, picturesque, literary Italy of the imagination, he is not unaware of that tendency, just as he is not totally blind to the realities and the material conditions of contemporary Italians. There is often tension between romance and reality. For example, describing a shepherd lying under a tree in a sketch dating from 1873, James frames the picture and adds a patina of romance to it. "Lying thus in the shade, on his elbow, with his naked legs stretched out on the turf and his soft peaked hat over his long hair crushed back like the veritable bonnet of Arcady, he was exactly the figure of the background of this happy valley." But having naturalized the shepherd, James undercuts his efforts, while at the same time holding on to his knowing privileged perspective. "The poor fellow, lying there in rustic weariness and ignorance, little fancied that he was a symbol of old-world meanings to new-world eyes" (150). Whether fixing the shepherd as a figure of romance or perhaps imagining a different role for him, James, from his strategic location, contains the rustic figure, representing him and speaking on his behalf. If the shepherd is not a symbol of Old World meanings, then what is he? James never says. Neither does the shepherd have his say.

In other passages, James more clearly demarcates romance and reality, past and present, art and life. In one anecdote dating from 1878, James recounts seeing a young man singing in Genoa. James wants to make of the figure "a graceful ornament to the prospect, an harmonious little figure in the middle distance," but in talking to the young man he instead discovers an "unhappy, underfed, unemployed" radical. "'Damn the prospect, damn the middle distance!' would have been all *his* philosophy," James writes. "Yet but for the accident of my having gossiped with him I should have made him do service, in memory, as an example of sensuous optimism!" However, if the young radical becomes an individual in this encounter (although we never actually hear *him* talk), James concludes that the fellow is exceptional in his misery and discontent. "I am bound to say however that I believe a great deal of the sensuous optimism observable in the Genoese alleys and beneath the low, crowded arcades along the port was very real" (107). This young man who resists James's picturesque aestheticizing is an exception in yet another way. He represents one of the few cases in *Italian Hours* in which we have some sense that James is actually talking to an ordinary Italian. We may not hear the young radical actually speaking, but we do learn a few personal details. However, not unlike many American travelers before him, James seems to have passed through Italy without ever really having had many human relations with the Italians. As Van Wyck Brooks says, "Of the Italians, [James] complained, besides the washerwoman, he knew only servants in hotels and custodians in churches, and, being neither a Dickens nor a Howells, he had nothing to say about such humble types."[18] Brooks is overstating the case. The fact is that James did have some things to say about such humble types, especially the picturesque *contadini*, but little of it seems to spring from any social contact beyond that required by the exigencies of travel, the needs of his literary profession, or the idle curiosity of the traveler.

It is rare in *Italian Hours* to hear an Italian talking, which is not the case in William Dean Howells's *Venetian Life*, published in 1866, some seven years before the first of James's Italian sketches. While Howells also talks of the difficulties of cracking Italian society and truly getting to know the people, his book is alive with Italian characters with whom he has interacted, including his neighbors, housekeeper, barber, and young Italian friends. Obviously, Howells had the advantage of a long sojourn in Italy, during which he was more than a tourist/writer. Serving as the largely ceremonial American consul in Venice, Howells consequently "saw Venice as a student of people, as a householder, besides, who had encounters with chimney-sweeps, with glaziers, chair-menders, upholsterers, fishermen, milkmen."[19] Howells not only lets his Italians speak, but attempts—if not very successfully—to capture the dialect of Italians speaking English. Howells's contacts are often on a business level, but some are more social than not. There is little of this type of interaction in James, or at least very little of it that makes its way into print. Howells could appreciate the Italian picturesque as much as James but is more interested in politics, commerce, and everyday life and customs. Although Howells is as interested as James is in the Italians' character traits, he inquires more deeply into the political, economic, and social influences on those traits.

James rarely has time to truly ponder the reality behind the sensuous optimism he wants to see in the Italian people. Illustrative is a tavern scene in the Campagna that James sketches in an 1873 essay. The scene is picturesque to a fault: "There is generally a rabble of infantile beggars at the door, pretty enough in their dusty rags, with their fine eyes and intense Italian smile, to make you forget your private vow of doing your individual best to make these people, whom you like so much, unlearn their old vices" (143–144). James's response is an interesting one: a case of the aesthetic tendency, the tendency ultimately to judge Italy and Italian life on aesthetic rather than ethical standards, clouding some vague humanitarian impulses James might have toward these particular Italians. Whatever reforming tendency James might have gets lost in the realization that the Italians' aesthetic virtues quite often just happen to derive from what James calls "their old vices"—their filth, their begging, their childlike acceptance of their fate. We have seen this same tendency, this urge to see picturesque value in the Italians' vices, in Jacob Riis. However, much more is going on here with James. Having accepted the beggars for their picturesque qualities, James undercuts that acceptance with a reference to the capture of Rome in 1870, which completed Italy's unification. He asks: "Was Porta Pia bombarded three years ago that Peppino should still grow up to whine for copper? But the shells had no direct message for Peppino's stomach—and you are going to a dinner party at a villa. So Peppino 'points' an instant for the copper in the dust and grows up a Roman beggar" (144). This passage is one of the few times James looks beyond Italy's poverty and misery to their potential causes. Quite rightly, as it turned out, the newly unified Italy did little to relieve conditions for the country's poorer classes, especially those of the South. The shells used to bombard the Porta Pia, as James realized early on, had no direct message for Peppino and others of his ilk. However, having ventured into political and social questions, James feels the need to pull back. His thoughts turn to the dinner party, where political and social issues might be inappropriate subjects. James's dismissal of Peppino as a future Roman beggar, while arguably a recognition of Italian "reality," closes off any possibility of change in Italy, and by inference posits a general, unspecified Italian failing as the cause of that inability to change.

A more abiding concern for Italy's dispossessed is shown by Mrs. Arthur (Katherine De Kay) Bronson, an American expatriate in Venice who often entertained James at her home on the Grand Canal. Mrs. Bronson loved "the engaging Venetian people, whose virtues she found touching and their infirmities but such as appeal mainly to the sense of humour and the love of anecdote," James writes. She wrote and staged short comedies, sometimes engaging as actors "children of the Venetian lower class, whose aptitude, teachability, drollery, were her constant delight" (75). Here we have humble Venetian children whose virtues of quickness and amiability are no more valuable than (or equally valuable to) their unnamed vices—"infirmities," James calls them—that give them the virtue of drollery and make them such fit subjects for short comedies and anecdotal storytelling. These children are not much different from the childlike adult peasants whose "infirmities" lend themselves to picturesque art.

In all these scenes, Italians—*contadini*, beggars, children, the lower classes in general—are aestheticized, made symbols of romance, elements of the picturesque, subjects of humor and anecdote, actors in small comedies. Again, however, James is aware that his travel abroad was an exercise in such aestheticizing. He wrote in a *New York Daily Tribune* column on December 11, 1875, "We most of us transact our moral and spiritual affairs in our own country. . . . We wander about Europe on a sensuous and aesthetic basis."[20] As Alan Holder says, James's approach to Europe was to see it as spectacle, material for satisfaction of the senses, imposing no involvement with or responsibility for that which is observed. "Italy, and Venice in particular, elicited from James an aesthetic response in which there was something unfeeling."[21]

We can perhaps best see this unfeeling romantic attitude in a passage from the essay "Venice: An Early Impression." On a visit to the island of Torcello near Venice, James encounters some begging urchins. "They were very nearly as naked as savages, and their little bellies protruded like those of infant Abyssinians in the illustrations of books of travel," James writes. Having turned the children into near-savage Africans, James proceeds to idealize them before turning them into an argument for innocence and poverty. "[G]rinning like suddenly translated cherubs," the urchins "suggested forcibly that the best assurance of happiness in this world is to be found in the maximum of innocence and the minimum of wealth." One small urchin who had "a smile to make Correggio sigh" was running wild "among the sea-stunted bushes, on the lonely margin of a decaying land, in prelude to how blank, or to how dark, a destiny?" The irony of this picturesque, angelic, but poor urchin is not lost on James, who compares the Italian boy with an imagined American child. "An infant citizen of our own republic, straight-haired, pale-eyed, and freckled, duly darned and catechized, marching into a New England school-house, is an object often seen and soon forgotten; but I shall always remember, with infinite tender conjecture, as the years roll by, this little unlettered Eros of the Adriatic strand" (53–54). Despite James's professed preference for the Italian, at least as an object of aesthetic nostalgia, the comparison sets up a stark racial/national dualism. The American boy is a duly-darned Anglo-Saxon citizen of a solid republic that values education; the Italian boy is an ignorant creature of the senses running wild "on the lonely margin of a decaying land" that presumably does not value education. These two boys will reappear in different incarnations in *The American Scene*. There, however, the "little unlettered Eros of the Adriatic" is now a young man—"a flagrant foreigner" and "remorseless Italian"—and the American boy is a much more appealing and memorable child who serves for James as an antidote to the disconcerting Italian.

As we have seen, James is aware of and sometimes critiques his aestheticizing and patronizing attitude. This occurs most dramatically in the essay "Italy Revisited," which appeared in *The Atlantic* in 1878. Here James draws a sharp distinction between heroic, artistic Italy and modern, commercial Italy. Returning to Italy, James is struck by the fact that the race of Michelangelo, Raphael, Leonardo, and Titian was now best known for producing "third-rate *genre* pictures and catchpenny statues" (102). But having disparaged contemporary Italy in favor of some heroic golden past, James catches himself and returns to the present. "After thinking of Italy as historical and artistic it will do no great harm to think of her for a while as panting both for a future and for a balance at the bank; aspirations supposedly much at variance with the Byronic, the Ruskinian, the artistic, poetic, aesthetic manner of considering our eternally attaching peninsula," James cautions, perhaps adding by inference the modifier "Jamesian" to these conventional ways of considering Italy. Initially irritated by this modern Italy, James tries to accept it. "For, if we think, nothing is more easy to understand than an honest ire on the part of the young Italy of to-day at being looked at by all the world as a kind of soluble pigment. Young Italy, preoccupied with its economical and political future, must be heartily tired of being admired for its eyelashes and its pose" (102–103). Focusing on the eyelids and pose not only aestheticizes but feminizes Italy and Italians. So, here James seems to be asking why we cannot see young Italy, modern Italy, and by extension modern Italians, as masculine beings concerned with the masculine pursuits of economics and politics. As an example of this misplaced admiration of picturesque Italy, James mentions the young artist in one of Thackeray's novels who sent to the Royal Academy a picture representing "A Contadino dancing with a Trasteverina at the door of a Locanda, to the music of Pifferaro." "It is in this attitude and with these conventional accessories that the world has hitherto seen fit to represent young Italy, and one doesn't wonder that if the youth has any spirit he should at least begin to resent our insufferable aesthetic patronage." It is interesting that now, as "young Italy," the country is a he, masculine. Turning his attention to the new tram-line in Rome, James foresees "a new Italy in the future which in many important respects will equal, if not surpass, the most enterprising sections of our native land." James does not specify what those important respects are, other than to simply say that in passing through Italian cities, "we" see a vision of the coming years that represents "Italy united and prosperous, but altogether scientific and commercial" (103–104). Italy's history in the late nineteenth and early twentieth centuries obviously proved James wrong. Unification did not bring a prosperous, scientific, and commercial South, the result of which will be James's shocking encounters with Italian immigrants in a radically changed America.

Having taken what, for James, passes as a cold hard look at contemporary Italian realities, he lets these thoughts dissipate and soon finds himself in Genoa, "up to his neck in the old Italian sketchability." But even here, James ruminates a bit on the reality behind the romance, even while meditating on his own artistic temperament. He concedes that there is "something heartless in stepping forth into foreign streets to feast on 'character' when character consists simply of the slightly different costume in which labour and want present themselves." However, "at least to the foreign eye," the Italians accept their "extreme and constant destitution" with "an enviable ability not to be depressed by circumstances." These accepting Italians, supremely able to bear their degraded conditions, anticipate Riis's docile, unambitious Italian immigrants. In yet another reversal, James, aware that he may be rationalizing, speaking utter nonsense, acknowledges the possibility that the Italian smile may be masking "a sullen frenzy of impatience and pain." Finally, James concedes, as Mark Twain himself would point out, that it is presumptuous for an observer to think he can truly understand a foreign country and a foreign people: "Our observation in any foreign land is extremely superficial, and our remarks are happily not addressed to the inhabitants themselves, who would be sure to exclaim upon the impudence of the fancy-picture" (106).

Having said that, a few years later James is back at creating fancy-pictures, the fanciest of all about Venice, which for James was the most sensual of Italian cities. In his 1882 sketch "Venice," James says of the city: "You desire to embrace it, to caress it, to possess it; and finally, a soft sense of possession grows up, and your visit becomes a perpetual love affair" (11–12). Still, in his perpetual love affair with a Venice that is both aesthetic and carnal, James is not blind to the problems of the Venetian people, whose habitations are decayed, taxes heavy, pockets light, and opportunities few. James is aware of the social and political problems, many of which are similar to those Howells had seen some two decades earlier, but again, unlike Howells, he does not dwell on the causes. Instead his focus is on the Italian's adaptability and sensuous optimism, his willingness to make do, to make the best of a bad situation. These same traits, transplanted to the New York ghettos, would be criticized by Jacob Riis as the Italian's tendency to fall behind other immigrant groups in material progress. James says that there may not be enough to eat in Venice, but "the rich Venetian temperament may bloom upon a dog's allowance." The "painfully large" numbers of Venetians who go hungry have for sustenance the sunshine, beautiful views, leisure, and "eternal *conversazione*." "It takes a great deal to make a successful American, but to make a happy Venetian takes only a handful of quick sensibility," James writes, with a rather cold-blooded patronizing tone. "Not their misery, doubtless, but the way they elude their misery, is what pleases the sentimental tourist, who is gratified by the sight of a beautiful race that lives by the aid of its imagination. The way to enjoy Venice is to follow the example of these people and make the most of simple pleasure" (9).

When commenting directly on the Italian character, James echoes Howells, but without Howells's urge to inquire, in more than cursory fashion, into the sources of that character. The Italian race, as exemplified by the Venetians, is gentle, polite, polished in manners, but wanting in morality, virtue, and industry. These are the very qualities that (for James, Riis, and many others) make an American an American. But only Howells wonders whether the Venetians' politeness and gentleness, which he contrasts with American rudeness and haste, is not the "vice of servile people" that have a history of subjugation.[22] James, on the other hand, essentializes the Venetians in a long tortured passage that is vague, sometimes contradictory, and perhaps ultimately impossible to pin down. Venetians/Italians inspire fondness, James says, because of their frank, sweet, and ingratiating manners. That is, they know their place. Their identity is in their race; their blood makes them what they are. Their race has "a long and rich civilization in their blood," which time has polished to a high gloss. But, beneath the pleasing surfaces of manners, address, and a desire to please, the Venetian/Italian is lacking in the American/Anglo-Saxon values of bravery, industriousness, and morality. The biggest lack is "stiff morality": the race is grasping and crooked in its business dealings, loose with its love, and too sensual in its approach to life. "But it has an unfailing sense of the amenities of life; the poorest Venetian is a natural man of the world," James concludes. "He is better company than persons of his class are apt to be among the nations of industry and virtue—where people are also sometimes perceived to lie and steal and otherwise misconduct themselves." This is a curious sentence, and raises a question: Is the poorest Venetian any different from a cultured upper-class Venetian? James does not say. However, he does say that the poorest Venetian is better company (because he is natural, or because of his manners?) than his counterparts in "nations of industry and virtue" (presumably America and England, among others). And even in these Anglo-Saxon nations, "people" are "also sometimes perceived" to lie, steal, and misbehave, just like the Venetian/Italian. Who these "people" are, whether they represent all classes or are limited to the poor class, James does not say. The phrase "also sometimes perceived" is slippery. Is this perception, which is only sometimes applied to these people, the reality—or is it a misconception? If the latter, then are the accusations of crooked dealings against the Italian race little more than false accusations, too? Not likely, for James is unequivocal when he says the Italian race "hasn't a genius for stiff morality" (19).

Having said all that, James fails to examine why the Italian is the way he is perceived to be. James may be interested in Italian history, but not that portion of Italian history that had helped to create a people whose virtues are associated with surface manners, social graces, and a sensual approach to life, and whose vices are a disregard for values such as bravery, morality, industriousness, and austerity. James in not interested in contemporary political and social conditions, or in any influence they may have on the Italian people. Two decades earlier, Howells had made similar comments about the Italians, noting their indolence and loose morals. However, living among them and showing a keener interest in social history and current events, he saw the Italians' defects not as something apparently intrinsic to the race, but rather the product of centuries of foreign oppression and other material conditions. For Howells, Italian indolence came from the enervating climate and lack of opportunity. The lying, cheating, and duplicity originated in the country's political and religious oppression. James might be aware of these connections, but apparently does not think them worth further exploration.

And yet, Sara Blair, one of the more provocative of James's critics, reads the "deliberately aestheticized essays" of *Italian Hours* within the broader context of Anglo-Saxon orientalism and emerges with a subversive James who avoids the conventional roles of both the dominating orientalist and the commodifying tourist. Blair says that James, unlike professional orientalists who are deeply ambivalent about their identification with the so-called feminine, occult races, explores "rather more 'queer' forms of racial identification and response." James's "'queer' identification with orientalized passivity and feminization" afford him "'peculiar' possibilities of 'floating,' not only beyond conventional gender divides but across boundaries of history, nation, and race." Blair argues that James's essay on Venice explicitly redirects Anglo-Saxon and American styles of acquisition and response. "James in Venice is never intent on becoming the putative other, but rather in constructing a cultural position from which otherness can be more pleasurably and freely experienced, and against which the limits of conventional filiations—of family, gender, nation, culture, race—can be tested and contested." Ultimately, Blair argues, James is trying to "revise racial and national typologies, to construct an open-endedly modern, internationalist, self-consciously shifting style of cultural subjectivity and response." As we will see, Blair carves out a very similar role for the James who appears some twenty years later in *The American Scene*.[23]

Although Blair makes a painstakingly nuanced and sometimes persuasive argument, I would argue that she is overstating her case. Yes, there is some of the subversive in James. He does make halting efforts at carving out a new position vis-à-vis Italy/Italians, one that goes beyond the usual aestheticizing, possessing, containing, othering, and otherwise dominating stance attributed to orientalists, tourists, and antimodernists. And from this position maybe he is critiquing Anglo-Saxon/American character and conventional notions of family, gender, nation, race, and culture. But is James the traveler really much more than a supremely sensitive upper middle-class *flaneur*, one who is in a privileged position that allows him to distance himself from America while playing the role of man of the world? Susan Sontag's description of the photographer as middle-class *flaneur* fits James nearly perfectly. "The photographer," Sontag writes, "is an armed version of the solitary walker reconnoitering, stalking, cruising the urban inferno, the voyeuristic stroller who discovers the city as a landscape of voluptuous extremes. Adept of the joys of watching, connoisseur of empathy, the *flaneur* finds the world 'picturesque.'"[24] Like the photographer, James is armed, not with a camera, but with a mental canvas; his pictures are word pictures. And what are these word pictures like? The fact remains that many of the images, tropes, ideas, and attitudes that James attaches to Venice/Venetians, Italy/Italians parallel Orientalist representations of the Orient/Orientals. Italy, like the Orient, is seen as a place of degradation, decay, and sensuousness, at best a stage for spectacle, at worst a moribund museum. Like the Orient, Italy has long ago seen its greatest days. The Italians themselves, like the Orientals or any other Others, possess some attractive qualities, but generally they have low morals, are lethargic and childlike, and approach life fatalistically. Like the Orientals, the Italians are essentially premodern primitives (albeit sometimes graceful ones with polished manners). But to give James his due, he is sympathetic enough to understand that there were some self-aware Italians who aspired to modernity, or were at least aware that such an outlook existed. We will see this Italian groping toward modernity in at least two of James's fiction works, "The Last of the Valerii" and *The Golden Bowl*.

Many of the same images, tropes, tensions, and themes that we see in James's travel writing are reprised in his early fiction. Here we again note the clash between romance and reality, between an Italy that is aesthetically pleasing but morally troubling. And it is here that we begin to see dramatized the oppositions between America/northern Europe and Italy, and between northern Italy and southern Italy.

In the early stories that emerged from James's first two trips to Europe in 1869–1870 and 1872–1874, James continues his love affair with Italy and the Italian landscape, which for him were the essence and meaning of the picturesque. But beneath Italy's pleasing aesthetic surfaces, James finds images of danger, poverty, and moral bankruptcy lurking in the background. In many ways, the conflicting images of James's stories are conventional ones. "The picture of Italy as the land of art, of passion, and of the survival of the pagan past conforms to traditional American images, and so does the undertone of social or political criticism contained in occasional allusions to the 'heavy heritage' of the past, to the profligate alliance of 'arts and vices,' and to the daily misery of common people hidden behind the holiday show of the picturesque."[25] James's antithetical images of Italy embody not only conventional American notions, but also typically Anglo-Saxon perceptions dating as far back as the Renaissance. On the one hand, Italy was seen "as a venerable relic of the Roman Empire, as purveyor and exemplar of culture and civilization, a land of carefree sensuous enjoyment and sunny skies." At the same time it was an Old World, Roman Catholic "sink of elegant vice and luxurious corruption, of subtle treachery with dagger and poison, of cynical sensual indulgence and Machiavellian casuistry, a moral hothouse pullulating with Jesuits, assassins, and courtesans." We are reminded that if James Russell Lowell saw ancient Italy as a political and cultural soul mate for America, earlier in life his image of contemporary Italy was of monks bearing poison and "bravos" wielding stilettos. James's treatments of Italy and Italians in Italy often deal with three complex motifs or broad thematic areas: romance, treachery, and sensuousness. We begin to observe all three themes in his early tales.[26]

In the three years following his first visit to Italy, James wrote five tales with Italian settings. The first two, "Travelling Companions" (1870) and "At Isella" (1871), are essentially fictionalized travelogues featuring narrators experiencing Italy for the first time. Despite any shortcomings these stories may have as literature, each begins to lay out in some concentrated fashion James's attitudes toward Italy. In "Travelling Companions," the narrator is a Mr. Brooke, a young American living in Germany who had long dreamed of making an "Italian pilgrimage."[27] Once in Italy, the narrator immediately begins making the kind of racial and geographical distinctions that would be more schematically laid bare by Jacob Riis, Edward Steiner, and other race-conscious observers of the late nineteenth century. Brooke calls da Vinci's *Last Supper* in Milan the "most strictly impressive picture in Italy" because it is the first Italian masterwork one encounters "in coming down from the North," and because of the "very completeness of its decay" (171). These observations by the narrator conflate Italy, high art, and decay, and implicitly contrast Germany and Italy, North and South, Anglo-Saxon/Nordic and Mediterranean/Latin. The North is where one lives and makes a living. The South, on the other hand, is where one visits to satisfy the senses, both aesthetic and sensual. Milan has for Brooke "a peculiar charm of temperate gayety,—the softness of the South without its laxity." He tells Charlotte Evans, the American woman he meets: "It's the South, the South . . . the South in nature, in man, in manners" (181). Brooke says that northern Italian towns "exhaled the pure essence of romance," even if they are "shabby, deserted, dreary, decayed, unclean" (184). When Charlotte speaks of Venice's "bright, sad elegance of ruin," Brooke replies that the city's reality exceeds its romance, saying that it is "romance enough simply to be here" (194). But it is not enough simply to be in Italy; one must also possess it. Standing atop the cathedral in Milan, Brooke, the northern traveler and "monarch-of-all-he-surveys," feels a "vague delicious impulse of conquest" stirring his heart (179). However, there is always the risk of being possessed by that which one seeks to possess, and Italy threatens a reverse conquest. Rejecting Brooke's marriage proposal, Charlotte says she hopes she will not see him in Rome. "I had rather not meet you again in Italy," she tells Brooke. "It perverts our dear good old American truth" (218). In other words, do not let Italian romance/falsity overwhelm American reality/truth.

However, if Charlotte wants to draw a line between clear-eyed American truth and blinding (untruthful) Italian romance, Brooke seeks instead to dissolve the distance between the Italian reality and the Italian romantic picturesque. The reality of an Italian woman praying "such bitter, bitter tears" in the Milan cathedral becomes for Brooke the stuff of romance. "This poor woman is the genius of the Picturesque," Brooke tells Charlotte. "She shows us the essential misery that lies behind it" (183). This fleeting awareness of the grim reality behind the picturesque is typical of James's own response to Italy in his travel essays.

It is not only the oppressed poor who are aestheticized in "Travelling Companions." Spotting a group of young Venetian gentlemen who are "glorious with the wondrous physical glory of the Italian race," Brooke says that they need only "velvet and satin and plumes" to be "subjects for Titian and Paul Veronese" (195). However, for all their pleasing aesthetic qualities, the Venetian gentlemen are seen as inferior to a young man, a gentleman, and a lady who are "all genuine Anglo-Saxons." The young Anglo-Saxon man is "not beautiful" but instead "handsome," Charlotte says, contrasting him to the "exceedingly beautiful" Venetian gentlemen. Here, not only Italy but also its men are gendered as feminine, pleasing to look at, but without the

Anglo-Saxon's more virile "handsome" manhood. And while the Venetians are passive subjects fit only for a picturesque painting, the young Anglo-Saxon is something altogether different. "The young man's face was full of decision and spirit; his whole figure had been moulded by action, tempered by effort. He looked simple and keen, upright, downright." When Charlotte inquires whether the young man is English or American, Brooke, like many of the Anglo-Saxonists of the late nineteenth century, dismisses any difference between the two. "He is both," Brooke tells Charlotte, "or either. He is made of that precious clay that is common to the whole English-speaking race" (196). Charlotte's father is also characterized in contrast to the passive, picturesque Italians. Mr. Evans is a "perfect American" who has a "shrewd, firm, generous face, which told of many dealings with many men, of stocks and shares and current prices" (173). Although Mr. Evans may lack taste, culture, and polish, he "nevertheless produced an impression of substance in character, keenness in perception, and intensity in will, which effectually redeemed him from vulgarity" and made him rather "aristocratic" (198).

There are some Italians in "Travelling Companions" who, like the Americans/Anglo-Saxons, are active, decisive, willful, but they too stand in contrast to Mr. Evans and the handsome young Anglo-Saxon man. There is, for example, an Italian family that tries to persuade Brooke to buy a painting that the family attempts to pass off as a genuine Correggio. The mother of the family plays on the narrator's sympathies with a sad tale about her poor, ailing daughter. Comparing Charlotte to the Italian daughter, Brooke says: "How she seemed to glow with strength, freedom, and joy, beside this somber, fading Southern sister!" (189). Brooke buys the painting and leaves the family "with a painful, indefinable sadness. So beautiful they all were, so civil, so charming, and yet so mendacious and miserable!" (191). Like Charlotte's father, these Italians are shrewd dealers, but they lack his character. They are essentially false in their business dealings, and false in their appearances, especially the daughter, who is a pale southern version of Charlotte and her northern/American/Anglo-Saxon health and freedom.

Traveling to Naples, Brooke discovers what he realizes is "the real South—the Southern South,—in art, in nature, in man, and the least bit in woman," a description that virtually echoes phrases he had applied to the Italian North (220). In Naples, Brooke meets an Italian woman recommended to him by a German lady friend. "She assured me on my first visit that she was a 'true Neapolitan,' and I think, on the whole, she was right. She told me that I was a true German, but in this she was altogether wrong." Brooke spends four days with the unnamed woman. On the last day, she takes him to Capri, where she has an infant. On the return to Naples, as the lady sings a song, Brooke realizes his mistake in assuming that northern Italy could have the "softness of the South without its laxity." Now he sees the more fundamental difference between northern and southern Italy. "As I looked up at Northern Italy, it seemed, in contrast, a cold, dark hyperborean clime, a land of order, conscience, and virtue" (220).

This distinction between northern and southern Italy was one that many Americans would make later in the nineteenth century as they tried to balance long-held notions of romantic, heroic Italy with negative images of Italian immigrants. The distinction, which eventually would be racially codified in an official American immigration document, allowed Americans to continue to admire Italy in its ordered, virtuous, heroic incarnation in the North, while recoiling from the supposedly disordered, dirty, morally lax southern Italy represented by southern Italian immigrants. Whatever "Travelling Companions" may lack in literary merit, the short story schematizes certain attitudes concerning geography, race/nationality, and human character that would have their full flowering later in the century. The story contrasts not only America and Italy, but also Northern Europe and the "South," northern Italy and southern Italy, and the northern Italian and the southern Italian. America is allied with northern Europe, and northern Italy is tied, if more tenuously, to northern Europe. Only southern Italy, the real "South," stands alone as something truly different and exotic. Americans and their cousins from northern European are shrewd, firm, decisive men of action; Italians in general are civil and charming, but soft, lax, mendacious, miserable. However, northern Italians, seen from the perspective of the real "South," look more like Americans and northern Europeans: people of order, conscience, and virtue. The woman from Naples, with her whiff of sexuality and scandal (a child living somewhere else, no mention of a husband), is, as Brooke says, a "true Neapolitan." And what of Brooke himself? He demurs when the Neapolitan woman describes him as a "true German." But is the woman that far off-base? The American Brooke lives in Germany, and as nativist race thinkers would point out more and more toward the turn of the century, Anglo-Saxon Americans were descendants of the Germanic race.

In "At Isella" (1871), another young American narrator who is intoxicated with the romance of the Italian picturesque is making his first descent into Italy. While still in Lucerne, Switzerland, he imagines "a great wave of Southern life" rolling down the mountains into that city's lake (2:308). Climbing the mountains into Italy, he wants "to trace the soft stages by which those rugged heights melt over into Southern difference" and begins "to watch for the *symptoms* of Italy." Here, "it was not absurd to fancy a few adventurous tendrils of Southern growth might have crept and clamored upward" (317). At Isella, the narrator thanks heaven that the inn was not "fastidiously neat, scrubbed" in Swiss fashion, but instead in need of "a wet cloth and broom" (319). Jacob Riis would echo these sentiments in *How the Other Half Lives*, when he says that Chinatown is "clean to distraction" and therefore disappointing as spectacle, compared to the lively, colorful "picturesque filth and poverty" found in the Italian Mulberry Bend.[28]

The narrator finds romance not only in the dirt but also in his encounter with a mysterious Italian lady who is fleeing her native land. "Of what romance of Italy was she the heroine?" the narrator wonders (322). He sees the "beautiful, pale, dark-browed, sad" signora as "an incorporate image of her native land" (327). But the lady scoffs at his romantic notions. "'The charm of Italy!' cried the Signora, with a slightly cynical laugh. 'Foreigners have a great deal to say about it'" (326). Undeterred, the narrator tells the signora that he has come on pilgrimage from a land "barren of romance and grace" to the "home of history, of beauty, of the arts." Italy is a "magic word," he says. "We cross ourselves when we pronounce it" (327–328). The narrator's image of a magical Italy worthy of worship is utterly conventional. But what are we to make of his claim that presumably Protestant Americans employ the Catholic sign of the cross when pronouncing the country's name? This may simply mean that Italy's magic is a kind of religion for dull, unromantic Americans who worship the country in the same fashion that Italians pay homage to their God. And yet Italians also cross themselves as a way to ward off the devil or the *mal'occhio* (evil eye). Does this then imply that, for the Americans, Italy's magic may also have an element of evil, of black magic, of superstition, in it? Italy's attractions are also its *"symptoms."* Its waves and tendrils, so alluring at a distance, can also drown or strangle you. The passage seems to be saying that Italy was both a god (or goddess) to be reverenced and a she-devil to be feared.

We see this same ambivalence toward Italy at the end of the tale, when the signora flees Isella one step ahead of her pursuing husband, leaving the narrator to ponder his first (defining) experience of Italy. "I returned along the winding footpath more slowly, a wiser, possibly a sadder man than a couple of hours before," he says. "I had entered Italy, I had tasted a sentiment, I had assisted at a drama. It was a good beginning" (338). A good beginning maybe, but in describing himself as "a wiser, possibly a sadder man," the narrator reminds us of Nathaniel Hawthorne's Young Goodman Brown, the Puritan who emerges from his night in the evil forest "a sad, a darkly meditative" man. If nothing else, "At Isella" conjures up contrasting conventional images of Italy as alluring, but a bit disheveled (needing a "wet cloth and broom"), mysterious but slightly sinister.

"The Madonna of the Future" (1873) extends these conventional images of Italy. The story's protagonist is the young artist Theobold, an American ("He must have been, to take the picturesque so prodigiously to heart"), who values Italy as a source of the type of inspiration that he, like James himself, sees lacking in America. "'We are the disinherited of Art!' he cried. 'We are condemned to be superficial! We are excluded from the magic circle.... We lack the deeper sense. We have neither taste, not tact, nor force'" (3: 14–15). Theobold's vocabulary echoes that of the narrator of "At Isella." Of Florence, where all his "profane desires, all mere worldly aims, have dropped away" (16), he says: "She's the sole true woman of them all; one feels toward her as a lad in his teens feels to some beautiful older woman with a 'history.' It's a sort of aspiring gallantry she creates" (24). Again the gendered language: Florence/Italy as a woman, on one hand sacred, on the other a more secular older woman "with a 'history'" (sexual pun intended?).

There is a second, more human woman in Theobold's life, one that will serve as the model for the ideal Madonna that he hopes to but never paints. The artist describes his model as "the most beautiful woman in Italy." However, the unnamed narrator of the story, whose perceptions have not been distorted by Italy and art, sees only an aging woman now growing stout. "She was neither haggard nor worn nor gray; she was simply coarse" (30–33). While the woman humors Theobold in his illusions, the narrator does not. By destroying Theobold's illusions, the narrator puts the finishing touches on the destruction of the would-be artist that Italy herself had begun. The deceptive, sometimes destructive influence of art-laden Italy on Americans who are "disinherited of Art" was a theme that James would take up and extend in his novel *Roderick Hudson*, published two years after "The Madonna of the Future." Roderick Hudson drinks too deeply from the cup of Italy's experience and becomes another American artist who is figuratively and literally destroyed by the country's seductions.

If "The Madonna of the Future" points to *Roderick Hudson*, "The Last of the Valerii" (1874) is a sort of early dress rehearsal for *The Golden Bowl*. In each, an American woman marries an Italian nobleman, with dubious results. In "The Last of the Valerii," the narrator is initially skeptical about his goddaughter marrying any foreigner whatsoever. However, "from the picturesque point of view (she with her yellow locks and he with his dusky ones)," the narrator concedes that the union between his ward and Count Camillo Valerio made for a "strikingly well-assorted pair" (3:89). The narrator considers the Count surprisingly honest for an Italian, but stupid and dull, and a sensualist. The Count "had no beliefs nor hopes nor fears,—nothing but sense, appetites, and serenely luxurious tastes." In short, the Count is an embodiment of "the natural man," primitive, picturesque, and essentially harmless (89, 94–95). Harmless, that is, until an ancient statue is discovered buried on his property.

Conceding that he is superstitious, the Count at first resists his wife's desire to excavate their property in search of buried ruins. Soon, however, he takes an interest in the excavations. When a Juno is discovered and unearthed, the Count begins to treat the statue as a sacred deity to whom he pays solitary visits, while now ignoring his wife. This only confirms the narrator's earlier misgivings about the Count. "Give us some wholesome young fellow of our own blood, who'll play us none of these dusky old-world tricks," the narrator says. "Painter as I am, I'll never recommend a picturesque husband!" (106). Like the three earlier stories, "The Last of the Valerii" meditates on the limits of the romantic picturesque, and the trouble that lurks when it is pursued too blindly. Here, it is a painter, no less, who learns that the picturesque is downright dangerous to practical domesticity. Interestingly, the narrator racializes the Italian picturesque: the corrupt, picturesque Valerio, with his Old World tricks, is inferior to some "wholesome" young fellow of the narrator's own American/Anglo-Saxon blood. The narrator continues his criticism of the Count with a lengthy peroration on the corrupting influences of Italian history, ancestry, and race, which he blames for Valerio's worship of a pagan statue and his cruel indifference to his wife. The Count becomes for the narrator "a dark efflorescence of the evil germs which had implanted in his line. . . . The unholy passions of his forefathers stirred blindly in his untaught nature and clamored dumbly for an issue" (107). James would employ a similar diatribe about Italian racial history in *The Golden Bowl* thirty years later, but there the catalogue of Italy's corrupting influences would be put into the mouth of an Italian, Prince Amerigo. However, if Prince Amerigo seeks to rise above his racial heritage, Count Valerio is mired in the ancient past. When the Count speaks of persecution, it is not of Christians by the pagans, but of pagans by Christians. Hearing this, the narrator meditates on "the strange ineffaceability of race-characteristics" and the undreamed strength of the Count's sturdy Latinness (111). In the end, Valerio accedes to his wife's desires to rebury the Juno. Yielding, the Count falls on his knees, buries his head in his wife's lap, and becomes a good dutiful husband. However, the narrator concludes, Count Valerio never becomes "a thoroughly modern man" (122). There is no reason to believe the count even desired any such thing. In this he is unlike the would-be modern, Prince Amerigo.

In "Adina" (1874), we encounter an American, Sam Scrope, who is not a sentimental lover of the picturesque. "The truth was that the picturesque of Italy, both in man and in nature, fretted him, depressed him strangely" (3: 212). The narrator of the tale does not share Scrope's disdain. When the narrator "breathed poetic sighs over the subjection of Italy to the foreign foe," Scrope swore "that Italy had got no more than she deserved, that she was a land of vagabonds and declaimers, and that he had yet to see an Italian who he would call a man." When the narrator quotes Alfieri's assertion that the "human plant" grew strongest in Italy, Scrope retorts that "nothing grew stronger there but lying and cheating, laziness, beggary and vermin" (212).

One day in the Roman Campagna the two men encounter a young rustic who has dug up a precious antique stone intaglio and Scrope tricks the man into giving him the stone. Realizing the injustice done to him, the rustic Angelo is tempted to strangle Scrope. However, "that saving grace of discretion which mingles with all Italian passion had whispered to the young man to postpone his revenge" (235). When the narrator discovers Angelo skulking like a burglar around Scrope's lodging, he offers the Italian the chance to go to America to "do some honest work" in his brother-in-law's hardware business. But Angelo will not give up thoughts of revenge and "be treated like a dog." Instead, he sees his experience with Scrope as a form of divine intervention in his life, an indication that perhaps he had been "too simple, too stupid, too contented with being poor and shabby" (243). Angelo's revenge does bring a sort of divine satisfaction: He steals Adina's love from the American Scrope, which only confirms the narrator's picturesque notions about the young rustic. The Italian appears "quite the proper hero of his romance," but he remains a mystery, his character "as great an enigma as the method of his courtship." In the end, the narrator concludes that Angelo has already forgotten how his good fortune came to him. He sees Angelo as "basking in a sort of primitive natural, sensuous delight in being adored. It was like the warm sunshine, or like plenty of good wine." Angelo seems to take his good fortune in stride, for "at the bottom of every genuine Roman heart,—even if it beats beneath a beggar's rags,—you'll find an ineradicable belief that we are all barbarians, and made to pay them tribute," an attitude the narrator dismisses as made up of "grotesque superstitions" (255). As for the imperial topaz, Scrope tosses it into the Tiber and the narrator is content to "let it return to the moldering underworld of the Roman past" (257).

As a revenge story, "Adina" introduces, twists and inverts a number of conventions and stereotypes. If Sam Scrope is Yankee enterprise perverted, Angelo is the injured, vengeful, yet discrete Italian. Rather than resort to the stiletto, the simple but enigmatic Italian steals the Anglo-Saxon girl, this "blonde angel of New England origin" (236). Angelo's revenge is sexual conquest, the tribute he expects from the barbarian others. Why should he go work in a hardware store in America when plenty of Americans would come to Italy to admire him?

It is not until the 1890s, with "The Real Thing" (1892), that James imagines an Italian character outside of an Italian setting, a theme to which the author would return a decade later with Prince Amerigo in *The Golden Bowl*. In both cases, the Italian character finds himself in England, James's adopted home, but there the similarity ends. Where Prince Amerigo is an expatriate, a member of Italy's fading aristocracy, Oronte in "The Real Thing" is an immigrant, an itinerant Italian adventurer who has "wandered to England in search of fortune" and "embarked, with a partner and a small green handcart, on the sale of penny ices. The ices had melted away and the partner had dissolved in their train" (8: 249). Consequently, Oronte appears at the studio of a commercial illustrator, seeking work as a model. The illustrator/artist, who narrates the tale, easily perceives Oronte to be a foreigner and soon discovers that the young man is an Italian who speaks no word of English beyond the artist's name. The narrator considers Oronte as not "meanly constituted—what Italian is?"—an assessment made without the benefit of the narrator's ever having been to Italy. The artist initially discourages Oronte's job request, but reconsiders when he sees "pictures" in the Italian's attitude and actions, and the sense of wonder with which he looks at the studio. "He might have been crossing himself in St. Peter's," the narrator says. "Before I finished I said to myself: 'The fellow's a bankrupt orange-monger, but he's a treasure'" (248).

The illustrator engages Oronte as a model, adding the Italian to three others already in his employ. One is a Miss Churm, a "freckled cockney" (239) who, like Oronte, has a chameleonlike ability to assume whatever characters the illustrator required. Dressed in some old clothes, Oronte "looked like an Englishman. He was as good as Miss Churm, who could look, when required, like an Italian." The narrator's other two models are a down-at-the-heels English couple, Major and Mrs. Monarch, who were hired more out of sympathy than any ability to serve the artist's professional needs. The couple, particularly Mrs. Monarch, is puzzled by Oronte's appearance as a model. "It was strange to have to recognise in a scrap of a lazzarone a competitor to her magnificent Major" (249).

Commissioned to do some drawings for a series of novels, the illustrator decides that the Major and Mrs. Monarch will not do as models for the hero and heroine. Instead he secretly substitutes Miss Churm and Oronte. The Monarchs believe that Miss Churm is modeling some low-life character and that Oronte is being done as an organ-grinder. But the truth soon emerges, and the illustrator publicly adopts Oronte as his hero for the book work. When the illustrator also rejects the Major in favor of Oronte for a figure in a magazine illustration, the Major turns pale and asks: "Is *he* your idea of an English gentleman?" (256). Undeterred, the Monarchs continue to come to the studio, where they begin to perform menial service for the illustrator. "They had bowed their heads in bewilderment to the perverse and cruel law in virtue of which the real thing could be so much less precious than the unreal; but they didn't want to starve," the narrator says. "If my servants were my models, my models might be my servants" (258). However, unable to watch the Monarchs continue to empty his slops, the narrator finally bribes them to disappear. Oronte apparently remains in the illustrator's employment, but we are given no hint as to his future.

Although "The Real Thing" may seem much different from the earlier stories I have discussed, in ways it is in dialogue with those stories, just as the earlier stories play off each other. In one way or another, the earlier stories deal with the romantic picturesque approach to Italy and Italians, and its attractions, limitations, and dangers. On the one hand, the picturesque perspective heightens Italy's values, its beauty, history, and culture, its softness and warmth, its magic. Seen through the romantic picturesque lens, the Italians themselves become civil, charming, sensual, and innocent. But at the same time, this romantic picturesque approach can trick and lure. It threatens marriages and may wind up destroying the very art it is seen to inspire. While some of the early stories seem to perpetuate conventional national/racial/social dichotomies and stereotypes, "The Real Thing" appears to critique that tendency, if not subvert the categories themselves. The artist narrator has a romantic image of Italians. Having never been to Italy, and presumably having never encountered many Italians, he says that Oronte is typically Italian in being not "meanly constituted." The Monarchs feel otherwise. Although they try to separate themselves from Oronte and Miss Churm on a class basis, the Monarchs also categorize Oronte in racial/national terms. To the Monarchs, Oronte is a "scrap of a lazzarone" (249) and the perfect model for the stereotypically Italian organ-grinder, images of Italians that colored American attitudes toward Italian immigrants. The Monarchs consider Oronte constitutionally incapable of playing an English gentleman, disqualified by both his social and racial status. However, for the illustrator, Oronte not only can model an English gentleman, but can also act like a "gentleman at a party" when served tea by Mrs. Monarch (255).

Obviously, James is playing around with and questioning class distinctions, and any relation they may have to "the real thing." Why cannot lower-class Cockneys and peddlers be ladies and gentlemen, and ladies and gentlemen be servants? However, there is also a racial/national element here: Why cannot a poor young Italian be more of "the real thing" than an English gentleman major? James seems to be suggesting that maybe different classes and races are really interchangeable, at least in the realm of art. But can an Oronte pass for a Major Monarch outside the confines of the narrator's studio? Finally, what does James mean by "the real thing"? The Monarchs see themselves as the victims of the "perverse and cruel law" through which "the real thing could be so much less precious than the unreal." For the Monarchs, being "the real thing" means being the genuine article, having the social and racial characteristics of their class: breeding, manners, and respectability. Oronte and Miss Churm represent the "unreal" thing because they lack the Monarchs' cultivation. However, the narrator/artist sees it differently. For him, Oronte and Miss Churm's "unreal" chameleonlike qualities make them the genuine article. It is they and their unreality that inspires the narrator's artistic imagination in much the same way that Italy inspires the characters in James's earlier stories. Ultimately, however, the romance of Italy and Italians exists in the mind of the beholder. For Oronte, the reality of romantic Italy is that he apparently could not make a living there. Emigrating, he finds success in England, if only as a figment of the narrator's imagination and the subject of his art—the second-rate art of illustration, at that. Prince Amerigo in *The Golden Bowl* has higher ambitions than Oronte, but he too will be aestheticized, albeit as a much more precious objet d'art than the young Italian model of "The Real Thing."

Chapter 4

Henry James's "Flagrant Foreigners": Whose Country Is This Anyway?

His life would be full of machinery, which was the antidote to superstition, which was in its turn, too much, the consequence, or at least the exhalation, of archives.

—Henry James, *The Golden Bowl*, 1904

Is not the universal sauce essentially *his* sauce, and do not we feel ourselves feeding, half the time, from the ladle, greasy as he chooses to leave it for us, that he holds out?

—Henry James, *The American Scene*, 1907

The types and faces bore them out; the people before me were gross aliens to a man, and they were in serene and triumphant possession.

—Henry James, *The American Scene*, 1907

Since its publication in 1904, *The Golden Bowl* has come to be considered one of James's most hermetic creations, a novel whose ambiguity is nearly legendary despite all that has been written about its meaning. The plot is a simple one: Maggie Verver, the daughter of a rich American, marries Prince Amerigo, an Italian living in London. Maggie's father, Adam, marries his daughter's friend, Charlotte Stant. The Prince and Charlotte have an adulterous affair. Maggie discovers the betrayal and tries to deal with it. Much of the critical literature about *The Golden Bowl* has focused on moral assessments of the four main characters, with conflicting conclusions the norm. For example, Maggie Verver, arguably the most important character, is variously described as a healing "saint" and a manipulating "witch." Other critics have focused on the outcome of the marriage of Maggie Verver and Prince Amerigo, seeing in it either a harmonious social or cultural union, or a case of appropriation, possession, and domination.[1] Although those issues are important to my discussion, my main concern is Prince Amerigo's relations with the Ververs and, to a lesser extent, with Charlotte Stant.

Amerigo is the only continental European in the entire James canon who is depicted from the inside. The Prince is doubly unique, at once James's "most carefully and fully developed European character and the most extended and profound expression of what [James] understood Italy and the Italian ethos to be."[2] Amerigo is very much an *Italian* prince. In Amerigo's opening dialogue with Fanny Assingham, "he lives up to widely held assumptions by confessing his lack of 'moral sense,' assumptions underlined by Fanny's bursting out, 'Oh you deep Italians!' and calling him, more succinctly, 'Machiavelli.'" Thomas Galt Peyser rightly connects James's characterization of the Prince with his characterization of the Venetian race in *Italian Hours*, where James says, "It hasn't a genius for stiff morality.... It scruples but scantly to represent the false as the true.... It has been accused further of loving if not too well at least too often."[3] Also of interest is the fact that Amerigo is one of the few Italians whom James imagines outside of Italy. In that way he serves as a bridge between the stay-at-home Italians of James's *Italian Hours* (personified by the rustic Angelo of "Adina," who chooses revenge over the opportunity to go to America to "do some honest work") and the Italian immigrants of James's *The American Scene*. And, while James places the Prince in England, just as he had Oronte of "The Real Thing," Amerigo is more ambitious than the young model. In fact, Amerigo has dreams of going to America, to the very land that took its name from the Prince's explorer ancestor, Amerigo Vespucci. To a large extent, as Jonathan Freedman has perceptively pointed out, the "racial drama" of *The Golden Bowl* "centers on the racially ambiguous figure of Amerigo, a figure represented as an emblem of racial and cultural degeneracy, whose task is understood to be nothing less than a successful assimilation of the norms and even the identity of the dominant Anglo-Saxon order."[4]

Beyond his self-confessed lack of moral sense, just what kind of Italian is Prince Amerigo, and how typical an Italian is he (if there is such a creature)? In many ways, Amerigo is not very representative at all. As an aristocrat, albeit an impoverished one, he certainly is very different from the type of Italian immigrant that James was to encounter and chronicle in *The American Scene*. Amerigo also seems to be atypically Italian in appearance, with dark blue eyes, dark brown mustache, and a facial expression "no more sharply 'foreign' to an English view than to have caused it sometimes to be observed of him with a shallow felicity that he looked like a 'refined' Irishman."[5] Unlike the Italians in America who speak no English, Amerigo not only speaks English, he sometimes thinks in English, all of which is part and parcel of his "Anglomania." In fact, his command of English is altogether too good for Maggie's liking. "Miss Verver had told him he spoke English too well—it was his only fault, and he had not been able to speak worse even to oblige her." Amerigo himself thinks that he does not speak American well enough and "was practising his American in order to converse properly, on equal terms as it were, with Mr. Verver" (31).

Amerigo is also right at home in the English country manor, that quintessential English institution and setting. His many trips to the country had taught him "to do the English things, and to do them, all sufficiently, in the English way." And although he did not particularly enjoy country house activities, still he was capable of going through the motions of shooting, riding, golfing, walking, billiards- and bridge-playing, and tea-drinking (247). Furthermore, there is nothing clannish about Amerigo's family, a charge that was repeatedly leveled at Italians in America. Amerigo marries the American Maggie, his younger brother had already married a woman "of Hebrew race," and his sister and her husband were "the most anglicised of Milanesi" (39). Amerigo and his family are cosmopolitan Italians, people of the world, even if they found themselves in reduced circumstances.

But for all his Anglomania and surface assimilation into English society, Amerigo remains a relatively trivial and useless outsider. In England, he is often "reminded how, after all, as an outsider, a foreigner, and even as a mere representative husband and son-in-law, he was so irrelevant to the working of affairs that he could be bent on occasion to uses comparatively trivial." He senses that he is, "among all these so often inferior people, practically held cheap and made light of" (265). There are no worthy personal services he can perform for them, acts such as plotting, lying, wielding a dagger, or preparing the poisonous cup. "These were the services that, by all romantic tradition, were consecrated to affection quite as much as to hate. But he could amuse himself with saying—as much as that amusement went—that they were what he had once for all turned his back on" (238). Here we see that Amerigo is caught betwixt and between. He is not modern enough or practical enough to be of any real service to the English or to the Ververs. However, the traditional abilities that Amerigo might offer by virtue of being Italian—lying, plotting, assassination with dagger or poison—are the very activities that he hopes to transcend in his life outside of Italy.

Having escaped his country, Amerigo now hopes to shed the stereotypes of his race, symbolized by the cup of poison and the stiletto, which characterized Italy for the young James Russell Lowell and many other Americans.[6]

Amerigo concedes that he understands neither the British nor the Ververs. Despite all the time he had spent with them, still "the number of questions about them he couldn't have answered had much rather grown than shrunken" (265). Amerigo's befuddlement is never fully explained. Is it the result of an individual failure, the product of a personal obtuseness, or is it a sign of an unbridgeable cultural/racial gulf between Italians and the British? From the Prince's perspective, the answer appears to be the latter. He is not so obtuse that he cannot frame the questions or offer at least one possible explanation for his puzzlement. If Amerigo is sure of one thing only, it is that the English "didn't like *les situations nettes*," what the English themselves complacently called "their wonderful spirit of compromise." It was this predilection for complexity and compromise that "had been their national genius and their national success," what in effect made the English English (265). Amerigo knows that much, but as a simple Italian he does not profit much from the knowledge; it explains their motivation, maybe explains their behavior, but ultimately makes it hard to really pin them down. Amerigo sees the Ververs themselves as an entirely different species, thereby hinting at distinct racial differences. "Those people—and his free synthesis lumped together capitalists and bankers, retired men of business, illustrious collectors, American fathers-in-law, American fathers, little American daughters, little American wives—those people were of the same large lucky group, as one might say; they were all, at least, of the same general species and had the same general instincts; they hung together, they passed each other the word, they spoke each other's language, they did each other 'turns'" (223–224). In fact, Amerigo sees himself as racially and morally the odd man out. "You're of the same race, at any rate—more or less; of the same general tradition and education, of the same moral paste," he tells Charlotte, before concluding, "I can't help seeing it—I'm decidedly too different" (236). Oddly enough, here Amerigo sounds like the turn-of-the-century race thinkers who conflated race, education, tradition, and character in efforts to draw distinctions between racial/national groups.

Amerigo is too different—too Italian—not only in his presumed lack of moral sense but also in his history, which forms, as he tells Maggie, but one part of him. That part is composed of his family's history, "the doings, the marriages, the crimes, the follies, the boundless *bêtises* of other people," things that are "written—literally, in rows of volumes, in libraries," and "are as public as they're abominable." Part of that history includes an "infamous Pope" and Amerigo's namesake, Amerigo Vespucci, whom Fanny Assingham calls an ersatz explorer. However, Amerigo claims another part, "very much smaller doubtless, which, such as it is, represents my single self, the unknown, unimportant—unimportant save to *you*—personal quantity" (33). This is the part of him that among other things does not dissemble or deceive. "Personally, he considered, he hadn't the vices in question—and that was so much to the good," James writes. "His race, on the other hand, had had them handsomely enough, and he was somehow full of his race. Its presence in him was like the consciousness of some inexpugnable scent in which his clothes, his whole person, his hands and the hair on his head, might have been steeped as in some chemical bath: the effect was nowhere in particular, yet he constantly felt himself at the mercy of the cause" (37–38). In other words, Amerigo's racial identity *is* his history.[7] Again we have here the popular idea of race as some combination of history and culture that gets into the bloodstream and is handed down from generation to generation. This racial chemical bath in which Amerigo seems to have been steeped will be echoed in James's *The American Scene*, when James talks about immigrants who spread their sauce over everything and are like a sponge saturating everything. It is his history, his culture, his race, and that inexpugnable scent that Amerigo seeks to escape. He hopes that his "single self," his "personal quality"—that is, his individuality—can help him transcend his race. And yet, he suspects that it will not happen. More promising may be his marriage to Maggie Verver and union with Adam Verver's millions. "What was this so important step he had just taken but the desire for some new history that should, so far as possible, contradict, and even if need be flatly dishonour, the old?" (38).

Ultimately, Amerigo's dream is to assert his individual self, escape the past, and slip into the modernity of a "scientific" future. It was this same scientific future that James saw unified Italy aspiring to in *Italian Hours*. Amerigo "was allying himself to science, for what was science but the absence of prejudice backed by the presence of money? His life would be full of machinery, which was the antidote to superstition, which was in its turn, too much, the consequence, or at least the exhalation, of archives" (38–39). In his desire to become modern, Amerigo is in some sense trying to become more of a modern Anglo-Saxon—practical, individualistic, able to redirect, if not transcend his racial past—and less of a premodern, primitive Italian entangled in the limitations of prejudice, superstition, and that racial past. It is this very machinery of science that has the potential to transform Amerigo's weak moral sense, or what passes for that quality in his "poor dear backward old Rome." Amerigo says that the Italian moral sense is like a tortuous, half-ruined stone staircase in some *quattrocento* castle, while the American version is like the "lightning elevator" in one of Adam Verver's fifteen-story buildings. "Your moral sense works by steam—it sends you up like a rocket," Amerigo tells Fanny Assingham. "Ours is slow and steep and unlighted, with so many of the steps missing that—well, that it's as short, in almost any case, to turn around and come down again" (48).

However, Amerigo himself knows that he has undertaken a risky voyage. He identifies himself with Edgar Allan Poe's marine adventurer A. Gordon Pym, who "found at a given moment before him a thickness of white air that was like a dazzling curtain of light, concealing as a darkness conceals, yet of the colour of milk or of snow. There were moments when he felt his own boat move upon some such mystery" (42). Having connected with Pym, Amerigo again raises the image of a great journey across an unknown sea. Everything is ready, he tells Fanny Assingham, but he cannot sail alone and needs her to show the way because he does not know the points of the compass (45). As the descendant of a dubious discoverer, Prince Amerigo, without compass, moral or otherwise, knows that both he and Charlotte are kept afloat in Adam Verver's boat. Without that boat, the Prince knows that he would sink to the deepest depths—"away down, down, down" (206). Fanny sees that Amerigo repays the Ververs by being beautiful, "by continuing to lead the life, to breathe the air, very nearly to think the thoughts, that best suited his wife and her father" (207). Consequently, if the Prince expects the Ververs' boat to carry him to a brave new modern world, he is sadly mistaken.

Maggie, for one, desires Amerigo for the very past that he seeks to escape. If Amerigo wants to be a less typical Italian, Maggie wants him to be an even more conventional one. She is not interested in Amerigo for his "single self," but rather for his colorful history—for his "archives, annals, infamies" (33). The Ververs seek to appropriate Amerigo's family history much in the same way that it has been appropriated by the British Museum, where the family's archives now reside. Like the British Museum, the Ververs have the economic power to appropriate Amerigo's family history for their own uses. They can, for example, secure aristocratic associations and purchase for Maggie's son a historical identity, summed up in the child's name, "the Principino."[8] Amerigo is the last in a long Jamesian line of Italians who are paid by Americans to be colorful, picturesque and romantic. "There is in the end hardly any other sort of Italian in Jamesian fiction, for the good reason that nearly all his Americans in Italy are both wealthy and yearning to be deluded."[9]

Amerigo is more than just picturesque. Maggie tells the Prince that, for Adam Verver, he is "a rarity, an object of beauty, an object of price. You're not perhaps absolutely unique, but you're so curious and eminent that there are very few others like you—you belong to a class about which everything is known. You're what they call a *morceau de musée*" (35). In fact, it is Adam Verver's sharpened appetite for collectibles that had served as a basis for his acceptance of the Prince's suit (121). Verver, although a surprisingly passive and vulnerable plutocrat from the "Darwinian jungle of American capitalism," is a shrewd connoisseur of people as objects. As Peter Conn says, "The idea of beauty, followed by its appropriation, governed Adam's existence. In such an ethical world, reciprocity must yield to the demands of possessorship, generosity must give way to calculation, and love to taste."[10] Adam Verver's attitude toward the Prince also characterizes his relationship with his grandchild, who is the most precious of all the "precious small pieces" that Verver has handled (126). If Amerigo is aestheticized, turned into an object of art, he is a valuable piece that keeps on giving, much like a bank check that is perpetually paid in, subject to infinite endorsement. At least that is the way the Prince sees it. As a result, Amerigo has no wish to see his value diminish. "He himself, after all, had not fixed it—the 'figure' was a conception all of Mr. Verver's own" (245–246). However, if the Prince is a valuable museum piece, in essence a blank check for Verver, he is also flesh and blood, a child of the sensual South we see figured so often in James's tales and travel essays. He is, as his affair with Charlotte Stant shows, one of those Italians who are accused of "loving if not too well at least too often, of being in fine as little austere as possible."[11] In Prince Amerigo, therefore, we see the limits of the aestheticizing tendency, just as we will see those limits in *The American Scene*.

Thomas Galt Peyser places Adam Verver's mercantile aestheticism and museum-building—his desire to create a "museum of museums" in American City—within the context of late nineteenth-century American imperialism, which in turn raises questions about assimilation. "By treating his subjects as if they were exhibits in a museum, apparently shorn of their historical determinants, James manages the problem of the alien in a time that witnessed both the peak of immigration to the US and the success of American imperialist ventures in the Pacific," Peyser writes. "Far from being an escape from history, James's manner of treating the world as a museum and its inhabitants as curators and exhibits joins his artistic labor to the assimilative labor that lay ahead for his native country." But the Italian Prince's marriage to the American Maggie raises other disturbing questions concerning imperialism, appropriation, and assimilation. In *The Golden Bowl*, the international theme in American politics takes on the character of a marriage plot. The questions here become, who is appropriating and colonizing whom, and where will assimilation lead for those who are doing the assimilating? These questions are tied up with other questions and fears about Anglo-Saxon superiority and purity and the threat posed by alien races. "Throughout the period, the strident faith in the superiority of Anglo-Saxon blood was shadowed at times by an almost tragic conception of racial fragility in an increasingly promiscuous population," Peyser writes. "As [Henry Cabot] Lodge had warned from the senate floor, 'If a lower race mixes with a higher in sufficient numbers, history teaches us that the lower race will prevail.' "[12]

We see these questions dramatized in *The Golden Bowl*. At the very beginning of the novel, the Prince fantasizes about recapturing his imperial past. This image of the Prince as imperialist balances/contests Adam Verver's own image of himself as John Keats's "stout Cortez" on the peak in Darien, realizing that "a world was left him to conquer and that he might conquer it if he tried" (122). In the opening paragraph, we are told that the Prince was "one of the modern Romans" who "had always liked his London," and who found there "a more convincing image of the truth of the ancient state than any they have left by the Tiber.... If it was a question of an *Imperium*, he said to himself, and if one wished, as a Roman, to recover a little the sense of that, the place to do so was on London Bridge, or even, on a fine afternoon in May, at Hyde Park Corner" (29). Later, Amerigo, having spoken of practicing his American to better converse on equal terms with Adam Verver, now tells Maggie: "Well, I'm eating your father alive—which is the only way to taste him. I want to continue, and as it's when he talks American that he *is* most alive, so I must cultivate it, to get my pleasure. He couldn't make one like him so much in any other language" (32). As Peyser says, "Even in the course of their playful banter this quip has a vaguely ominous ring to it, but the context of contemporary debates about the fate of northern European stock in America gives it specifically racial undertones."[13]

It is not only Adam Verver whom Amerigo threatens to consume. The Prince's adulterous affair represents an alien challenge that threatens to engulf Maggie's arranged and ordered life. This is expressed when Maggie ponders her betrayal by Amerigo and Charlotte. "This situation had been occupying, for months and months, the very centre of the garden of her life, but it had reared itself there like some strange, tall tower of ivory, or perhaps rather some wonderful, beautiful, but outlandish pagoda" (301). Peyser says the heterogeneous ivory pagoda is an apt symbol in light of fears about the Asiaticization of America at the turn of the century. "Recalling the alien presence in *The American Scene*, we can see that the threatened Asiaticization of Maggie's life is paradoxically what makes her an American, what shows her fantastically exceptional situation to be nevertheless the representative story of the US."[14] Interestingly, Maggie's encounter with the adultery is described in language that echoes James's encounter with the alien in *The American Scene*. "[I]t had met her like some bad-faced stranger surprised in one of the thick-carpeted corridors of a house of quiet on a Sunday afternoon; and yet, yes, amazingly, she had been able to look at terror and disgust only to know that she must put away from her the bitter-sweet of their freshness" (459).

However, if the Prince is a threat, he is a paradoxically mild, even bland character. He is a flexible, gallant, consummate gentleman—in essence, one of James's typical European Italians. Amerigo is a hedonist who enjoys life, but does not wholly trust it. "He is, in short, a classic Italian fatalist, and his fatalism renders him constitutionally incapable of initial action and constantly alert to the abyss of irony that yawns beneath all human endeavor."[15] With typical irony, he seems to accept the role imposed on him by the Ververs, saying, "I shall be one of the little pieces that you unpack at the hotels, or at the worst in the hired houses, like this wonderful one, and put out with the family photographs and the new magazines" (36). Christof Wegelin argues that the early Amerigo is like an irresponsible, innocent child who willingly accepts the role that the Ververs have assigned him.[16] Despite the Prince's initial passivity, Amerigo is not self-satisfied in his graceful hedonism, detachment, and inaction, but instead has a restless curiosity and openness to new stimuli.[17] *The Golden Bowl*, then, may appear to be the story of Amerigo's growth. In this reading, the difference between the early and later Amerigo is striking. But is it really? Amerigo's "good faith was the good faith of the unmoral child. That is why what he finally acknowledges is not his past fault, but his new awareness of what Maggie has done for him.... The reason for Amerigo's passivity is that Maggie is the one who guides and rules their relationship and the moral awakening it involves for him."[18]

However, is not that really the point? Maggie in fact may come to realize that the Prince is more than just a museum piece, more than just a stock romantic Italian. She may, as Maves argues, learn to live with Amerigo's "sensuous pessimism." But it is Maggie, and her superior Anglo-Saxon genius for order and organization, that finally controls and arranges the relationships. Where does that leave the others, especially Amerigo? Roslyn Jolly argues that Maggie ultimately encloses the others in "glass cages of consciousness." These then become "the glass cases of Maggie's museum, which is the product of a fiction so powerful that it ceases to be fiction and attains the status of history." Maggie's powerful subjective vision changes reality but only at the expense of the subjectivity of the others. Ultimately, "Amerigo and Charlotte are punished for their wish to see life from their own point of view, and it is in this punitive role that Maggie's imaginative power is expressed."[19] Mark Seltzer offers a twist on this interpretation, arguing that Maggie controls the novel's resolution by fusing power and love, control and sympathy. Rather than seeing Maggie's triumph in either/or fashion—as the triumph of a creative "sympathetic imagination" that affirms the "imaginative autonomy" of the others, or as the intelligent control of others by denying "vital interchange with others"—Seltzer views the two readings as interchangeable. "Control and sympathy are not opposed here; in fact, Maggie controls precisely through a power of sympathy."[20] It is the same dynamic that characterized an imperialist nation's relations with its colonies, and the same dynamic that could be said to have motivated reformers such as Jacob Riis in their relations with America's poor immigrants: We are controlling you because we love you and want to help you. Peyser puts it another way: "The very fact that these peoples could be made into exhibits was precisely what required that they *be* made into exhibits for their own protection."[21]

That, in fact, appears to be exactly what happens in the final scene involving the four main characters, when the Ververs take stock of their belongings, before Adam and Charlotte depart for America. Adam Verver fixes his gaze on a picture, an early Florentine religious subject that he had given Maggie for her wedding. Maggie interprets her father's leaving the picture behind as his "doing the most possible toward leaving her a part of his palpable self" (541). The Italian picture, of course, is not the only thing that Adam has purchased and left behind for his daughter. There is also the Italian Prince who was bought with Verver's money, as well as all the other objects in the room—"the other pictures, the sofas, the chairs, the tables, the cabinets, the 'important' pieces." Adam and Maggie's "eyes moved together from piece to piece, taking in the whole nobleness," which includes lastly, but not leastly, their respective wife and husband. "Mrs. Verver and the Prince fairly 'placed' themselves, however unwittingly, as high expressions of the kind of human furniture required, aesthetically, by such a scene. The fusion of their presence with the decorative elements, their contribution to the triumph of selection, was complete and admirable; though, to a lingering view, a view more penetrating than the occasion really demanded, they also might have figured as concrete attestations of a rare power of purchase" (541). The Prince becomes here a piece of furniture, more aesthetic than functional, which contributes to the domestic scene. Adam tells Maggie, "You've got some good things," but he might just as well have said, "We've got some good things." Maggie responds by saying, "Ah, don't they look well?" Hearing this, the Prince and Charlotte—encaged, aestheticized, commodified, domesticated—give the Ververs "an attention, all of gravity, that was like an ampler submission to the general duty of magnificence; sitting as still, to be thus appraised, as a pair of effigies of the contemporary great on one of the platforms of Madame Tussaud" (542).

The Golden Bowl ends with Maggie and the Prince alone. In an attempt to put closure on the adulterous episode, Maggie pronounces the safely departed Charlotte "too splendid." When Amerigo seconds Maggie's assessment, his wife, to underscore her moral, says, "That's our help, you see." This is followed by James's curious concluding paragraph: Maggie's comment—her moral—fixes Amerigo. "'See?' I see nothing but *you*," Amerigo replies. The truth and force of Amerigo's reply had so strangely lighted his eyes that, "as for pity and dread of them," Maggie buries her own eyes in the Prince's breast (547). This act of reconciliation recalls the reunion of the Count and his American wife in "The Last of the Valerii." Both the Prince and the Count have been adulterous, the Count with an ancient pagan deity cast in marble, the Prince with the flesh-and-blood Charlotte. Both aristocrats are particularly Italian in their adultery, the Count motivated by superstition, the Prince by sensuality. "The Last of the Valerii" ends with the Count yielding, falling on his knees, and burying his head in his wife's lap. In *The Golden Bowl*, however, it is Maggie who buries her head in the Prince's breast. The Count's act is obviously one of submission, a casting off of his ancient superstitions, which, however, still fails to make him a modern man. But what about the Prince?

Several critics see the Prince's rapprochement to Maggie as a simple parable of fusion and harmony. Wegelin sees it as a double conversion, a social interfusion of "the discipline of Maggie's spiritual energy by Amerigo's form, the quickening penetration of his form by her spirit—possible only to the high intelligence on which their love is based."[22] Maves argues that *The Golden Bowl*, as James's last extended treatment of the international theme, represents his resolution of the lover's quarrel between Europe and America. Maggie learns to live with Amerigo's "sensuous pessimism" and the Prince fathoms and tempers Maggie's "passionate moralism," thereby creating a spiritual and physical union, "a fusion of knowledge and fancy, Europe and America."[23] Freedman takes these ideas of conversion and fusion one step further. Amerigo had initially represented "an image of the unassimilated, unassimilable alien" whose full integration into the Anglo-Saxon sphere was as questionable as that of the immigrants in New York's Lower East Side. By the book's end, Freedman says, both Maggie and the Prince have been altered "to produce a new order—a new marital, a new genetic, and thus ultimately a new racial order—of identity." The union of Maggie and Amerigo, Freedman argues, regenerates Amerigo's degenerate race, saves Maggie's regenerated race from falling into decline, and creates "a successful racial admixture (that) will lead to a revitalization first of the family order, then of 'the West' itself."[24]

However, the language of the book's concluding paragraph indicates that these interpretations are too optimistic, too pat. In one sense, Amerigo is still the typical Italian of James's *Italian Hours*, too eager to please and to be pleasing in his attempt to accept what Maggie is offering. As a result he *sees* only her. And, if Maggie ultimately controls the relationship through "a power of sympathy," as Mark Seltzer says, we are nevertheless left with the contradictory images of Amerigo "enclosing" Maggie and of Maggie burying her eyes in Amerigo's breast. Amerigo may see nothing but Maggie, but the Prince's eyes, the windows to his soul, inspire her with pity and dread. If, in one sense, Amerigo is a romantic aesthetic object appropriated and possessed by the Ververs, he is also now a flesh-and-blood creature who possesses Maggie with pity and dread. These are the same two conflicting emotions Americans will have when masses of formerly picturesque Italians succeed, unlike Amerigo, in crossing the Atlantic in an effort to become modern American immigrants. Maggie's attraction to, pity for, and dread of Amerigo will be developed in James's own reaction to these Italian immigrants in *The American Scene*. James may in fact hold out the possibility of assimilation and union for the Italians, but it is a prospect for which he holds highly ambivalent feelings, as we will see in *The American Scene*.

Henry James had completed what is traditionally known as the "master phase" of his career when, in 1904, and now in his sixties, he returned to the United States for a ten-month tour after an absence of twenty-one years. James had just published his final masterwork, *The Golden Bowl*, to sharply mixed reviews. He was now undoubtedly at the height of his achievement as an artist, but nevertheless there was critical debate about the value of his work.[25] Still, the trip was to be a triumphant tour for James. His itinerary included lunches and dinners with President Theodore Roosevelt, old friends Senator Henry Cabot Lodge and Secretary of State John Hay, and Samuel Clemens. There was also a very strong personal element inscribed into the trip, as there would be with any return home by a longtime expatriate, especially one who had never stopped thinking of his native land. The homecoming "was professedly a voyage of discovery, and James hoped it would prove a voyage of recovery as well."[26] Ultimately, it was James's personal, interior journey—not the triumphant professional tour—that came to dominate *The American Scene*, his record of the 1904–1905 trip, which was collected in 1907 from pieces already serialized in *The North American Review*.

The book, like his late fiction, received mixed reviews. Critics complained about the overly ornate rhetoric and wearisome verbiage of James's later style, while *The North American Review* defended that same style as an expression of the subtleties of James's thought. Some critics accused James of snobbery, of being "a novelist of the aristocracy," a corrupted expatriate who was now looking down his nose at his countrymen.[27] *The Nation* praised the book for highlighting the defects and shortcomings of American civilization, but criticized James's inability to sympathize with the common man. "Mr. James is fundamentally incapable of getting inside the skin of the average American or of realizing that the outlook to such a citizen is by no means so dreary and 'common' as to himself."[28]

The American Scene was soon relegated to a minor position in the James canon and thereafter treated as an oddity, the "eccentric travelogue of a reactionary aesthete."[29] In recent years, however, critics have returned to the work with renewed interest, in the process revising the prevailing view that *The American Scene* represented the final note of a genteel aesthete whose destiny, as John Carlos Rowe said, "always seems to end in the intricacies of his late style and its retreat from life into the palace of art."[30] As John Sears says, "*The American Scene* provides both a critical vision of America at a crucial turning point in its history and a portrait of a profound observer of the scene, whose fears and prejudices, hopes and enthusiasms are themselves a telling revelation of the complex fate of being an American."[31]

That James had returned to America at "a crucial turning point" in its history is incontestable. These were years of "peculiar turbulence" marked by accelerating urbanization and industrialization, revolutionary technological changes, centralization of business and politics, and sometimes-violent social struggles. In the years leading up to James's visit, the United States had experienced the assassination of President William McKinley, the last of the Indian wars, the imperialistic Spanish-American War, the bloody repression of the Filipinos, violent labor battles and sharpened class conflict, hundreds of lynchings and periodic race riots, and a wave of immigration unprecedented in American history. These events, especially the unprecedented "new immigration," had caused a cultural revolution that transformed turn-of-the-century America into "a border town, a region poised between contending facts and images of past and future."[32]

James's visit also coincided with a frenetic period in the muckraking and reform movements. Almost daily, books and magazine articles exposed the political corruptions and economic disruptions of American society. This was the time not only of Jacob Riis, but also Lincoln Steffens, Ida M. Tarbell, Upton Sinclair, Eugene V. Debs, and W.E.B. DuBois, among others. However, as Peter Conn points out, "Almost nothing of this national ferment appears in *The American Scene*." There is, he says, a "typical absence of politics—of current 'topics' generally—from his book."[33] But Conn overstates his case, for at least one social/political topic is very much on James's mind and very much present in *The American Scene*: the issue of immigration. *The American Scene* may be highly personal literary journalism, but it does engage with important contemporary issues, particularly questions of race, immigration, assimilation, and their relationship to national character. In fact, many of the "fears and prejudices, hopes and enthusiasms" expressed by James centered around the masses of immigrants who went a long way toward making the turn of the century a crucial turning point in American history. James returned to an emergent industrial nation in which "Americanization" of the immigrant had become a definitive cultural project. As masses of new immigrants threatened to mingle alien "strains of blood" with those of native-born Americans, nativists, progressives, and James himself struggled to define and redefine the nature of nationality and cultural filiation. "In (James's) own extensive observation of American manners, institutions, and public life in *The American Scene*, the restored American absentee records numerous scenes in which the making of Americans—of American 'race,' of American culture, of American civic fate—is enacted."[34] The Henry James of *The American Scene* has been seen as everything from a genteel, patrician, Anglo-Saxon nativist recoiling from the threats of the "alien" immigrant, to an activist, subversive, Whitmanian multiculturalist who embraces American heterogeneity.[35]

It is within this context that I want to examine several critical passages in which James encounters Italian immigrants, who along with the Jews made the greatest impression on him. These passages, like much of *The American Scene*, are dense, impressionistic, meditativè. They are alternately vague, contradictory, and polyvocal. James routinely assumes the personae of the "mooning observer," the "lone visionary," the "restless analyst," and, perhaps more tellingly, the "repentant," "repatriated," and "reinstated" absentee. These chameleonlike changes are one indication that James is unsure of his identity in his relation to both Europe and America. James's role-playing goes beyond the personae to other more subtle narrative techniques involving point of view. In critical episodes with foreigners/the alien, James slips in and out of different points of view and often constructs his attitudes and impressions along an oppositional I/we versus he/they axis. Examples of this, and their importance, will become apparent as we look at the passages.

James's experience at Ellis Island sets the stage for what follows. The brooding, restless analyst visits what Italians called the "Island of Tears" on a day of "dense raw fog" and "ice-masses" in New York harbor, an appropriate atmosphere, as he says, for witnessing a scene that ultimately puts a chill in his heart. It is here that James sees the immigrants "marshalled, herded, divided, subdivided, sorted, sifted, searched, fumigated," a process he refers to as "an intendedly 'scientific' feeding of the mill," one that gives "the earnest observer a thousand more things to think about than he can retail."[36] The accumulation of classificatory verbs and the quotation marks around the word "scientific" seem to indicate an ironic critique of the social science approach to the immigrants, an approach that Jacob Riis had criticized, but sometimes employed, in *The Battle with the Slum*.

James's visit to the immigrant-processing center comes courtesy of the "liberal hospitality of the eminent Commissioner of this wonderful service." James is referring to William Williams, the New England patrician (Yale, Harvard) and Wall Street lawyer appointed by President Roosevelt in 1902 to bring honesty and efficiency to the occasionally corrupt operation at Ellis Island, then in its tenth year. As commissioner of immigration for the port of New York from 1902–1905 and 1909–1914, Williams oversaw the process of categorizing and controlling that was a necessary part of the work. However, James's impressions of the process are diffuse, general. For James, all those people passing through the gates of Ellis Island are immigrants, aliens—not individual Italians, Jews, or Slavs. These masses are part of a "poignant and unforgettable" drama, a "visible act of ingurgitation on the part of our body politic and social" as amazing as "any sword-swallowing or fire-swallowing of the circus." This ceaseless drama of ingurgitation unsettles James, as it would "any sensitive citizen" who cannot help coming away from the scene a changed person. "He has eaten of the tree of knowledge, and the taste will forever be in his mouth." James may have known in the abstract that it was the American's fate "to share the sanctity of his American consciousness, the intimacy of his American patriotism, with the inconceivable alien; but the truth has never come home to him with any such force" as in "the lurid light projected on it by those courts of dismay." The shock of Ellis Island is such that James says he *has* to think of the visitor as ever afterwards exhibiting "the outward sign of the new chill in his heart. So is stamped, for detection, the questionably privileged person who has had an apparition, seen a ghost in his supposedly safe old house" (66).

We can see that James begins the Ellis Island scene with the personal I/eye, from the privileged perspective of a guest of the eminent immigration commissioner. However, the perspective soon shifts to "any sensitive citizen," which presumably includes James and the reader, and gives James a civic relationship to America. It is this typical sensitive citizen who will leave Ellis Island chilled to the heart. The Ellis Island scene reads like an account of demonology, with its references to chilled hearts, ghosts, and possession. The language echoes that of James's tale, "The Jolly Corner," where the narrator, also a returning expatriate, comes face-to-face with an apparition or ghost who represents what the expatriate might have become had he never left America. At Ellis Island, James encounters what America/Americans might become as a result of these new immigrants. But other things are also going on here. The word "home" ("the truth has never come home to him with any such force") appears to have a double meaning: The truth hits home not only in the individual heart, but also may strike deep into the heart of James's other home, America. Does this imply that foreigners, among them Italians (and perhaps especially Italians), were fine when they stayed at home and did not invade James's presumptive American home? There is another marvel of Jamesian ambiguity in his reference to the "questionably privileged person who has had an apparition, seen a ghost in his supposedly safe house." Was seeing the ghost a questionable, unsettling privilege? Or is the person's privileged position itself rendered questionable by the influx of aliens? It is interesting that the trip to Ellis Island begins with the narrator in a privileged position, as the guest of the facility's commissioner, and ends with him questionably privileged in having had the experience.

Although James's experience at Ellis Island lasted no longer than a few hours and claims little more than a page of *The American Scene*, he says that the "after-sense of that acute experience" would grow and grow wherever "I turned." It is telling that James here uses the personal pronoun rather than the impersonal third-person, which he so often employs. Most likely, this signifies the intensely personal nature of the experience. Elsewhere, James writes that the "affirmed claim of the alien, however immeasurably alien, to share in one's supreme relation was everywhere the fixed element, the reminder not to be dodged." Having shifted from the personal "I" to the impersonal, but inclusive pronoun "one," James then posits that one's (an American's?) "supreme relation" is one's relation to one's country, meaning in large measure one's countrymen and one's countrywomen. Given that logic, the aliens—one's "however immeasurably alien" future countrymen and countrywomen—are seen as forcing a "profane overhauling" of "the idea of the country itself," through which it (and, presumably one) "appears to suffer the indignity of change." But, James asks, is it not "our instinct" to want to keep the idea of the country "simple and strong and continuous, so that it shall be perfectly sound?" However, the aliens, in their "free assault upon it," seemed to insist on a readjustment of the idea in "*their* monstrous, presumptuous interest," James says, completing the "we"/"they" opposition of the passage. Describing the immigrants, James says: "The combination of their quantity and quality—that loud primary stage of alienism which New York must offer to sight—operates, for the native, as their note of settled possession, something they have nobody to thank for, so that *un*settled possession is what we, on our side, seem most reduced to— ... We must go, in other words, *more* than halfway to meet them; which is all the difference, for us, between possession and dispossession." Here, the impersonal "one" becomes "the native," who in turn is quickly transformed into the plural "we": "We," not "they," must make reorienting surrender; "we" must meet them more than halfway. However, James feels this sense of dispossession in personal terms. He says *he* is "haunted" by it, so much so that "the art of beguiling or duping it became an art to be cultivated." James here enviously imagines an alternative to this dispossession—"the luxury of some such close and sweet and *whole* national consciousness as that of the Switzer and the Scot." But, having moved on to the area around Washington Square, a place of fond memories where he hopes to artfully evade the unsettling question of the immigrant, James concludes: "There was no escape from the ubiquitous alien into the future, or even into the present; there was an escape but into the past" (67–68).

The pronoun progression in the preceding passages shows a subtle transition not only in James's literary point of view, but also a shift in the writer's own position vis-à-vis Americans and the aliens. James's highly personal reaction to the aliens at Ellis Island eventually is subsumed into his and his American countrymen's "instinct" to keep the country a certain way. It is as if there has been a circling of the wagons here, with James as the trail boss. This progression has the effect of turning the expatriate, absentee James back into an American, but just what that means remains unclear. If meeting the alien *more* than halfway is the difference between possession and dispossession, does James's "we" lose possession if they do not meet the alien halfway, or if they go more than halfway? The sense of dispossession that already haunts James seems to make that question moot. He tries to deal with that haunting loss by cultivating a "beguiling" or "duping" art, in that way hoping to find something enchanting in that dispossession, yet realizing that such a response is tantamount to duping himself. And what exactly did James's "we" originally possess? Is it that "fond alternative vision"—the envy of Americans—of that "close and sweet and *whole* national consciousness" embodied by the relatively racially pure Scots and Swiss? Faced with the ubiquitous alien, James knows that Scotland and Switzerland are impossible ideals for polyglot America. And yet what seems to be implied here is that, before the new immigration, before the arrival of Italians and other truly different nationalities/races, the ideal of a close, sweet, whole national consciousness—America/Americans as essentially Anglo-Saxon—was not only possible, but perhaps extant. It is the new immigrants, then, who destroy any possibility of that ideal. However, James never says what it is that made these new immigrants more alien, so different from, and so much more of a threat to unified national consciousness than the earlier immigrants had been. The implication is that the new immigrants are non-Anglo-Saxon, non-Germanic, non-northern European.

Sara Blair argues that James was initially drawn to Ellis Island by a voyeuristic urge for the picturesque, but ended up increasingly aware of the "need to manage otherness in the service of an inclusive social body and progressive modes of culture building."[37] Posnock, meanwhile, speaks of James's "intimate response" to Ellis Island.[38] There may be some truth to what they say, but both critics seem to ignore the language of possession, dispossession, ghosts, and chills found in James's ruminations over his Ellis Island experience. Clearly, James responds to Ellis Island in an intensely personal way. And, yes, what he saw there revealed the limitations of his picturesque urges. But to claim that this terribly unsettling experience began to turn him into a multiculturalist is, I believe, overstating the case.

James earlier mentioned Ellis Island during a visit to Harvard Yard, which had recently been enclosed with a fence and gates. Ruminating on the enclosure and the young men passing through the yard, he says that he had not yet visited Ellis Island (itself a fence and a gate) to witness "the ceaseless process of the recruiting of our race, of the plenishing of our huge national *pot au feu*, of the introduction of fresh—of perpetually fresh so far it isn't perpetually stale—foreign matter into our heterogenous system" (50). James concludes with a discussion of "our vast crude democracy of trade," which is characterized by "the new, the simple, the cheap, the common, the commercial, the immediate, and, all too often, the ugly." He offers as an antidote "any human product," "any creature," "any form of suggested rarity, subtlety, ancientry, or other pleasant perversity" (53). The implication here is that the immigrant, the alien, is of this order. This is underscored by the Ellis Island section, which, for all its shocking aspects, is no more unsettling (and perhaps less so) than the frenzied, almost apocalyptic vision of Wall Street and the financial district that immediately precedes it. At the very least then, the immigrants may be for James an antidote to the new, ugly, insolent "great commercial democracy" that he again decries after his Ellis Island visit. Tellingly, he takes refuge from this "great commercial democracy" in the Ascension Church on Fifth Avenue, where he makes reference to an Old World Italian *piazzetta* (72).

James extends his meditations and speculations on the alien in a later chapter when, making some observations on New York, he conjures up images of unity and continuity, of "hanging together"—images that seem to echo the close, sweet, whole national consciousness held up as the ideal in the Ellis Island passages. Oddly enough, James is applying these images of stability and wholeness to what was then clearly the most heterogenous, most rapidly changing, and, some might say, most fragmented city in the United States, if not the world. James's New York, contrary to the atomized, out-of-control city represented by Riis and other reformers, initially seems to be held together by "the general queer sauce of New York, " which is presumably a native sauce, perhaps the native character. But James quickly confesses his inability to see "the common element in the dense Italian neighborhoods." He wonders at his failure when he recollects "charming afternoons of early summer, in Central Park, which showed the fruit of the foreign tree as shaken down there with a force that smothered everything else." The Italian neighborhoods were at least a fifteen-minute walk away from the park, but still "the alien was as truly in possession, under the high 'aristocratic' nose, as if he had had but three steps to come." Not only had the alien come, he had placed himself in the foreground, making a "singleness of impression." When James begins speculating about this singular impression made by the alien, he attributes his speculations to the second person—"the alien still striking you as an alien"—in effect making his impressions also the reader's. James asks about the alien: "Is not the universal sauce essentially *his* sauce, and do we not feel ourselves feeding, half the time, from the ladle, as greasy as he chooses to leave it for us, that he holds out?" (90). Here, as in the Ellis Island passages, James's "I" and his reader finally merge into a "we" and "us" that stand in opposition to the alien. Peter Conn, among others, sees the "greasy" ladle as not only a symbol of revulsion on James's part, but as an example of the vulgar stereotyping that "is unhappily typical of James's treatment of the immigrant throughout *The American Scene*."[39] Other examples include James's reference to the Jews' "overdeveloped proboscis" and his comparison of the Jewish immigrants to worms, snakes, monkeys, and squirrels (100–102). The immigrant's ladle is revolting, not only dirty, but specifically greasy and intentionally left so. The alien not only has possession of the park, but also possession of the ladle. And greasy as the alien's sauce is, it is becoming the American sauce, having perhaps already displaced/dispossessed the native New York sauce.

James's thoughts and questions occupy him for about an hour, but he concedes that he is reluctant to deal with his speculations "at the expense of a proper tribute" to the park over which the immigrants "swarmed." However, the "brooding visitor," and even more so the "restored absentee," could not help being "conscious of the need of mental adjustment to phenomena absolutely fresh" (90). Although James wants to keep social questions separate from his aesthetic enjoyment of Central Park, he is unsuccessful. During a subsequent scene in Central Park, which will be discussed later, James will describe an entirely different episode involving immigrants, an encounter he seems to enjoy, perhaps because he has imposed a mastery over the scene. For now, however, this encounter with the Italians in Central Park seems to unsettle him.

In another scene, James encounters some diggers and ditchers while walking with friends through a large new residential development on the New Jersey shore. Under normal circumstances "everywhere," the natural inclination would have been to pause out of instinctive interest in the labor, and perhaps the encounter would have led to further interaction, James says. However, "whatever *more* would have been anywhere else involved had here inevitably to lapse" (90–91). What lapses is what James calls "the element of communication with the workers," which in Europe would have operated "as the play of mutual recognition, founded on old familiarities and heredities, and involving, for the moment, some impalpable exchange." Here, however, the diggers and ditchers are Italians, "of superlatively southern type," and any impalpable exchange is unthinkable, although we are never fully told why. "It was as if contact were out of the question and the sterility of the passage between us recorded, with due dryness, in our staring silence," James says. What follows is worth quoting at length:

> This impression was for one of the party a shock—a member of the party for whom, on the other side of the world, the imagination of the main furniture, as it might be called, of any rural excursion, of *the* rural in particular, had been, during years, the easy sense, for the excursionist, of a social relation with any encountered type, from whichever end of the scale proceeding. Had that not ever been, exactly, a part of the vague warmth, the intrinsic color, of any honest man's rural walk in his England or his Italy, his Germany or his France, and was not the effect of its so suddenly dropping out, in the land of universal brotherhood—for I was to find it drop out again and again—rather a chill, straightway, for the heart, and rather a puzzle, not less, for the head? (91)

This encounter, and James's handling of it, raises many questions that speak to his troubled, conflicted relationship with "the alien." For example, how important is it that the aborted encounter is with a group of Italians specifically described as of "superlatively southern type"? The demographics of Italian immigration to America's eastern seaboard at the turn of the century make it very probable that these manual laborers were in fact from southern Italy. But how could James be sure, except through conversing with them or their boss, or hearing and being able to place their dialect? James gives no indication that he did either. And what does James mean by "superlatively southern type"? Was he in fact attracted to their southern sensuousness? And was it their type, or was it something else, that made any exchange impossible? James does not elaborate. It is interesting that James uses the conjunction "and" to connect the workers' type to impossibility of any exchange. It is almost as if we are meant to read the conjunction in one of two different ways. If we accept James's assertion that an exchange would have been natural in Europe, then the "and" could be read as "despite the fact that"; however, because the encounter takes place in America, we can read the "and" as "because," as cause and effect: because the diggers were "superlatively southern" Italians in America, an exchange was unthinkable. Would an exchange have been more thinkable had the workers been "superlatively northern" middle-class Italians, or, more tellingly, had they been German or Irish? And had there been an exchange, would James have recorded it in light of Peter Conn's observation that *The American Scene* eradicates human speech and replaces it with monologues delivered by buildings?[40] Interesting that we rarely hear any of the aliens talking, when not only skyscrapers and hotels, but also rivers and entire cities are given voice in *The American Scene*. Also telling is that James can engage in dialogue with buildings, but repeatedly experiences communication breakdown in his encounters with the aliens/Italians. It is as if James at least understands all the new buildings, even if he does not particularly like their commercial message, but he cannot comprehend the aliens and what they ultimately mean to him and to America.

Speech and language are important here because, for James, they are an index of the broader culture. In his 1906 essay on "The Speech and Manners of American Women," James essentially says that speech equals manners equal morals equal civilization. "Conversation thus becomes a force for preserving the entire structure of American culture from ignorant foreigners," Kevin McNamara writes. McNamara also notes that in his commencement address to Bryn Mawr graduates, James "exhorted them to become 'models and missionaries, perhaps a little even martyrs of the good cause' of protecting the tone of American speech from the destructive forces of those 'innumerable aliens [who] are sitting up (*they* don't sleep!) to work their will on their new [linguistic] inheritance and prove to us that they are without any finer feeling or more conservative instinct of consideration for it.' "[41] In this same speech James said that "we have simply handed over our property," the English language, to "the American Dutchman and Dago," among others.[42] In *The American Scene*, James says: "The accent of the very ultimate future, in the States, may be destined to become the most beautiful on the globe and the very music of humanity (here the 'ethnic' synthesis shrouds itself thicker than ever); but whatever we shall know it for, certainly, we shall not know it for English—in any sense for which there is an existing literary measure" (106).

Speaking of the sterility of the encounter on the Jersey shore, James invokes as his ideal alternative previous encounters in Europe, which, with its "play of mutual recognition, founded on old familiarities and heredities," offered the excursionist a "social relation with any encountered type, from whichever end of the scale proceeding." This "social relation," what James calls "the main furniture" of any rural excursion, is "part of the vague warmth, the intrinsic color, of any honest man's rural walk in his England or his Italy." Again, James is vague. What does he mean by a social relation, and why does he talk about it first in utilitarian terms ("the main furniture") before reverting to rather aesthetic terms ("the intrinsic color")? We are reminded that at the conclusion of *The Golden Bowl*, Prince Amerigo is figured as a piece of furniture. James's problem seems to be that he cannot aestheticize the Italian diggers and ditchers in his America, when it had been so much easier to frame them from his privileged position in "his Italy." In Italy, James was a bourgeois traveler in a land of established social forms; in the United States, he is a native son returning to a fluid democratic society. He had a definite, if limited, relationship with the peasants he encountered in his rural rambles in Italy. There, the lower classes knew their place, were even content with their place, as James implies in *Italian Hours*. There, the *contadino* was a small but important detail in the middle ground of a picturesque landscape. However, here on the Jersey shore, James the "restored absentee" has no such established relationship with the laborers he encounters. These diggers and ditchers do not know their place; James himself does not know their place. Furthermore, James is not even sure of his own place. This makes it hard, if not impossible, for James to aesthetically frame the laborers and the other Italians he meets. They have no understood place and there are simply too many of them. James is obviously troubled that his vaguely warm "Italian hours" have been transformed into a sharply chilling "American scene." The loss of this social relation in "the land of universal brotherhood" (the same ideal invoked by Riis and Steiner) creates for James a "chill" in the heart, the same sensation that he felt during his trip to Ellis Island.

In the scene with the diggers, James seems to be unsuccessfully trying to transform a disquieting American scene into a more comforting Italian/European one. He is more successful during another visit to Central Park much different from the earlier one in which he had encountered and been disquieted by all the Italians. This time, James apparently revels in his encounter with a diverse population of "polyglot" voices. This rather utopian moment, as well as James's sometimes-sympathetic accounts of the Jewish ghetto in New York's Lowest East Side, may be seen as proof of his identification with the alien Other. However, McNamara does not see a change in James's sympathies away from his recoiling from the immigrants at Ellis Island. Instead, McNamara argues that during this visit to Central Park, James is able to put the "social question" behind him by aesthetically framing the urban pastoral scene, which is exactly what he failed to do with the diggers in New Jersey. In Central Park, James in essence "transformed New York into a *European* space," McNamara writes. "James's ability in Central Park to imagine that he was looking out upon the once stable world of European manners and classes answered his social question in two ways: his waving of the authorial wand created a world that contested the dominance of money as manners and, adding a final twist to the dizzying place of aliens and alienation, effected his repatriation by producing an image of a foreign culture in which he felt at home."[43] McNamara's assessment seems to me rather astute.

Not long after his encounter with the Italian diggers, James segues into another rural encounter that leaves him even more unsatisfied. This time James is already disoriented—geographically, if not psychologically, lost in the New Hampshire hills. He appeals for help from a young man who has emerged from a neighboring wood, but is met with a blank stare of incomprehension. Noticing that the man had "a dark-eyed 'Latin' look," James concludes that he is a French Canadian. James tries asking for directions in French, and, when that does not work, he tries Italian with no better result. Exasperated, James asks the fellow, "What *are* you then?" The man replies that he is an Armenian, "as if it were the most natural thing in the world for a wage-earning youth in the heart of New England to be" (91). James's assumption that the man is French Canadian is a natural one in the hills of New Hampshire. His second-best guess also makes sense given the man's dark-eyed Latin look. However, when the man turns out to be even more alien, James concludes that the best he can do with the encounter is to profit from its lesson. What that lesson might be he never specifies. Did he learn the pitfalls of using physical appearance to determine nationality or race? Or was it impressed on him that no place in America was out of bounds for immigrants of virtually any country? Whatever the lesson, James soon realizes that the encounter would yield nothing more. "I could have made it better, for the occasion, if, even on the Armenian basis, he had appeared to expect brotherhood; but this had been as little his seeming as it had been that of the diggers by the Jersey shore" (92). James concludes by equating the alien Italian diggers of the Jersey shore with the even more alien Armenian of the north woods. In both encounters, the question for James is not *who* these people are, but *what* they are, and *what* they are seems to determine what their relation—or lack of relation—will be to James. Had the man been a French Canadian, would the encounter have been more productive and more satisfactory for James? As a Frenchman and a Canadian, would the fellow have appeared to be more expectant of brotherhood than an Italian or Armenian? And would James have tended to see this French Canadian as more of a brother, if not as more of a countryman, than the Italian or Armenian? It is telling that James calls the man a French Canadian, but the presumed Italian is not an Italian American, just as the Armenian is not an Armenian American, in James's eyes.

Invoking again the sense of "chill" produced by such encounters with the alien, James explains "that there is no claim to brotherhood with aliens in the first grossness of their alienism." They are being "dressed and prepared" for brotherhood, James says, clearly implying that brotherhood is conditional and achieved rather than inherent. Most of the aliens will not attain that state in their lifetimes, but their children probably will because the "colossal" machinery of assimilation will see to that, James says, echoing Riis's hope for the second-generation immigrant. However, having said unequivocally that assimilation will eventually lead to brotherhood for even the grossest of aliens, James now enters into an extended meditation on what he calls "the great 'ethnic' question" and its relation to "the cauldron of the 'American' character." What, he wants to know, will assimilation of these alien immigrants wreak or reap? "What meaning, in the presence of such impressions," James wonders, "can continue to attach to such a term as the 'American' character?—what type, as the result of such a prodigious amalgam, such a hotch-potch of racial ingredients, is to be conceived as shaping itself?" James takes "refuge" from the question and finds relief in concluding that there are no answers, solutions, or conclusions to his questions (92–93). And yet James does not let the matter rest there. Unable to define the American character in the making, James turns his thoughts to the "process of the mitigation and, still more, of the conversion of the alien" (94).

James sees the country as "the hugest thinkable organism for successful 'assimilation,'" but one that still has to deal with a "residuum." That, however, is of less concern for the moment than a more fundamental question: "Who and what is an alien, when it comes to that, in a country peopled from the first under the jealous eye of history?—peopled, that is, by migrations, at once extremely recent, perfectly traceable and urgently required.... Which is the American, by these scant measures?—which is *not* the alien, over a large part of the country at least, and where does one put a finger on the dividing line, or, for that matter, 'spot' and identify any particular phase of the conversion, any one of its successive movements?" James tries to imagine seeing enacted in an immigrant group or in an individual "the dawn of the American spirit while the declining rays of the Croatian, say, or of the Calabrian, or of the Lusitanian, still linger more or less pensively in the sky." He wonders whether there is any foreign spirit "that the American does not find an easy prey." These concerns, if concerns they are, seem to be allayed (and other concerns raised) by the crowds of foreigners who overwhelm the electric trains and cast a "sense of isolation" over the observer. "The carful, again and again, is a foreign carful; a row of faces up and down, testifying, without exception, to alienism unmistakable, alienism undisguised and unashamed.... It was not for this that the observer on whose behalf I more particularly write had sought to take up again the sweet sense of his natal air" (95–96). The aliens, James says, were more at home in America than they had ever been in their native countries, and as much at home (if not more so) as James himself, creating an "equality of condition" that makes things strange for him. A similar disquieting sensation assaults James in the American South, in Richmond, but now it is not the aliens but other Others, the Negroes, who are in possession. Now it is the black teamsters who emphasized for James "with every degree of violence that already-apprehended note of the negro really at home" (278). James seeks relief from the "the great equalizing pressure" by sometimes "intimate surrender to it," "getting away from one's subject by plunging into it for sweet truth's sake, still deeper" (96).

What strikes James most is that of the aliens "not being what they *had* been." Instead, they seem to have been glazed over with the "wholesale varnish of consecration" by a "huge white-washing brush." James sees as a "sizable step in the evolution of the oncoming citizen, the stage of his no longer being for you—for any complacency of the romantic, or even verily of the fraternizing, sense in you—the foreigner of the quality, of the kind, that he might have been *chez lui*. Whatever he might see himself becoming, he was never to see himself that again, any more than you were ever to see him." For James, this phenomenon turns the foreigner into a "creature promptly despoiled of those 'manners'... by which one had best known and, on opportunity, best liked him." In fact, the foreigner appeared "as wonderingly conscious that his manners of the other world, that everything you have there known and praised him for, have been a huge mistake" (97). The process of whitewashing, of making the foreigner colorless, is curious in light of James's other pronouncements about the alien spreading his sauce over the American mixture. It is also a very curious term, a perhaps unintentional pun on race that came at a time when some Americans were contesting the Italians' whiteness. Furthermore, it seemed to imply that racial characteristics were not inherent but rather the result of environment, as Steiner had tried to argue.

James speaks of "categories of foreigners" who might be thought to be more resistant to this bleaching, who might require "a mechanism working with scientific force" to make them colorless. However, even the Italians do not seem immune to whitewashing. The Italians he sees serve only to make him ask what has become of that "element of the agreeable address" that made them so interesting and pleasurable in Italy. "They shed it utterly, I couldn't but observe, on their advent, after a deep inhalation or two of the clear native air; shed it with a conscientious completeness which leaves one looking for any faint trace of it. 'Colour,' of that pleasant sort, was what they had appeared, among the races of the European family, most to have." The effect, James says, is of a brightly colored garment losing its color in a washtub, but without in its turn coloring the rest of the clothes in the vat. "If this property that has quitted him—the general amenity of attitude in the absence of provocation to its opposite—could be accounted for by its having rubbed off on any number of surrounding persons, the whole process would be easier and perhaps more comforting to follow." James wonders what happens to the foreigners' "various positive properties," again giving as an example their "good manners." Are they truly extinguished, or is there the possibility of a "final efflorescence"? James does not say (97–99). However, in the same way that James complains about the Italian's loss of manners, later, in the South, he will lament the disappearance of mannerly service among the black porters and servants (312). The parallels between Italy and the Old South and between Italians and blacks are hinted at in a suggestive experience James has in Charleston, South Carolina. Searching for a friend and for "some small inkling" of "'the South before the War,'" James knocks on a wrong door and is greeted by an elderly mulatress who gives him a glimpse of the past and a "vanished order." But, before James can see more, the woman shuts the door in his face. James connects this scene to one in Italy, with the role of the mulatress now played by "the ancient sallow crones who guard the locked portals and the fallen pride of provincial *palazzini*" (297).

As John Sears points out, James complains about the Italian immigrants on two somewhat contradictory fronts. In America, the Italians become both "crude" and "neutral" by losing the good manners and the "colour" that made them so appealing in the Old World. "No longer related to him through established hierarchies and traditions like the peasants he was accustomed to dealing with in Italy, their new-found independence and mobility creates a chasm in his relationship to them."[44] But, in reality, how independent and mobile were Italians in the New World? Yes, they could be found in many cities and even in rural areas. And yes, the Italians could easily walk from their tenements to Central Park or to Boston Common. If that is

James's measure of independence and mobility, then that is itself telling. The reality, however, was that Italians in America were neither truly independent nor truly mobile. Many led dependent, rooted lives in the slums. Perhaps James is not so much offended by the modicum of independence and mobility they enjoyed in America's democratic society, but by the fact that their limited movement, and, perhaps more important, their sheer numbers, made it just that much harder for him to fit these teeming masses into an aesthetic frame.

James has two more encounters with Italians in New England, one in Boston and one in Salem. Near the Boston Common on a "benignant" Sunday, he sees a parade of couples that appear to be simple wage earners in their Sunday best. James notes that "no sound of English, in a single instance, escaped their lips; the greater number spoke a rude form of Italian, the others some outland dialect unknown to me—though I wanted and waited to catch an echo of antique refrains." The laborers' speech marks them as doubly different: They are neither American nor fully Italian. With their "rude form of Italian" and "outland dialect," they lack the manners, morals, and civilization of those Italians who speak the Tuscan tongue immortalized by Dante as the national language. James describes the people as "gross aliens to a man" who "were in serene and triumphant possession" of what James calls "'my' small homogenous Boston of the more interesting time." The scene gives James a vision of "a huge applied sponge, a sponge saturated with the foreign mixture and passed over almost everything I remembered and might still have recovered." James seeks refuge in the nearby Athenaeum, his "temple of culture." However, that shrine to the mind is "rueful and snubbed," humiliated by the tall buildings that surround it, just as James is overwhelmed and dispossessed by the masses of Italians who have taken over Boston Common and the waves of immigrants who threatened to take over the entire country (171–172).

Later, James is in Salem, again searching for "the New England homogenous." Unable to find Hawthorne's House of the Seven Gables, he asks directions from a stranger. This stranger, like the one in the New Hampshire hills, turns out to be a "flagrant foreigner" who responds with a blank stare. This young man is not an Armenian, but instead "a remorseless Italian—as remorseless, at least, as six months of Salem could leave him." James is shocked and "put off" by the encounter and the young man's ignorance of Hawthorne's American monument. However, the Italian leaves James "with the interest of wondering how the native estimate of it as a romantic ruin might strike a taste formed for such features by the landscape of Italy" (196–197). Just as with the diggers on the Jersey shore, there is no possibility of communication. Still, in this scene James at least imagines a common ground in the possibility that the young Italian might share his assessment of the House of the Seven Gables as a romantic ruin. If nothing else, James and the young Italian might be united by the romantic picturesque, which of course had been the basis of much of James's relationship to Italians in Italy. If James and the Italian boy can meet, it will be on an aesthetic level. However, more substantial links connect James and the "dear little harsh, intelligent, sympathetic American boy" who appears, like a deus ex machina, to guide him to the House of the Seven Gables. The American boy is confident, knowing, "the master of his subject," and James and the boy form a close alliance on the spot. "He made up to me for my crude Italian—the way they *become* crude over here!—... he was exactly what I wanted—a presence (and he was the only thing far or near) old enough, native and intimate enough, to reach back and understand" (200).

This scene in Salem is the flip side of the encounter on the strand in Venice in *Italian Hours*, when James aesthetically transformed a wild Italian urchin into a "little unlettered Eros of the Adriatic strand." That Italian boy had been memorably picturesque when compared to a better dressed, better educated "infant citizen of our own republic" marching into a New England schoolhouse. But in Salem, the Italian boy becomes a "a flagrant foreigner" and "my crude Italian," while the forgettable American youth becomes a memorable, confident, knowing "master of his subject" who bonds with James and rescues him from the alien with whom there is little hope of any communion. In Italy, the Italian can be aestheticized, romanticized, can be made an object of "infinite tender conjecture." In America, that same Italian is simply a very real ignorant, crude urchin—a flagrant foreigner.

What is interesting in these encounters with the Italians in America is James's shifting attitude as expressed in his image making. The preceding passages and meditations represent classic Jamesian ambiguity and subtlety so refined that James appears to be speaking with multiforked tongue. In one scene, the Italians are spreading their sauce over the New York scene, imparting to the city its distinctive flavor, but intentionally forcing the native-born Americans to eat from a greasy ladle. In another episode, the alien/Italian sponge is saturating everything James "remembered and might have recovered." Later, the foreigners, even the so pungent, pervasive, and colorful Italians, are being bleached of their color, threatened with American whitewashing and uniformity. In some passages, James longs for homogeneity and order, but in others he speaks of maintaining margins and distinctions, resisting America's leveling tendencies toward the "common mean" and the "great grey wash" (325, 335). On the one hand, James praises the Italians and other foreigners for refusing to be what Americans thought they were or want them to be; on the other hand, he criticizes them for losing their Old World charm and becoming, in the New World, crude and gross. James tells Americans: Do not expect the foreigners to be as they were in their native lands, do not expect the Italian immigrants to be the romantic, picturesque

Italians-in-Italy that I myself helped to construct in my travel narratives. Here, James seems to be renouncing his earlier aestheticizing tendencies. He is implying that Italians and other immigrants, by throwing off American perceptions of them, take a significant step toward citizenship, if not brotherhood, with American natives. But having said that, James regrets that the Italians-in-America are not what he imagines Italians-in-Italy to be: mannerly, courteous, agreeable in their address, romantic, and picturesque.

Finally, there are James's images of possession and dispossession. On one hand, the aliens are triumphantly taking possession, dispossessing James and other native-born Americans, and forcing James to wonder: What will the aliens make of us? On the other hand, it is the aliens who are being possessed, with James now asking: What is America making of the aliens? It is as if James is offering up two diametrically opposed forces: alienism and assimilation. Both are ubiquitous, voracious, almost inexorable. Assimilation is a single-minded machine or a giant organism. Alienism is gross and crude, if sometimes colorful and vital. What is it that makes the aliens so gross and crude and threatening? Is there anything besides their native color, their native manners, and their vitality that is worth saving from assimilation? Are the aliens overwhelming American society, or is it the other way around? The eternally ambiguous James will not be pinned down.

Nor surprisingly, what can be said with any degree of certainty is that James has deeply conflicted attitudes toward the Italians and the other so-called new immigrants. He both recoils from and is attracted to them. He seems to have little doubt that they can eventually be assimilated, but questions the wisdom of that goal. Does that, however, make him a cultural pluralist who rejects Anglo-Saxon hegemony, as Posnock and Blair argue? Posnock claims that "James's questions insist on honoring the dynamic reality of American heterogeneity that is muffled by that fabled ideological instrument of pseudounity, the 'American character,' so dear to the identity logic of progressivism."[45] Blair says: "'Beguiling' and 'duping' his own anxiety of dispossession—his own capacity, we might say, for racial distaste—James relocated assimilation as a social act from the corporate to the individual body, figuring a newly American 'being' in whom the requirements of American citizenship—active incorporation of difference as the grounds of culture-building—will contend with the 'universal will' of capitalist assimilation and its 'appetite at any price.'"[46] There is some validity in what Posnock and Blair argue, but they are clearly overstating their cases, relying on an oversubtle analysis that simply fails to account for James's shock and horror over the threat posed by the gross and crude alien. James does try to identify and empathize with Italians on both sides of the Atlantic, but ultimately he cannot transcend the prejudices of his age and class.

Ultimately, James is left with a question that he himself poses, and for which he has no answer: "What meaning . . . can continue to attach to such a term as the 'American' character?—what type, as the result of such a prodigious amalgam, such a hotch-potch of racial ingredients, is to be conceived as shaping itself?" (92). We cannot say with any certainty just what it is that James wants America and the American character to become, and the role the alien may play in that process. The ground becomes a little more firm when we look at James's attitudes toward what America and the American character *has* become, and the alien's position vis-à-vis that character.

James's main quarrel is, I believe, with American capitalism and American democracy, two terms that he often conflates. Throughout *The American Scene*, James rails against America's passion for change, growth, size, and money-making, all of which are most apparent in New York, which he calls his "terrible town" and the "miscellaneous monster" (57, 40). He speaks disparagingly of "the monstrous form of Democracy" and "the huge democratic broom"; he ridicules the "great commercial democracy" and "our vast crude democracy of trade" (44, 72, 53). He says America's energy and commercial spirit and its mania for change fail to create beauty, and that they account for the "great grey wash" that dissolves color and results in bourgeois uniformity and sameness of type (328, 335). As Larzer Ziff says, "The dominant picture painted in *The American Scene* is one of a crassly materialistic society that young as it may be is nevertheless committed to the systematic elimination of whatever is not new rather than the nurturing of continuity, so that a sense of the past—of tradition, shared manners, inherited values—is ruthlessly obstructed."[47] In opposition to commerce, James offers beauty, taste, manners, distinctions. The tall commercial buildings of New York are ugly; Giotto's bell tower in Florence is beautiful.

The aliens/Italians and Europe/Italy become, in part, pawns in James's quarrel with commercial democracy. Ideally, their heterogeneity, their picturesqueness, taste and manners, and sense of the past make them an antidote to what James sees happening to America and the American character. But to be an effective antidote, the immigrants have to stay the same, have to bring Europe with them to America. As Kevin McNamara says, James wanted to preserve the aliens' pleasing diversity from "ingurgitation" by the machinery of Americanization. "But he was put off balance by the mobility of the aliens, who seemed out of context and troubled his view as they would not were they still European peasants with whom the American on tour delights to chat, and he often treated them as objects of unadulterated, unchanging culture, his seeming pluralism relaxing into a 'soft focus' appreciation of exotic poverty."[48] James (and other Americans) thus put the Italian immigrants in a bind. He wanted the Italians to preserve their color, to resist the racial whitewashing so necessary for Americanization. However, many Italians came to America to escape their exotic poverty, if not to become modern in the way that Prince Amerigo had hoped to become modern. They came to do what James perhaps hated most about modern Americans—to make money, and as much of it as possible. Those Italians who wanted more, who wanted to become Americans, were held back by their color, which could be both pleasing and repellant. James, it seems, wanted his Italians to be both colored and white. He wanted to retain enough of the Italians' color to serve as an antidote to American uniformity, but he also wanted to bleach out the color that made Italians alien and gross and threatening. And in fact, to become Americans the Italians *had* to become white. Ultimately, the Italian immigrants, along with industrialism, capitalism, and materialism, not only threatened James's already tenuous position in American society, but also his American past, his American memories, and his American associations. That is, they threatened those very things that might help remake the expatriate James as an American.

Chapter 5

Mark Twain: Racism, Nativism, and the Twinning of Italianness

How can men, calling themselves men, consent to be so degraded and happy?

—Mark Twain, *The Innocents Abroad*, 1869

Italians! How romantic! Just think, ma—there's never been one in this town, and everybody will be dying to see them, and they're all *ours*! Think of that!

—Rowena, in *Pudd'nhead Wilson*, 1894

Judge Driscoll, an old and respected citizen, was assassinated here about midnight by a profligate Italian nobleman or barber on account of a quarrel growing out of the recent election. The assassin will probably be lynched.

—Newspaper notice, *Pudd'nhead Wilson*, 1894

If we are foolish enough to believe Mark Twain, he performed a simple "kind of literary Caesarean operation" on the unruly tale of Siamese twins that was giving him such a struggle in the early 1890s. Dr. Twain saw the procedure as a simple one: Remove, from the main story line, the farce involving Aunt Patsy Cooper, Rowena, and the Italian Siamese twins. Preserve the tragedy of Roxana, Tom Driscoll, and David "Pudd'nhead" Wilson. Deliver, through this editorial surgery, literary Siamese twins: *The Tragedy of Pudd'nhead Wilson and the Comedy of Those Extraordinary Twins* (1894), a "tragic" novel and a "comic" short story that are separate and yet linked. Twain, in typically self-deprecating fashion, called the operation the performance of a "jack-leg" author. "Also I took those twins apart and made two separate men of them," he says. "They had no occasion to have foreign names now, but it was too much trouble to remove them all through, so I left them christened as they were and made no explanation."[1] Many critics have too readily agreed with Twain. They see him as a sloppy obstetrician who botched the operation by leaving remnants of the Italian twins in *The Tragedy of Pudd'nhead Wilson*, in much the same way a surgeon might leave a gauze wipe inside a patient. Consequently, these critics have dismissed the twins as nothing but freaks/grotesques who destroy the unity of the novel.[2]

In this reading, the fact that Twain's twins are Italians named Luigi and Angelo Capello means little or nothing. Luigi and Angelo might have been inspired by an exhibition of the Tocci brothers Siamese twins in 1891, but they might just as well have been named Frank and John Smith, or Chang and Eng, as they were in an earlier Twain tale.[3] This traditional reading was established in an early English review in *The Idler*, which praised Twain's novel for its construction and characterizations, but singled out "one false note" in "the two alleged Italian noblemen" who "are as little like Italians as they are like Apaches."[4] However, the twins' race/nationality is as important as the fact that they are twins. I will argue that Twain's "extraordinary twins" are extraordinarily "Italian," as intensely Italian as Henry James's Prince Amerigo or the Italian immigrants who filled Edward Steiner's steerage and Jacob Riis's tenements. That Twain should downplay the twins' race/nationality should alert us to its significance. Whether or not Twain truly wanted to banish the twins from the work that became *Pudd'nhead Wilson* is irrelevant; the fact is that he could not shed the Italian twins and all they represented, just as Twain's countrymen could not shake the reality of the Italian presence in America in the 1890s. As Eric Sundquist has shown, *The Tragedy of Pudd'nhead Wilson and the Comedy of Those Extraordinary Twins* engages with the period's unsettled discourses on immigration, race, and assimilation. Sundquist links the twins to anti-immigrant and anti-Italian thought and action, in particular the lynching of the eleven Italians in New Orleans in 1891.[5]

Building on Sundquist, I will argue that the twins serve as the locus for America's bifurcated attitudes toward Italy, representing as they do a number of dualities then current or emerging in the national discourse. These dualities include: northern Italians versus southern Italians, old Italian immigrants versus "new" Italian immigrants, romantic visions of a timeless, idealized Italy versus realistic fears of the Italian immigrants pouring in from "modern" Italy. As we will see, Twain's representations of Italy/Italians in *Pudd'nhead Wilson* and in his travel writing sometimes reflect, sometimes refract, and often resist prevailing American attitudes and depictions. Consciously or unconsciously, Twain explores these dualities and other themes, including the limitations of the picturesque aesthetic, the connections between Italians and blacks, and the notions of brotherhood invoked at various times by Riis, Steiner, and James.

Before looking at *Pudd'nhead Wilson and Those Extraordinary Twins*, it will be worthwhile to examine Twain's attitudes toward Italy and Italians, and then his opinions on immigration. It is in *The Innocents Abroad or The New Pilgrims' Progress* that we find Twain's most extended treatment of people and things Italian. As one of the pilgrims on the "Holy Land Pleasure Excursion" organized by Henry Ward Beecher's Plymouth Church in 1867, Twain immediately saw he was part of a larger social movement involving the American middle class's discovery of Europe. If the century's earlier travelers had gone to Europe to absorb its culture and observe its customs and manners, sketching and journalizing their way through the Old World, the new tourists went to consume it and in that way to affirm the respectability of their class and race.[6] Twain had mixed emotions about his fellow pilgrims, but delighted in his membership in this social movement in a way that Henry James would have found distasteful. Twain mocked the pilgrimage, while still expressing true pilgrimhood.[7] Twain's narrator assumes various roles: innocent, vandal, humorist, satirist, realist, romantic. He is often indignant, sometimes sentimental. And although he often ridicules his fellow tourists, "he began to convert some of their baser attitudes—their outrage at bureaucracy and beggars, at the wealth of the Church, at superstition and the veneration of relics, their raucous irreverence and impatience with the past, their conviction that Europe was a sell, a swindle, a fraud—into a flexible, joyously inconsistent view that was wholly his own."[8]

While not altogether ignorant or unappreciative of Italy's attractions, Twain's narrator sees the country as "one vast museum of magnificence and misery" and "the wretchedest, princeliest land on earth."[9] Very often he burlesques the old gushing guidebooks, but more than once his own "guidebook" is sentimental and romantic. Like James and many other American travelers, Twain seems to reserve some of his greatest admiration for Italy's arcadian landscape. He may disparage the Arno as a river short on water and describe Lake Como as "a bedizened little courtier in [the] August presence" of Nevada's Lake Tahoe (145), but he often rhapsodizes, with apparent sincerity, over the enchantments of certain Italian landscapes. The same second-best Lake Como is described in a passage that, with its sense of wonder, echoes Twain's writing about the Mississippi River in *Adventures of Huckleberry Finn*.[10]

Like many another American traveler to Italy, Twain's narrator is both attracted to and repelled by the country and its people. Much of the attraction comes from the Italian picturesque, which Twain tries, with varying success, to dissociate from the fraudulently romantic. Outside of Milan, "Troops of picturesque peasant-girls, coming from work, hooted at us, shouted at us, made all manner of game of us, and entirely delighted me," the narrator writes. "My long-cherished judgment was confirmed. I always did think those frowsy, romantic, unwashed peasant girls I had read so much about in poetry were a glaring fraud" (139). Behind the romance of these peasant girls is the reality of poverty and dirt. However, not all efforts to debunk the romance of the picturesque are as successful. Despite his initial disenchantment with a "mangy, barefooted guttersnipe" of a Venetian gondolier named Roderigo Gonzales Michael Angelo (155), the narrator concludes that the gondolier is a romantic and "picturesque rascal" despite his less-than-romantic material reality. "His attitude is stately; he is lithe and supple; all his movements are full of grace. When his long cane, and his fine figure, towering from its high perch on the stern, are cut against the evening sky, they make a picture that is very novel and striking to a foreign eye" (166).

When the narrator looks closer into the broad picturesque canvas, he sees decay, degeneration, poverty, dirt, sloth, and superstition. Most of it is blamed on the Catholic Church, an attitude representative of many Protestant Americans who equated Catholicism with Italy and Italianness, blamed it for many of the Italians' character flaws, and saw it as a threat to American ideals such as individualism, democracy, and republicanism. On the way to Bergamo, the narrator thinks, "We were in the heart and home of priestcraft—of a happy, cheerful, contented ignorance, superstition, degradation, poverty, indolence, and everlasting uninspiring worthlessness. And we said fervently, It suits these people precisely; let them enjoy it, along with the other animals, and heaven forbid that they be molested" (148). Decay is everywhere and serves as the symbol of a fallen culture, a once glorious civilization now in declension. For Twain, the decay is perhaps most noticeable in the paintings of the Old Masters, whose faded and weathered works are now less handsome than those of the ubiquitous copyists. The Italian cities also have deteriorated, thanks in great measure to their degraded populations. Genoa has "degenerated into an unostentatious commerce in velvets and silver filigree work" (118). Venice, the "haughty, invincible, magnificent Republic," now "is fallen a prey to poverty, neglect, and melancholy decay... a peddler of glass beads for women, and trifling toys and trinkets for schoolgirls and children" (154). Venice's only poetry is nocturnal, when its realities are not exposed by the "glare of day" and "treacherous sunlight" (157–158).

If Venice is best seen in moonlight, Naples is beautiful only from a great distance, from far up the side of Vesuvius. Then only did the maxim "See Naples and die" truly apply. Do not, however, go within the city walls, the narrator warns. "That takes away some of the romance of the thing. The people are filthy in their habits, and this makes filthy streets and breeds disagreeable sights and smells." In Naples, "the contrasts between opulence and poverty, and magnificence and misery, are more frequent and more striking ... than in Paris even" (236–237). Another city, the Roman port of Civita Vecchia, is barely European. It "is the finest nest of dirt, vermin, and ignorance we have found yet, except that African perdition they call Tangier, which is just like it" (191).

Images of dirt and disorder appear over and over in *The Innocents Abroad*, recapitulating a trope that runs through much American writing about Italians in both Italy and America. Jacob Riis and Edward Steiner seemed obsessed with the image of the dirty Italian, and their obsession mirrored the American's general preoccupation with the Italian immigrant's threat to Anglo-Saxon cleanliness, health, and order. For Twain's narrator, the Italian's obsession with fumigating and quarantining foreign visitors is misdirected: It is the Italians themselves who need fumigating. Still, Twain's narrator says he will try to pray for these dirty "fumigating, macaroni-stuffing organ-grinders" (141), these Italians who elsewhere are depicted as tobacco "stub-hunters" (113) and "garlic-exterminating" mouths (129). In the interior regions of Italy, the people are characterized as content in their ignorance. "*They* have nothing to do but eat and sleep and sleep and eat, and toil a little when they can get a friend to stand by and keep them awake. *They* are not paid for thinking—*they* are not paid to fret about the world's concerns.... How can men, calling themselves men, consent to be so degraded and happy?" (148).

If the Italians of *The Innocents Abroad* lack American initiative and ambition, they are not indifferent to the lure of money. Near Mount Vesuvius, the narrator encounters dirty Italians who grasp for money for every service imposed on the tourist, while carrying a subtle threat of disease and infection. "They crowd you—infest you—swarm about you, and sweat and smell offensively, and look sneaking and mean, and obsequious. There is no office too degrading for them to perform, for money" (231). In one shape or another the money-grubbing charge was be linked to Italians throughout the nineteenth and into the twentieth century. Early travel accounts of Italy often speak of carriage drivers, cicerones, guides, and small tradespeople always on the alert for an opportunity to squeeze the traveler. In time, these same grasping Italians from the south of Italy would be transformed into the grasping Italian immigrants who will do anything for a wage.

Like his acquaintance Henry James but unlike his good friend William Dean Howells, Twain rarely stops to examine the causes behind the decay, degeneration, and degradation. Twain's narrator professes the same ignorance about Italy's history and society as he does for its art. He is puzzled that such a financially bankrupt nation, in the throes of unification, can afford "palatial railroad depots," "marvels of turnpikes," and an unnecessary navy. "Italy has achieved the dearest wish of her heart and become an independent state—and in so doing she has drawn an elephant in the political lottery," the narrator says. "She has nothing to feed it on. Inexperienced in government, she plunged into all manner of useless expenditure, and swamped her treasury almost in a day" (186–187). Here, Italy is figured as a vain, profligate woman who overextends her credit on impractical toys and luxuries even while her children go hungry and shoeless. With no other recourse, the government "in effect" confiscated the church's domains, those immense riches that had been lying idle while the people were "ground to death with taxation to uphold a perishing government" (188). The narrator heartily applauds these measures. "As far as I can see, Italy, for fifteen hundred years, has turned all her energies, all her finances, and all her industry to the building up of a vast array of wonderful church edifices, and starving half her citizens to accomplish it." Finally, it is the Catholic Church that has made Italy "one vast museum of magnificence and misery" and the "wretchedest, princeliest land on earth" (188–189). Like the cultural pilgrims who came before, Twain's narrator had prostrated himself before the Duomo in Florence and "worshiped it." However, "when the filthy beggars swarmed around me the contrast was too striking, too suggestive, and I said, 'Oh, sons of classic Italy, *is* the spirit of enterprise, of self-reliance, of noble endeavor, utterly dead within yea? Curse your indolent worthlessness, why don't you rob your churches?'" (189).

As we can see, the picture of Italy and Italians that emerges from *The Innocents Abroad* is a typically Twainian mixed-bag that deflates, exaggerates, and often denigrates in humorous fashion, making it all but impossible to cut through to Twain's real feelings about the country and her people. There is some sincere appreciation for the land itself, but Twain's narrator feels compelled to qualify that praise with chauvinistic comparisons to American scenery. For the most part, the country—its art and commerce and people—is seen as a degenerate shell of its former self, a culture that long ago experienced its glory days. Heroic Italy is in the past. Now, all is decay and deterioration, from the faded Old Masters paintings to the once powerful cities. Newly independent Italy is still oppressed by superstitious, relic-revering religion, held back by foolhardy, impotent leaders, and endured by a dirty and ignorant people who show initiative only in begging from and otherwise fleecing tourists. Twain's Italy in *The Innocents Abroad* retains some of its picturesqueness, but has been shorn of much of its romance. Negative images that were somewhat more muted in earlier American travel accounts become, with Twain, more pronounced, more exaggerated. In stripping Italy and Italians of their romance, Twain both satirizes America's romantic notions of Italy/Europe and provides an admittedly exaggerated but cold-eyed "realistic" view of Italy and its people. It is obviously difficult to determine just how seriously Twain is to be taken. To some extent, as Larzer Ziff says, Twain may intend for his attacks and stereotypes to be read as examples of his comic irascibility rather than as objective truths. "Yet even granting this somewhat doubtful contention, the heaped-up diction of derision goes beyond comic intent or even scorn to convey an almost violent abhorrence of other peoples because they are not clean, not sensible, not industrious, not modern—not, in a word, American."[11]

Following *The Innocents Abroad*, Twain's writings have little to say about Italians. There are a few brief chapters on Italy in *A Tramp Abroad* (1880), but these do not often engage in the type of national and racial generalities found in *The Innocents Abroad*. One striking exception is all the more startling becomes it seems to come out of nowhere. Describing a boat trip in Germany, Twain recounts how the excursionists are bombarded by Italian workers blasting away at a new railbed along the river. Twain reports that Italians handled most of the heavy work in quarries and on railway gradings. "That was a revelation," he writes. "We have the notion in our country that Italians never do heavy work at all, but confine themselves to the lighter arts, like organ-grinding, operatic singing, and assassination. We have blundered, that is plain."[12] Twain here compactly captures a strain of mid-nineteenth-century American thinking that saw Italians as either feminized artists of both high and low culture (organ-grinding, opera), or masculine assassins (not unlike Luigi Capello in *Pudd'nhead Wilson*). However, "the multitude of Italian laborers" in Germany (immigrants blazing one of the many migratory trails away from Italy) gives the lie to America's "notion" that Italians shun heavy work. In the years immediately following publication of *A Tramp Abroad*, Americans would see more graphic evidence that Italians were certainly capable of heavy work.

There are other sporadic mentions of Italy and Italians in Twain's notebooks and autobiographical writings, but they add little to our understanding of his attitudes.[13] Although there is even less on Italian immigrants, Twain must have had some firsthand experience with them in the Northeast. He lived briefly around New York State (New York City, Buffalo, and Elmira), before beginning a twenty-one year residence in Hartford, Connecticut, in 1871. His publishing company, Webster and Company, eventually had offices on New York's Union Square, not far from the Lower East Side, which was filling to bursting with new immigrants. Although Twain left the United States in June 1891 and lived in Europe for most of the next decade, he made numerous trips back to the United States, usually to New York City, in frantic attempts to shore up his troubled literary and business interests. And although Twain lived but briefly in New York City, he had extensive ties with it. He had moved to the city in 1867 as a correspondent for the *Alta California*. In search of copy, he made a tour of the Five Points and the city's worst slums, areas that would figure so heavily in Jacob Riis's career. Twain's biggest coup in New York City, a public lecture on the Sandwich Islands on May 6, 1867, survived a challenge from an Italian actress who symbolized America's continuing mania for things Italian. Despite a repertory that was exclusively in her native tongue, the Italian tragedienne Adelaide Ristori had filled houses across the country and was giving her farewell performance the same night as Twain's speech. Twain found Ristori's popularity amazing, and must have wondered if he could compete with her in the face of his countrymen's Italophilia.[14] As we will see, like Adelaide Ristori, the twins of *Pudd'nhead Wilson* charmed and dazzled Americans with their prodigious musical talents.

Twain also would have been exposed to the Italians found in William Dean Howells' *Venetian Life* (1866) and *A Hazard of New Fortunes* (1890), two books he greatly admired.[15] Having read *Venetian Life* as a young man, Twain must have been struck by the book's generally sympathetic account of the Italians, which could not help but give the young Sam Clemens a greater appreciation for the Italian people. In *A Hazard of New Fortunes*, Twain would have encountered numerous Italian immigrants in New York City as seen through the eyes of the transplanted Bostonians, Basil and Isabel March. Usually the Marches are little more than tourists among the city's immigrants, enjoying the foreigners' foreignness and appropriating their immigrant culture. The Marches see the Italian immigrants as raggedly picturesque and seemingly content with their rather mean lives in the tenement districts, images that are similar to, if not as stark as, the ones we get in Riis's *How the Other Half Lives*, published the same year as *A Hazard of New Fortunes*. While Riis sought to shock, titillate, and ultimately reassure, Basil March, the editor of a new magazine, thinks more of working up the sights "very nicely," as his wife suggests, for a feature not unlike a long touristic piece, "The Italians of New York," which appeared in the January 1888 issue of *The Cosmopolitan*. Like James's and Twain's *contadini* in Italy, Basil March's Italians in New York are figures for aesthetic treatment. Basil, like Howells himself, is broadly sympathetic toward the Italians and other new immigrant groups, but he does not stop long enough to examine the cause of the Italians' condition, as Howells the American consul did in *Venetian Life*. Basil March generally sees more of the Italians' positive attributes than does Riis. Still, Basil March does wonder vaguely what effect the Italians and other immigrant groups will have on America. However, his dreamy approach to the issue may indicate that in the 1880s, some people did not yet see the immigrant question as the immigrant problem. Although *A Hazard of New Fortunes* presents the main conflict as one between socioeconomic classes, between producers and laborers, between the "haves" and the "have-nots," it touches on the new immigration as an emerging problem. And Twain, as an admirer of the book, could not have failed to notice.[16]

If Twain's post-*Innocents* writings speak little about Italians, general ideas about race and racial differences—issues that went beyond black and white—seemed to be on Twain's mind beginning in the 1880s, just as the new immigration was starting to make itself felt. A notebook entry dated August 15, 1885, finds Twain making simple stereotypical assessments of various nationalities and races of Europe. Twain here conflates not only race and nationality, but also religion. He provides no context for the entry, which is a straightforward listing of the various groups and their presumed traits. In Twain's taxonomy, Americans constituted the "material nation," the same one that would distress James in *The American Scene*. Twain lumps together as the "ignorant nations" the Roman Catholic countries of Europe (including of course Italy), describing them as "hot-blooded, kind-hearted." It is interesting that Twain distinguishes these Roman Catholic countries by religion, not race or nationality, and consigns them all to ignorance, with the connotations of superstition, degradation, powerlessness, and primitivism that we saw in *The Innocents Abroad*. Three years later Twain again plays with national/racial traits in his notebooks.[17]

It is difficult to say what Twain had in mind here or what his motivations are, especially in light of an essay and a sketch, both written some seven years later in the mid-1890s, in which he satirizes this very tendency to categorize, subdivide, and label peoples according to race or national character. Twain criticizes this approach to race in an essay on the French novelist, critic, and journalist Paul Bourget, who was a close friend of Henry James. Bourget had written about Americans, and Twain responded with his 1895 essay, "What Paul Bourget Thinks of Us," in which he compares the Frenchman to a specimen-collecting naturalist who groups, subdivides, and labels for study different species. It is "a pleasant System," Twain writes, "but subject to error"—especially when applied to humans, and particularly when applied to foreigners. Among his own people, an "Observer of Peoples" may prove competent to the task, Twain suggests. "But history has shown that when he is abroad observing unfamiliar peoples the chances are heavily against him. He is then a naturalist observing a bug, with no more than a naturalist's chance of being able to tell the bug anything new about itself, and no more than a naturalist's chance of being able to teach it any new ways which it will prefer to its own."[18] Obviously, this passage resonates with anti-imperialist sentiment. Additionally, it represents an attempt to subvert the segregationist, differentiating approach to nationality/race that was currently popular and showing signs of being used in the service of racism and race nativism. It was an approach that Riis and Steiner criticized but often employed. Needless to say, Twain the travel writer had himself engaged in classifying and generalizing about foreign peoples. However, while many commentators were beginning to see racial hierarchies as immutable, impervious to the influences of education, religion, and environment, Twain was beginning to see the shortcomings and the perils of such ideas about humankind.

Just as Twain may have started out as a racist and later overcome those prejudices, so too he may have entertained mild nativist attitudes before becoming more sympathetic to foreigners. Guy Cardwell argues that the young Sam Clemens was by some standards both a racist and a nativist, sharing mildly in the Know-Nothing suspicion of foreigners.[19] As late as November 18, 1878, Twain declared in a letter to Howells that disenfranchising blacks and barring immigration was "a mighty sound and sensible" remedy for dangerous tendencies in American life.[20] However, it is unlikely that Twain entirely meant what he wrote. At this stage in his life he was not hostile toward Negroes or foreigners. In a letter to Howells five months later, on April 5, 1879, Twain opposed limits to Chinese immigration. "I knew the President would veto that infamous Chinese bill," Twain wrote, referring to a move that would have barred shipmasters from bringing to America more than fifteen Chinese at any one time.[21] Seven years earlier, in the essay "Disgraceful Persecution of a Boy," Twain had vented his indignation at the mistreatment of the Chinese in California. The satirical piece deals with a real incident in which a well-dressed American boy stoned a Chinaman on his way to church. In the piece, Twain criticizes the Pacific Coast's system of justice where the typical response to any mysterious crime was, "'Let justice be done, though the heavens fall,' and go straightaway and swing a Chinaman"—yet another Twainian reference to lynching. Twain protests that the ten-dollar vaccination for entering Chinese was the equivalent of a "disabling admission fee" that kept "the poor and oppressed" of all nations from the "asylum" created by the Constitution.[22]

Despite his attacks on racial prejudice and nativism, Twain did not hold much hope for improvement. We see this in his 1899 essay, "Concerning the Jews," which offers a point-by-point defense of that oppressed group. In the essay, Twain disclaims any prejudice. "I am quite sure that (bar one) I have no race prejudices, and I think I have no color prejudices nor caste prejudices nor creed prejudices," he writes. "Indeed, I know it. I can stand any society. All that I care to know is that a man is a human being—that is enough for me; he can't be any worse."[23] In asserting his own blindness to color, race, class, and religion, Twain is dissociating himself from Americans who were increasingly dividing humankind according to racial differences.

This might seem to substantiate Twain's claim that the twins' Italianness in *Pudd'nhead Wilson* was of no account. However, for the race-conscious Americans that Twain is criticizing, the fact that the twins are Italian was of great importance. In the 1899 essay on the Jews, Twain says that although religious persecution of the Jews has ended, race prejudice against the group would continue. He tells the Jews: "You will always be by ways and habits and predilections substantially strangers—foreigners—wherever you are, and that will probably keep the race prejudice against you alive."[24] Here Twain is underscoring the intensity of the period's race thinking, even while acknowledging the cultural and social differences that were often being equated with racial differences. And it should be remembered that at this time, not only Jews but also Italians were being seen as the most pervasive and the most foreign of the European "new immigrant" groups who were second only to the Chinese as targets of nativism.

As Shelley Fisher Fishkin argues, Twain rejected racial determinism and the hierarchy of race/color, even if he did not launch full frontal attacks on racism in the manner of peers such as George Washington Cable. Fishkin cites a passage, ultimately deleted from *Pudd'nhead Wilson*, which shows that Twain went further than his white contemporaries, including Cable, in imaginatively subverting these racial beliefs. In this passage, the mulatto Tom ruminates over the realization that he is little more than a piece of property because of his one-thirty-second-part black blood. These few paragraphs express the notion that although human beings have varying degrees of virtue and talent, race itself is irrelevant. Fishkin also cites an unpublished sketch, probably dating from the 1890s, that shows Twain again parodying the racial discourse of the day. In this fantasy, "The Quarrel in the Strong-Box," different denominations of money, which represent the hierarchy of color (and, I would add, race/nationality), get into a nasty dispute over "matters of right & privilege." The case ends up in court, where the judge asserts that despite physical and intellectual differences, denomination (e.g., color/race) does not matter because all denominations earn the same interest rate.

I very much agree with Fishkin when she says that although Twain's writings on race are complex and ambiguous, it is untenable to conclude that Twain believed in a natural racial hierarchy, the biological inferiority of blacks, or, for that matter, the biological inferiority of other non-Anglo-Saxon races.[25] As the product of a slave culture, Mark Twain by training and custom probably grew up believing that skin color differences equated with caste and fundamental rights, but he certainly had begun to question those beliefs by the time he wrote *Adventures of Huckleberry Finn* in the 1880s. Few subjects energized Twain more than outrage over injustice. "His indictments of politicians who betrayed the public trust and his defense of oppressed minorities vitally informed his vision," Andrew Hoffman says, and by the

1880s Twain had a confirmed faith in human equality and a growing progressive belief in the effects of training.[26] Twain's growth is perhaps most evident in his travel book, *Following the Equator* (1897), which expresses contempt for the ways of white settlers, shame over his own complicity in racial discrimination, and an attraction to people of color.[27] Twain may have alternately loved and loathed the human race, but in his mature years he did not single out particular races for scorn. He ultimately seemed to believe in the essential unity and brotherhood of man, a faith that Riis and Steiner, if not Henry James, professed. As we will see, Twain had already begun playing with the idea of universal brotherhood—not only between whites and blacks, but between native-born Americans and immigrants—in *Pudd'nhead Wilson*.

By the time Twain came to write *Pudd'nhead Wilson*, both he and the country were in a state of flux, disorientation, and anxiety.[28] Although Twain was spending much of his time in Europe during the early 1890s, he kept in touch through regular transatlantic crossings to attend to business in the United States. Twain would have been aware of race relations and immigration as two issues uppermost in America's national consciousness. Nervous about his own life, Twain would have been tuned into America's nervousness about burgeoning cities, dizzying technological change, labor strife, social unrest, and economic recessions. He would have detected the varied concerns about American national character, its Anglo-Saxon racial purity, and the threats to that ideal from not only blacks, but also new immigrant groups such as the Italians. For blacks, the early 1890s meant intensified race hatred and segregation built on white supremacy, Jim Crow laws, and control through violence. For Italians and other immigrants from southern and eastern Europe, the early 1890s meant calls for immigration restriction and attacks, sometimes physical, from nativists.

During what Higham calls "the Nationalist Nineties," many journalists, academicians, and politicians began publicly arguing that the new immigrants from southern and eastern Europe were undesirable and should be barred from America. Most prominent was Henry Cabot Lodge, who in 1891 wrote three magazines pieces about the new immigration. One piece, "Lynch Law and Unrestricted Immigration," directly engaged with the lynching of the eleven New Orleans Italians that year and concluded that America's open gates, as much as the well-heeled mob, caused the killings.[29] Lodge and other influential leaders regarded the new immigrants as not much different from Negroes, saw them as other "Others" who could not be assimilated and thereby threatened America's racial purity and Anglo-Saxon-based national character. In the minds of some Americans, Italians and other new immigrants were seen as less than white, but it was generally the Italian (and the Jew) among the new immigrants who was most likely to be perceived as colored.[30] According to some historians, Higham being the most prominent, these "new" Italian immigrants suffered discrimination and racism second only to blacks in America. "The Italians were often thought to be the most degraded of the European newcomers. They were swarthy, more than half of them were illiterate, and almost all were the victims of a standard of living lower than that of any of the other prominent nationalities."[31] Because some Italians would work for next to nothing and were thought to be controlled by the ruthless *padrone*, with his image as a latter-day overseer, some commentators compared their status to a form of "slavery."[32] Furthermore, in the American imagination, Italian immigrants often bore the mark of Cain (just as blacks bore the mark of Ham), suggesting as they did the stiletto, violence, and the mafia. "That stereotype conditioned every major outburst of anti-Italian sentiment in the 1890s."[33]

Italians were mixed up with blacks in social relations, in the political maneuverings of the North and South, and in the public imagination. The most graphic of the similarities between Italians and blacks was that Italians, like blacks, were dismissed as a group worthy of lynching. The 1890s saw repeated lynchings of both Italians and blacks.[34] The worst incident—the New Orleans lynching of eleven Italians in March 1891—took place in a city and state that Twain knew well through his steamboating days. Although extreme, the lynching of the eleven Italians suspected of murdering the city's popular police chief is a locus for exploring links between Italians and blacks in the public discourse, and how those links relate to themes in *Pudd'nhead Wilson*. In "Lynch Law and Unrestricted Immigration," Henry Cabot Lodge absolved the New Orleans lynch mob of racism. "The killing of the eleven prisoners had in it no race feeling whatever," Lodge wrote. "There has been no hostility to the Italians in America, as such."[35] The facts indicate otherwise.[36] If lynching was used as a form of social control against both blacks and Italians, the rhetoric surrounding these lynchings was both similar and different. In both cases, the victims were depicted as subhuman, animal-like. However, while blacks were often represented as a sexual threat to American womanhood, the Italians were usually seen as a threat to the American working man, American society, and American national character.

The situation in Louisiana is particularly instructive in its tangle of relations between nativist white supremacists, blacks, and Italians—tangles not unlike those running through the subtexts of *Pudd'nhead Wilson and Those Extraordinary Twins*. Italians and blacks had mixed in New York City in the 1880s, much to the dismay of Jacob Riis, who saw "moral turpitude" in the "common debauch," but did not elaborate.[37] In Louisiana, with its sizable Italian population, contacts between Italians and blacks went back further and often were more extensive than in the North.[38] In New Orleans, Italians had started by peddling fruit on the street, but quickly had developed a fruit industry important to the local economy. Italians controlled both the dock and the market. And it was a suspected rivalry between the dock Italians and the market Italians that some people saw as the cause of the police chief's murder. Italians fared less well economically in the cotton fields, where, because of their reputation as good, but desperate farmers, they were recruited to displace the "allegedly shiftless, immoral, and unreliable black farm workers."[39]

The exact nature of the relationship between Italians and blacks in the South is not entirely clear, but some historians believe that initially Italians and blacks treated each other with a degree of mutual respect and tolerance in the workplace, if not in the social sphere.[40] This apparent lack of Italian prejudice against blacks is supported by a scene in *The Innocents Abroad*, when the narrator encounters a cultivated young American black, the son of a South Carolina slave, who grew up in Italy and had no desire to leave. "Negroes are deemed as good as white people, in Venice," Twain's narrator says, "and so this man feels no desire to go back to his native land. His judgment is correct."[41]

However, if Italians in the South were having relatively few problems with the blacks, as early as the 1880s they were becoming targets of racism and bigotry, contrary to Lodge's assertion that Americans exhibited no hostility toward the Italians.[42] In the decade prior to the New Orleans lynchings, Italians were being linked to murder and the stiletto not only in the popular imagination but in police work. A wave of anti-Italian bigotry prompted police to unfairly attribute many murders to Sicilians. In some cases police dishonestly Italianized the names of accused murderers. The New Orleans *Times-Democrat* would later describe the accused murderers of Police Superintendent David Hennessy as having "low, repulsive countenances," "brutal natures," and "slovenly attire"—a clear conflation of Italians and Negroes.[43]

Whatever the relationship between blacks and Italians, it alarmed white supremacists who were trying to consolidate their power in Louisiana. "In the South, the newcomer's 'in-betweenness' seemed a double threat. He might endanger not only the purity of the white race but also its solidarity."[44] One historian argues that there was in fact potential for a Populist solidarity between Italians and blacks, but that the lynching of Italians—whites resorting to violence against whites in a move for white solidarity and white supremacy—put an end to thoughts of camaraderie between the Italians and the blacks. Louisiana's efforts to disenfranchise blacks also had a lesson for Italians. "They had better adopt the customs, prejudices, and the way of life of white Louisiana as soon as possible. They must look with loathing upon everything that the native whites loathed. Once they did so, the Italians could gain acceptance among native whites, though at first not on the basis of complete equality."[45] The 1891 lynching of the New Orleans Italians and the ensuing diplomatic conflict between the United States and Italy may have further isolated blacks, even while putting Italians on a par with them. According to one historian, the war fever sparked by the Italo-American crisis was fanned by those hoping to patch sectional differences and pave the road to reunion for northern and southern whites.[46]

It is difficult to say just how much Twain knew about the racist/nativist climate in the South, particularly in Louisiana, during the late 1880s and early 1890s. One possible source of information was the southern writer George Washington Cable, with whom Twain had a close, sometimes bristly friendship. Cable took an intense interest in social, racal, and political relations in his home state of Louisiana, and was deeply committed to political and economic equity for America's blacks.[47] During the 1880s, Twain spent a fair amount of time with Cable and was influenced by Cable's attitudes on race and the fundamental equality of people. As an ex-Confederate who would soon go into Northern exile for his heretical racial beliefs, Cable "was in an excellent position to give Clemens an up-to-date liberal view of conditions in the postbellum South."[48] While on a reading tour with Cable in the mid-1880s, Twain recorded in his notebook the germ of a story set a century into the future: "America in 1985. (Negro supremacy—the whites under foot)."[49] In 1885, Twain would have seen that some American writers were beginning to compose a similar story, "America in 1985. (Foreign supremacy—the Anglo-Saxon under foot)."

Certainly, as Sundquist says, Twain would have known about the New Orleans lynching and its aftermath. The incident combined two subjects that Twain knew well, New Orleans and lynching. Twain had lashed out at lynching as early as 1869, in a piece for the *Buffalo Express*. He saw the practice as an act of moral cowardice, and dramatized it as such in the failed lynching of Colonel Sherburn in *Huckleberry Finn*. At the time of the New Orleans lynching and during the writing of *Pudd'nhead Wilson*, lynchings were reaching epidemic proportions. As Twain's indignation grew in the 1880s and 1890s, he began collecting incidents for a book on the subject.[50] Twain worked on *Pudd'nhead Wilson* while living in a villa in Italy and would have heard of the New Orleans lynching and the ensuing Italo-American diplomatic crisis. The Italian government's condemnation of the incident and the ill will it caused between the two countries certainly would have been the talk of Italy. Twain's Italian twins are threatened with lynching in *Pudd'nhead Wilson* and in fact are lynched in the tale of *Those Extraordinary Twins*. It is no coincidence that Twain was imagining the lynching of his Italian twins at about the same time that the citizens of New Orleans were following through on the idea by lynching eleven Italians.

It can be strongly argued then that in the early 1890s, blacks, Italians, and lynching were very much in/on Twain's mind, so much so that they helped shape *Pudd'nhead Wilson* in important, if sometimes unresolvable ways. As I will argue, Twain's Italian twins mirror the Italian immigrants of the late nineteenth century who were twinned with Negroes in tangled Siamese bonds of slavery, savagery, and social control through violence. As Sundquist says, *Pudd'nhead Wilson* and the attached tale of the twins mirrored both the "dilemma over national discrimination against blacks" and "the equally volatile issue of anti-immigrant nativism." The twins, coming from a non-Anglo immigrant race, blur the color line already blurred by the nearly white mulatto Roxy and her changeling "white" son, Tom. "The Italian twins, in their Siamese version, define the conjunction of black and white that Twain located in the bodies of Roxy and Tom," Sundquist writes. "As immigrant figures they simultaneously bridge the gaps between white and black, and between North and South, further segregating one pair while unifying the other."[51]

To some extent, the Italian twins are figures of parody and burlesque, an Italian Duke and Dauphin who parody romantic notions of Italy and serve as sham counterparts to the equally pretentious First Families of Dawson's Landing—Twain mocking both Old World and New World aristocratic pretensions. In this reading, Angelo's story of the twins' oppression, bad fortune, and exile is little more than a preposterous tall tale, two confidence men having a go at the local yokels.[52] Angelo's tale, told to a rapt audience of locals, certainly has all the hallmarks of parody and satire. However, read in another way it simply relates, albeit in inflated language, the lamentable Italian history of war, foreign domination, degradation, and immigration. Twice Angelo speaks of his and Luigi's "slavery" when working as freak attractions in a cheap museum after war destroys the noble family's fortunes.[53] If we look beyond parody, we see that the twin's "slavery" under foreign powers does indeed connect to Italy's "slavery" under foreign (and internal) oppression, which in turn has parallels to the American Colonies' "slavery" under Britain and to the slavery of blacks under white America. This type of slavery discourse was readily available in the United States. Writers as disparate as Margaret Fuller, Karl Marx, and William Dean Howells spoke in print of Italians "enslaved" by foreign oppressors.[54]

The twins generally represent Italian emigration to America and a flight from political and/or economic oppression in the Old World. The mid-nineteenth-century setting of *Pudd'nhead Wilson* would make the twins part of the earlier, mostly northern Italian immigration that included political exiles and artists, categories to which the Florentine twins belong. But I will argue that concurrently the twins represent the "new" Italian immigration of mostly poorer southern Italians in the late nineteenth century. As representatives of both the old and the new immigration, the twins incorporate two other dualities: the cleavages between northern and southern Italy and the clash between the idealized Italian and the one thought to be degraded. If, as one critic has argued, the twins can be seen as representing America's North and South, then it is an American North and South with strong social, economic, and political parallels to the Italian North and South. It is interesting that the southern Italians were governed by the Bourbons, a term often used to describe the South's aristocratic social and political structure. In Barbara Ladd's reading the contentious twins—Puritan Angelo and Cavalier Luigi—are atomizing tools that disassemble American pretensions toward postbellum reunion and reconciliation.[55] However, there is another narrative of (failed) national unification represented by the twins, that of the Italian North and South during the period of the Risorgimento and its aftermath. The twins undercut Italian pretensions toward national unity: The recalcitrant Luigi stymies the progressive Angelo, just as America's South stymies its North, and just as Italy's "backward" *Mezzogiorno* stymies the progressive North of Italy. And much in the same way that American northerners ascribed cultural, social and moral inferiority to southerners, so too did Italian northerners stereotype southerners as an inferior breed. If anything, Italian sectional differences were more fundamentally ingrained among the people than American differences were in the United States. The American North typically attributed the southerners' vices to the debilitating effects of slavery and saw southerners as lapsed Americans capable of rehabilitation. The Italian North, however, saw their southerners as an alien race, as something not quite Italian, as a people who needed to be assimilated, but might not be capable of it. At best, the Italian South was seen as "the other half" of Italy, the degenerate twin to Italy's more privileged North; at worst, it was seen as a foreign land, even a foreign continent. As the old (northern) Italian adage goes, "South of Rome is Africa."[56]

Northern Italian stereotypes of southern Italians were constructed on attitudes informed to some extent by scientific racism. And northern Italians tended to carry their prejudices against their countrymen to America, seeing the southerners as peasantlike, illiterate, unable to speak proper Italian, "an embarrassment that might prejudice the American establishment against Italians."[57] Many of the stereotypes that Americans applied to Italians immigrants had their roots in stereotypes developed by northern Italians against southern Italians. In time, Americans would focus these stereotypes on *southern* Italian immigrants in particular. We have seen these images in the writings of Jacob Riis, Edward Steiner, Henry Cabot Lodge, and other commentators.[58] Eventually, this distinction between north Italy and south Italy would be explained "scientifically" and be codified in a dictionary of American immigrant races compiled by a government commission on immigration. *The Dictionary of Races or Peoples* (1911), which would speak of impulsive, impractical south Italians and cool, practical north Italians, made official the types of distinctions anticipated some four decades earlier in Henry James's Italian tales and embodied in Twain's Italian twins.[59]

On one level, the twins Angelo and Luigi can simply represent America's perceived differences between northern (Nordic) Italy and southern (Mediterranean) Italy, the former white, the latter darker-skinned. The townsfolk of Dawson's Landing initially see the twins as "the most distinguished-looking pair of young fellows the West had ever seen. One was a little fairer than the other, but otherwise they were exact duplicates" (222). However, the people soon begin to notice differences much in the same way that Americans started to distinguish between the southern Italian immigrants and the artists, artisans, and political refugees of the earlier Italian emigrations to America. Both physically and morally, the twins become very different, if not polar opposites. Angelo, the slightly fairer of the twins, is the angelic one, the blond northern Italian with "kind blue eyes," "curly copper hair and fresh complexion," and "delicate pink" cravat. Luigi (a nice stereotypical Italian peasant name) is darker-skinned, with a "violent scarlet" cravat (125–127). Angelo is a teetaler who drinks tea; Luigi takes stimulating liquor and coffee. Angelo is a Methodist who reads *Whole Duty of Man*; Luigi is a Freethinker who reads Paine's *Age of Reason*, a volume to which Twain traced his own moral and religious sensibility.[60] Angelo shows his moral fiber by being baptized a Baptist, while Luigi shows his bravery in a duel. Angelo is a reform-minded Whig, Luigi one of the brawling, immigrant-loving Democrats. Each of these descriptives for Angelo and Luigi are culturally and politically charged to the point of suggesting dualities within dualities: northern versus southern Italy, the old versus the new Italian immigrant, and the broader duality of America's bifurcated views of Italy and Italians, one romantic, a product of the imagination, the other racist, a reaction to real conditions in America's cities and on her plantations. As representatives of the relatively modest Italian immigration before 1880 and symbols of romance, Angelo and Luigi are "musical prodigies"—cultivated, polite, noble, and exotic, but not menacingly alien. However, mixed into their personality are stereotypes of the new Italian immigrant of the late nineteenth century. Luigi is an assassin, carries a knife, and impulsively avenges an insult by assaulting Tom Driscoll.

Twain begins playing with these dualities in "A Whisper to the Reader" at the start of *Pudd'nhead Wilson*. He invokes Italy's glories with references to the ancient Roman republic, Dante and Giotto, and the incomparable arcadian landscape that surrounds the author's Tuscan villa outside Florence. Twain sits writing under "the busts of Cerretani senators," whom he adopts into his family for the "great and satisfying lift" their long history will give him (2). The writer's adoption of the Cerretani senators mimics the nineteenth-century American's readiness to appropriate Italy's stately culture and romantic, heroic past as a means of self-definition and self-elevation. Twain's authorial persona, like James's Maggie Verver and countless other Americans, seeks to absorb Italy's idealized past and traditions, the very past that Prince Amerigo wants to shed as representing little more than a series of follies and atrocities. But Twain injects some jarring notes into his "Whisper." He speaks of "Macaroni Vermicelli's horse-feed shed" near the Piazza del Duomo, near where Dante watched the building of Giotto's campanile and saw Beatrice "on her way to get a chunk of chestnut cake to defend herself with in case of a Ghibelline outbreak before she got to school" (1). Here, linked to Italy's art and romance (Piazza del Duomo, Giotto, Dante) is a hint of Italian folly and violence (the protracted wars between the Guelphs and Ghibellines)—the kind of historical events that Prince Amerigo is so sensitive about in his Italian past. But, if the Guelphs and Ghibellines retain a certain heroic stature, the same certainly cannot be said about a horse-feed shed owned by Macaroni Vermicelli, whose carnavelesque culinary name combines two varieties of the (southern) Italian's "national" dish.

The highbrow-lowbrow imagery continues when Twain mentions the Dawson's Landing barber pole. The candy-striped pole, which indicates "nobility proud and ancient" in Venice, here is merely the sign of a "humble barber-shop" (3). This alludes to the perceived degeneration of the Italian as he is transplanted from Italy to America, a theme that runs through the work of James and Riis. In Italy, a man with a "barber pole" owns a gondola. In America, the man with the barber pole is in fact a barber, one of the stereotypical trades that some new Italian immigrants pursued as a stepping-stone to upward mobility. The barber motif appears twice more in *Pudd'nhead Wilson*, first when Judge Driscoll refers to the twins as "back-alley barbers" (83), and later when a newspaper notice identifies the judge's suspected assassin as "a profligate Italian nobleman or barber" (95). Judge Driscoll's racist rhetoric turns the humble Italian barber into a vengeful razor-wielding "back-alley" barber who threatens the town. The circle is closed in the public notice, which conflates the two categories of Italians—the nobleman and the barber—into one stereotype, the vengeful assassin. Angelo and Luigi alternate—sometimes together, sometimes in opposition—between being idealized "noble" men and stereotyped back-alley barber-assassins. The townsfolk's perceptions of the twins take radical turns, a sign of not only America's fickle public opinion, but also its shifting, often conflicting attitudes toward Italy and Italians.

The twins' anticipated arrival in Dawson's Landing is truly an extraordinary event. "Italians! How romantic!" Rowena gushes to her mother. "Just think, ma—there's never been one in this town, and everybody will be dying to see them, and they're all *ours*! Think of that! . . . Think—they've been in Europe and everywhere! There's never been a traveler in this town before.

Ma, I shouldn't wonder if they've seen kings! . . . Luigi—Angelo. They're lovely names; and so grand and foreign—not like Jones and Robinson and such." The letter announcing the twins' arrival is read, reread, and discussed, and "everybody admired its courtly and gracious tone, and smooth and practiced style" (26). Rowena's act of possession, if giddy and slightly vulgar, is no more starry-eyed and no less utilitarian than Henry James's possession of his Italians and the impressions of them he so assiduously collects for his "mental sketch-book." Rowena's reaction recapitulates a typical American response to things Italian during the nineteenth century, when thousands of Americans went to Italy or read about the country in countless newspapers, magazines, and travel books.[61] Twain himself was part of that tradition in *The Innocents Abroad,* which if it critiqued American fawning over Italian culture, also engaged in transports not entirely different from those of Rowena.

The two Italians who arrive in Dawson's Landing also have a negative, darker streak. It is soon revealed that Luigi had assassinated a man "because he needed killing." Angelo calls it a "noble" act, but the townsfolk will come to see it another way. During a raucous meeting of the Sons of Liberty, Luigi's "southern" Italian blood again asserts itself when he kicks Tom Driscoll. The mulatto Tom, born a slave child, had been substituted after birth for the master's son. So there is irony when he later refers to Luigi as a "miserable hound," "murderous devil," and "that derned Italian savage" (60–62), epithets that had been hurled at Italian immigrants by nativists, and insults little different from those that racists used against blacks. We are reminded that New Orleans newspapers identified David Hennessy's alleged Sicilian killers as having "low, receding foreheads, repulsive countenances and slovenly attire," which "proclaimed their brutal natures."[62] By turning the twins into the Other and distancing himself from them, Tom tries to solidify his tenuous position within the town's ruling white structure. In much the same way, Italians in the American South and elsewhere found they had to distance themselves from American blacks, the quintessential American Other, if they were to have any chance for acceptance and assimilation into American society.

The contentious relationship between Tom and the twins is a curious one. It begins as a rivalry for the affections of Rowena, who dumps Tom for the superior, noble twins. Soon, however, the relationship becomes more complex. The twins initially see Tom Driscoll as a "rather handsome" and "graceful" young man. Later, where Angelo notes "a good eye" and "a pleasant free-and-easy way of talking" in Tom, Luigi sees "something veiled and sly" in the eye, and something "more so than was agreeable" in Tom's manner (48). Angelo's attitude reflects that of the Louisiana Italian immigrants who for a time had generally positive relations with American blacks. Luigi is more wary of Tom Driscoll because, despite their obvious differences, and despite Tom's racial imposture, Luigi sees something of himself in the black man passing as the white foster son of the town's leading citizen. In his first meeting with the twins, Tom talks Pudd'nhead Wilson into reading Luigi's palm, which reveals that Luigi had in the past killed a man. Pudd'nhead then tries to read Tom Driscoll's palm, but Tom snatches it away, blushing. When Luigi comments on Tom's reluctance, Tom responds: "Well, if I am, it ain't because I'm a murderer!" Seeing Luigi's "dark face" flushing, Tom quickly begs "a thousand pardons" (53). The exchange underscores Luigi's volatile nature in the face of dishonor. Luigi is insulted that Tom degrades as simple murder an act that Luigi considers noble. As the narrative progresses, Luigi the "murderer" is further transformed into Luigi the assassin, with its more sinister echoes of stealth, lawlessness, and disorder.

When the twins are invited to a mass rally of the local pro-rum faction, Tom follows uninvited. The Sons of Liberty greet the twins with "a prodigious explosion of welcome," and the chairman quickly proposes that the "illustrious guests" be accepted into the organization, which he describes as "the paradise of the free and the perdition of the slave" (54). Tom tries to undo the twins' assimilation by pointing out their freakish resemblance to each other and publicly calling them "a human philopena." Luigi's "southern blood" boils over. Not one to "let the matter pass, or to delay the squaring of the account," Luigi gives Tom a titanic kick and the Sons of Liberty meeting ends in a chaos of fighting and fire (56).

Tom becomes a social outcast when he turns to the law rather than to the gentleman's duel as a way to defend his honor against the assault from Luigi's southern Italian foot. Tom's act violates both the town's code and the honor of the "noble" First Families of Virginia, to which Tom is "heir." Tom's real mother, the mulatto Roxy, turns Tom's "hound" epithet on Tom himself. Roxy says that by refusing the duel and showing his cowardice, Tom has betrayed his own noble pedigree, including his white First Family father Cecil Burleigh Essex, Cap'n John Smith, Pocahontas, and "a nigger king outen Africa" (70). Roxy tells Tom that "de nigger" in him has made him "a ornery low-down hound" and little more than a "nigger" (70). Trying to turn the rival twins into murderous animal-like Others, Tom is himself turned into an animal-like "nigger" by his own mother despite being only one thirty-second black. Later, recounting the duel between Luigi and Judge Driscoll, Roxy refers to Luigi as "de brown one," which would presumably make Luigi darker than both Roxy and Tom, blacks whose skins are as white as that of many, if not most, of the town's whites. The differences in skin coloration between Angelo and Luigi, given their associations with both Americans and Italians North and South, suggest a different racial makeup. "Here Twain's image plays with the ideas of filial connection between races, a central component of the culture's debate over race."[63] All this talk about First Families, bloodlines, heredity, and color becomes more compelling when seen within the discourses of the late nineteenth century, when American-style ancestor worship and a "strident belief in Anglo-Saxon supremacy" reached its apogee, manifesting itself as "more comprehensively racist than merely Negrophobic."[64] It is clear that Twain is playing with ideas of nature versus nurture, heredity versus environment, in ways that maybe cannot be resolved. Ultimately, however, Twain seems to be saying that racial categories are frauds that disguise fundamental commonality between races.[65] Throughout *Pudd'nhead Wilson*, Tom and the twins compete for acceptance and assimilation in much the same fashion that blacks and new immigrants did at the turn of the century. However, the fortunes of Tom and the twins usually go in opposite directions. It is as if the citizenry and social structure of Dawson's Landing can accommodate either blacks or immigrants, but not both at the same time.

When Tom declines to honorably avenge Luigi's attack, Judge Driscoll steps in and challenges the Italian to a duel. By accepting the judge's challenge, Luigi overcomes his color—in essence, becomes white—by establishing himself as a man of honor. Luigi, as a southern Italian who hates northern Italian government/law, is not about to seek legal resolution of differences and grievances, as the cowardly Tom does. Luigi here recalls Riis's Italian immigrants, all those Pasquales who argue over cards on the Sabbath, then use revenge and the vendetta—a sort of petty assassination—to square their intramural disputes.[66] However, Luigi also connects to assassination as an act against oppression. Here, Luigi represents the downtrodden Italians rebelling against their Bourbon and Austrian oppressors, or the marginalized southern Italians resisting northern domination after the Risorgimento. Luigi and Judge Driscoll both have a code that disdains lawful justice in matters of honor. By giving up murder/assassination in favor of Driscoll's challenge to a duel, Luigi endears himself to Driscoll and his friend, Pembroke Howard. The two men shower the Italian with encomiums that stress his manhood, the very quality that Twain sees lacking in both duelists and lynchers. Driscoll tells Howard, "He's a darling! Why, it's an honor as well as a pleasure to stand up before such a man. . . . A rare fellow, indeed; an admirable fellow, as you have said!" (66). Luigi is also embraced by the townsfolk, who took great pride in the duel. "It was a glory to their town to have such a thing happen there. In their eyes the principals had reached the summit of human honor. Everybody paid homage to their names; their praises were in all mouths" (74). Twain himself saw dueling as a vestige of the cult of southern aristocracy not unlike lynching. Both were violent customs, involved a perverted code, and were followed slavishly by cowardly people.[67]

By giving up the concealed stiletto of the southern Italian vendetta for the visible pistol of the southern American duel, Luigi adopts the aristocratic code of chivalry and thereby assimilates into the town's social structure. Now, the twins are accepted not only as romantic heroes, but embraced as (Italian) Americans. "The twins were prodigiously great, now; the town took them to its bosom with enthusiasm." As their popularity grows, so too does their romantic Italianness—their incomparable charm, artistic talents, and other rare accomplishments. Even as they become more intensely idealized as Italian, the twins move closer to America and announce their intention to apply for citizenship, to become naturalized, that is made "natural," no longer freaks. They resolve to end their wanderings and "to finish their days" in Dawson's Landing. "That was the climax. The delighted community rose as one man and applauded; and when the twins were asked to stand for seats in the forthcoming aldermanic board, and consented, the public contentment was rounded and complete" (74). It is interesting that even before officially becoming newly minted citizens, the twins are quickly incorporated into the democratic system, not simply as franchised voters but as candidates for public office. Should we dismiss this as Twain simply satirizing flighty, gullible Americans that enfranchise unnaturalized foreigners while denying that same vote to native-born American blacks? Or can the twins' rapid assimilation into the town's social and civic life be seen as an admittedly exaggerated representation of mid-nineteenth-century America's relatively more inclusive approach to immigrants? Might we even see it as a critique of the move for more restrictive immigration policies that characterized the 1890s, when Twain was writing *Pudd'nhead Wilson*? If so, it would not be the first time Twain uses 1850s Missouri to comment on turn-of-the-century America.

The twins' popularity is, however, very short-lived. The outcast Tom soon turns the twins into outcasts by exposing Luigi—"that Italian adventurer"—as "a confessed assassin." If the honorable face-to-face duel had furthered Luigi's Americanization, outright murder or furtive assassination, with its intimations of anarchism, disqualify him from the same process. For Judge Driscoll, Luigi's self-professed "noble" act of killing is tantamount to ignoble premeditated murder/assassination—malicious, sneaky, ungentlemanly, and un-American in the manner of the Italians' suspected killing of David Hennessy in New Orleans. Now, Judge Driscoll restores Tom to his good graces and pledges revenge against Luigi. "That this assassin should have put the affront upon me of letting me meet him on the field of honor as if he were a gentleman is a matter which I will presently settle—but not now," Driscoll vows.[68] The judge says he will simply shoot Luigi—presumably in forthright, gentlemanly, American fashion—outside the field of honor. But first the judge plans to ruin the twins during the election campaign (77–79).

Tom also has an ally in the fickle-minded townsfolk. The twins' "popularity, so general at first, had suffered afterward; mainly because they had been *too* popular, and so a natural reaction had followed." Meanwhile, the twins placed all their hopes on the election, which, if successful, would solidify their civil standing in the community as well as give them power and perhaps restore their popularity. However, Judge Driscoll, the voice of supreme authority in Dawson's Landing, vents the people's adjusted attitudes in a mud-slinging stump speech against "both of the foreigners." On one level, Driscoll's classic campaign oration is simply a parody of standard election rhetoric. But the message here is a nativist one and the invective is colored with anti-immigrant, anti-Italian sentiments. The twins are not simply bad guys; they are bad Italian foreigners. The speech, which drowns the twins in "rivers of ridicule," proves "disastrously effective." Driscoll "scoffed at them as adventurers, mountebanks, side-show riff-raff, dime-museum freaks; he assailed their showy titles with measureless derision; he said they were back-alley barbers disguised as nobilities, peanut peddlers masquerading as gentlemen, organ-grinders bereft of their brother-monkey." Worst of all—he implies after a pregnant pause—they are liars and assassins. Driscoll delivered his "deadliest shot" with "ice-cold seriousness and deliberation," dismissing the reward for the knife Luigi claimed to have lost as humbug and suggesting that the owner could easily find it "whenever he should have occasion to *assassinate somebody*"(83).

Driscoll's speech turns the twins into stereotypical "low" Italians, freaks who expose the humbug of romantic old Italy, which is as much a sham as Luigi's heirloom knife and the "reward" he offered for its return. The judge's accusations are a double blow. They destroy the idealized Italian that Americans loved so well and wanted to appropriate/assimilate, while essentializing the pathetic, if menacing Italian who, because he threatens the character and order of American society, should be excluded from American life. According to Driscoll, the Italian gentleman and the Italian nobleman are a sham, little more than back-alley barbers, peanut peddlers, and organ-grinders. They are not only organ-grinders, but organ-grinders *manqués*, "bereft of their brother-monkey." They are subhuman, brother to the monkey, and brother, it is to be inferred, to the "monkey"-like black man, and as such inassimilable. The twins, now stripped of their glory, "withdrew entirely from society, and nursed their humiliation in privacy." As "back-alley" barber-assassins, the twins are now disqualified from Americanization. They are, in effect, assassinated socially and politically. Their new status also disqualifies Luigi from engaging in a second duel with Judge Driscoll, who declined to fight with an assassin in the field of honor (92).

The town's nativist fears are fed when Tom murders Judge Driscoll during a botched burglary, and the twins are accused of the heinous crime. "The town was bitter against the unfortunates, and for the first few days after the murder they were in constant danger of being lynched" (97). Having briefly become heroes and Americans-in-the-making through one form of extralegal conflict resolution (the duel), the twins now find themselves potential victims of a more contemporary American mode of extralegal conflict resolution: lynching. Tom, having fled to St. Louis, reads in the papers a brief telegram announcing that Judge Driscoll was assassinated by "a profligate Italian nobleman or barber," an "assassin (who) will probably be lynched" (95–96). Being an assassin makes Luigi a fit subject for lynching, just as it did for the Italians suspected of "assassinating" David Hennessy. If dueling is a noble, honorable practice for Judge Driscoll and Pembroke Howard, lynching is a noble, honorable expedient for the townsfolk of Dawson's Landing and New Orleans. In a sense, lynching is dueling's dark double or twin. Dueling defends one's individual purity, honor, and manhood; lynching safeguards the community's collective civic purity, honor, and patriarchal structure. We are reminded of Theodore Roosevelt's comment that the lynching of the eleven New Orleans Italians was "a rather good thing."[69]

As potential lynching targets, the twins retain only two loyal friends. One is the outsider Pudd'nhead Wilson, who serves as Luigi's attorney. From the start there had been a certain rapport between the twins and Wilson, all three of whom are outsiders and outcasts.[70] Also loyal to the twins is their "poor old sorrowing landlady," Aunt Patsy Cooper, the eternal romantic still caught up in the romance of fairy-tale Italy. However, Roxy, the realist, feels differently about the twins. Sitting in the "nigger corner" of the courtroom, the mulatta "hated these outlandish devils" for killing the kind Driscoll, and she would not "ever sleep satisfied till she saw them hanged for it" (99-100). During the trial, Pembroke Howard, the prosecutor, accuses the twins of not only murder, but of assassination "conceived by the blackest of hearts and consummated by the cowardliest of hands" (100). Pudd'nhead Wilson counters by referring to the twins as "those unfortunate strangers" (107)—an echo of the German conflation of the terms stranger and foreigner that Twain mentions in his sympathetic 1899 essay on the Jews.[71] Wilson's depiction of the twins ultimately prevails when his detective work exposes Tom Driscoll as the murderer. In carrying the day, David "Pudd'nhead" Wilson, long the social outsider in Dawson's Landing, sheds the "pudd'nhead" tag and is fully embraced as the town's golden-tongued genius. "His long fight against hard luck and prejudice was ended; he was a made man for good" (113–114). This is Pudd'nhead Wilson as Horatio Alger—the outsider who, through his pluck, native ingenuity, and defense of the poor foreigners, becomes an insider much in the manner of Jacob Riis. The townsfolk may have dismissed Pudd'nhead as somewhat eccentric and slow. He may have been a stranger/foreigner in the town. However, he was never a racial/ethnic outsider in Dawson's Landing, as the twins were. His last name is Wilson, one of those names "like Jones and Robinson and such" (26) that Rowena might think boring and lacking in grandeur, but one of those names that still represented the town's dominant Anglo-Saxon strain.

If Pudd'nhead Wilson's transformation is the typical American success story of the social outsider rising to the top, the flip side is the corresponding failure of the novel's racial/ethnic outsiders to fully integrate into the social fabric of Dawson's Landing. *Pudd'nhead Wilson and Those Extraordinary Twins* can be read, then, as an allegory of failed assimilation for both the twins and for Tom Driscoll, a trio who in many ways are twins. The mulatto Tom, now exposed as a slave changeling, is sold back into slavery to satisfy creditors despite his being one-thirty-second white. There is clearly no assimilation possible for blacks, even for those with but a drop of black blood, as long as they are still seen as slaves and "niggers." The Italian twins present a more problematic case. Acquitted of being back-alley barber assassins, Luigi and Angelo Capello, like Pudd'nhead Wilson, are turned into heroes. But, if Wilson "was a made man for good," a real American hero who will reap real material benefits, the twins essentially revert to being storybook heroes of the American imagination. "The Twins were heroes of romance, now, and with rehabilitated reputations." However, "weary of Western adventure"—weary, that is, of the vicissitudes of American attitudes and opinions; tired of their roles as symbols of romantic Italy; and most likely despairing of achieving the kind of assimilation and success open to the native-born Anglo-Saxon David Wilson—the twins, both strangers and foreigners, "straightway retired to Europe" (114). It was a return route taken by a sizable number of Italian immigrants.

The twins' fates are less happy in the tale of *Those Extraordinary Twins*. Here, Luigi the Democrat and member in good standing in the town's liquor interest, is elected an alderman. Unfortunately, he cannot take his seat because of his physical attachment to his Siamese brother Angelo, the teetotaler, who is not an elected official. This throws a monkey wrench into the town's legal and civic workings. The situation threatens the democratic process, drains the town's treasury, and makes a mockery of municipal government, all problems associated with the arrival of the Italians and other new immigrants in the late nineteenth century. In fact, the twins' disastrous effect on Dawson's Landing recall many of the problems the Rev. Theodore Munger of Hartford leveled against southern and eastern European immigrants in *The Century*. Like Munger's foreigners, the twins, singly or in unison, poison the local politics, block the wheels of industry and progress, feed the "drink-evil," and turn municipal government into "a farce and a shame."[72] The town's dilemma is handed over to the courts, which fail to resolve the issue. "As a result, the city government not only stood still, with its hands tied, but everything it was created to protect and care for went a steady gait toward rack and ruin." Taxes could not be levied and minor officials resigned rather than starve. Good old American capitalism, in the form of the liquor interest, was threatened. Private subscription was needed to defray the enormous legal expenses of the case. The townsfolk finally realize they should have listened to Pudd'nhead Wilson's original advice that Luigi be hired (i.e., bribed) to resign his post. But now the town cannot afford even that gambit. What the town does have is a halter with which to hire Luigi into resigning by hanging him.

With no other apparent options, the town turns to lynching. "That's the ticket," many of the townsfolk shout. "And so they hanged Luigi" (169) as a threat to the town's political, social, and economic health. Just as lynching is the dark twin of dueling, so too is lynching the dark, violent, desperate twin of other more socially acceptable forms of social control used on immigrants by writers, progressive reformers, and nativists. If Henry James wanted to aestheticize the Italian immigrants and make them more like his happy, courteous Italians-in-Italy, Jacob Riis and other reformers wanted to wash them up, teach them American ideals, and turn them into patriotic middle-class Americans. But when all else fails, lynch them. With Luigi disposed of, Angelo—or what remains of him ("Nobody said anything about hanging him.")—presumably lived on in the imaginations of Americans who preserved a romantic, heroic conception of Italy from earlier times.

Either way, the twins do not find a proper, satisfactory place in the town. Ultimately, they are comfortable with neither of the constructed identities imposed on them by Dawson's Landing. Being treated as idealized figures of romance finally proves wearying, a constant struggle to fit into an unrealistic image. And there was no guarantee that racist nativism would not threaten the twins once again as it had during the dark days of the political campaign and the subsequent murder trial. Conversely, even when they are allowed to stay in America, and voluntarily do so, with Luigi now firmly entrenched in local Democratic Party politics, they remain foreigners who threaten the social order with their difference and therefore are turned into targets of animosity, racism, and lynching.

Earlier in the nineteenth century, American writers and travelers had constructed a storybook Italy characterized by an enchanting pastoral landscape, glorious republicanism, and high art and music. When American observers looked closer at contemporary Italy, they saw little more than a degraded people of lost glory. The twin images of grandeur and degradation, of romance and "reality," had managed to coexist relatively peacefully in the American mind as long as Americans could bask in the warmth and splendor of a far-off Italy, while keeping the "degraded" Italians in Europe. But once the degradation arrived on American shores in the form of hundreds of thousands of supposedly dark, dirty, and ignorant Italian immigrants, these contradictory images clashed in the streets of New York's Lower East Side, the mines of West Virginia and Colorado, and the docks and plantations of the South. Before 1880, real Italian immigrants were too few to claim a great deal of space in the American consciousness and the public discourse. After 1880, Italians and other threatening "new immigrant" groups seized hold of a public mind that often twinned foreigners with the "black problem." In the 1880s and 1890s, race-based socially constructed twin images of both Italians and blacks became frozen in a portion of the American mind, blinding many native-born Americans to more realistic perceptions of Italians and blacks, thereby precluding a more productive relationship with these two groups of Others. Blacks were feared as savage, violent, and socially inferior, while at the same time romanticized as loyal, docile, and sympathetic. Italians were feared for many of the same reasons as blacks, while being romanticized as noble, artistic, and cultivated, or as simple and picturesque.

Twain, himself a twin, must have been attuned to America's twinned perceptions of blacks and immigrants. As other critics have reasonably argued, Twain's own attitudes combined sympathy for blacks and foreigners with some of the prejudices of his times. I suspect Twain struggled with the dichotomy, just as his country would, in the succeeding troubled decades of the early twentieth century. In one sense, theirs would be an effort to construct newer, more complex, and richer identities for blacks and foreigners, identities that would help native-born Americans to bridge the gap between romantic idealization and racist xenophobia. In the case of the Italians, this meant finding an image of Italy that went beyond Twain's earlier binary notions of "magnificence and misery."

Conclusion: The Fight for Whiteness

An Italian sociologist ... describes the South Italian as excitable, impulsive, highly imaginative, impracticable; and as an individualist having little adaptability to highly organized society.

—U.S. Immigration Commission's
Dictionary of Races or Peoples, 1911

Steerage passengers from a Naples boat show a distressing frequency of low foreheads, open mouths, weak chins, poor features, skew faces, small or knobby crania, and backless heads.

—Edward Alsworth Ross, professor of sociology, 1914

This study has been an attempt to look at American ideologies concerning Italy, Italians, and Italian immigrants during the decades from 1880 to 1910. My goal was to examine how those ideologies were represented, and to ask not so much what those representations say about Italy, Italians, and Italian immigrants, but rather to explore what they may tell us about America and Americans. In particular I was interested in what these representations had to say about American attitudes toward race, immigration, Americanization, and American national identity during this volatile period. Consequently, I did not inquire too deeply about the "historical truth" or the "material reality" of Italians in Italy or Italians in America. And I have said very little about the Italians themselves, how they contributed to or resisted

American representations, or what their own attitudes toward race, immigration, and Americanization may have been.

As Antonio Gramsci says in his *Prison Notebooks* (and here I'm stealing a page from Edward Said), the starting point for criticism is being fully conscious of what you really are and knowing yourself as the product of a historical process "which has deposited in you an infinity of traces, without leaving an inventory." With that in mind, Gramsci says, it is imperative at the outset to compile such an inventory. I confess I have just only begun to compile that inventory. Responsible for some of the most important traces in my life was the Italian immigrant Giuseppe Frustaci, my maternal grandfather for whom I was named. It was he who came to New York City around 1912, and it was because of that brave move that some forty years later I found myself transported from Calabria to America.

Having belatedly followed the trail of the immigrant blazed by Giuseppe Frustaci, I try to imagine what kind of world he found in New York City and the kind of life he ended up living there. As a newly arrived Italian in New York City, Giuseppe Frustaci certainly must have found strength in numbers and comfort among some of his countrymen in the tenements of the Lower East Side. However, America still must have seemed a threatening place to a poor uneducated young man from Calabria. In many ways, America circa 1912 was not much different from America of the three previous decades. Industrialization, urbanization, and disruptive change continued apace. Great clashes still characterized America's class, race, labor, and ideological relations. Nativism was again rearing its ugly head. Questions of national identity and assimilation still raged. Calls for immigration restriction were intensifying. And Italians like Giuseppe Frustaci still found themselves at the center of these events and debates, whose nerve center was still New York City.

Writing about "The Italians in the United States" in the January 1911 *Forum*, Alberto Pecorini said that "the Italian problem—if, indeed, an Italian problem exists—" could be said to be centered in New York City, where more than a quarter of America's two million Italians lived. Pecorini acknowledges some continuing problems—illiteracy, tenement overcrowding, the "Black Handers"—but says he is encouraged by the improvement in Italian immigration. "The day of the organ-grinder, once the only representative of his race, has passed forever, and that of the ignorant peasant is rapidly passing," he wrote. "Illiteracy is diminishing, and with it the evils of which it has been the principal cause."[1] However, if Italian immigration was improving and the immigrants' illiteracy diminishing, many native-born Americans both ignorant and educated failed or refused to see these changes. America's obsession with racial thinking, racial classification, and racial ranking had showed no signs of receding. In the previous three decades, nativism itself had waxed and waned, but by 1914 xenophobia exhibited many of the same signs of the hysteria and violence that characterized its peak years in the 1890s. In 1914, the Supreme Court ruled that unnaturalized Italian immigrants could be discharged from working on the New York subway. And, in the country's mining camps, Italians were being lynched.[2] Social control of the Italians was not always violent, however. It also took the form of education and social work, among other initiatives. In Connecticut, the Daughters of the American Revolution hired John Foster Carr in 1911 to write a *Guide for the Italian Immigrant in the United States*. While the guide urged Italians to settle on farms away from the urban centers of the Northeast, it acknowledged that many of the immigrants would probably remain in the cities. Consequently, the guide preached "public hygiene" in the urban setting and made a connection between cleanliness, wellness, and material prosperity. Included in the advice was the maxim, "A working man's capital is a strong, well body."[3] However, less enlightened commentators still attributed the Italians' supposedly sickly bodies to their race. In 1914, Edward Alsworth Ross, a professor of sociology at the University of Wisconsin, published *The Old World in the New*, in which he warned against subcommon immigrants, including those from southern Italy. He wrote: "Steerage passengers from a Naples boat show a distressing frequency of low foreheads, open mouths, weak chins, poor features, skew faces, small or knobby crania, and backless heads. Such people lack the power to take rational care of themselves; hence their death-rate in New York is twice the general death-rate and thrice that of Germans."[4] Many of the Italian stereotypes promoted by Riis, Steiner, and James were being given wider currency in the national discourse. Hostility toward Italians in New York City peaked in the years leading up to World War I, and Americans increasingly saw the Italian immigrants as ignorant, dirty, dishonest, violent, and criminal people who refused to assimilate. "Sicilians were specially singled out for scorn as swarthy Mafiosi, as transients who came and went at the beck and call of agents and padroni."[5] These images of Italians ran counter to prevailing discourses that promoted Americans as independent, strong, honorable, and self-controlled.

The mania for racial classification that we saw in Riis, Steiner, and others, and the race nativism that had been evolving over the decades, came together in the decade's leading nativist, Madison Grant. Neither a quack nor an extremist, Grant "represented a band of progressive opinion, one terrified of the consequences of unregulated monopoly capitalism, including the failure to regulate the importation of nonwhite (which included Jewish and southern European) working classes who invariably had more prolific women than the 'old American stock.' "[6] By 1916, Grant had published his masterful, widely read polemic, *The Passing of the Great Race or the Racial Basis of European History*. In it Grant argues that heredity, more than environment, shapes humankind, and warns that race mixing produces lower hybrids. Dividing Europeans into Nordics, Alpines, and Mediterraneans, the same general breakdown made earlier by economist William Z. Ripley in his *The Races of Europe* (1899), Grant exalts the Nordic/Anglo Saxon as the "Great Race" and "the white man par excellence."[7] He dismisses southern (or Mediterranean) Italians as a mongrel race of slaves and makes them less than white, saying they are racially identical to the Berbers of North Africa (71–72, 189). Nordic northern Italians are altogether different, Grant argues. It is the nordic blood that accounts for Rome's enduring political organizations and ideals, Italy's great men of classical times, and her great Renaissance artists (153–154, 215). In 1920, Lothrop Stoddard, a New England attorney with training in history, echoed many of Grant's claims in *The Rising Tide of Color Against White World-Supremacy*, which featured an introduction by Grant.[8]

In large measure, Grant was recapitulating distinctions that had been made by leading thinkers such as the Boston Brahmins as early as the 1880s. According to the Brahmins, the "Germanic blood" and artistic achievements of the northern Italians clearly distinguished them from the supposedly ignorant, uncultivated peasants of southern Italy.[9] These same Brahmins, among them James Russell Lowell, Henry Wadsworth Longfellow, and Charles Eliot Norton, were among the foremost proponents of Italian high culture and had helped focus America's image of things Italian. However, they, like Henry James and many other Americans, had deeply divided attitudes toward modern Italy and modern Italians, only occasionally recognizing the modern Italian "as the heir of the ancient, medieval, and Renaissance Italy." Consequently, "They contributed toward creating a climate of opinion on 'modern' Italy and so prepared for the misunderstanding of the Italian immigrants to the United States beginning in the 1880s."[10]

There were, of course, dissenters. One of the most prominent was Franz Boas, the Columbia University professor of anthropology and author of *The Mind of Primitive Man* (1911). Boas attempted to refute racial nativism by trying to demonstrate that America's environment was modifying the "racial characteristics" of the immigrants that nativists found detestable. Studying and measuring the slope of crania, Boas concluded that nutrition and other living conditions determined "racial characteristics" more than heredity. Boas's study purported to show that head form—traditionally considered stable and permanent—underwent significant change after immigrants moved to America from Europe. If bodily features changed, Boas concluded, the whole bodily and mental makeup of immigrants might change. Boas had trouble convincing the nativists, but his ideas surely must have appealed to someone like Edward Steiner, who also spoke of the mollifying influence of America. Boas's findings and conclusions were included in a forty-two-volume report issued in 1911 by the U.S. Immigration Commission, which was appointed four years earlier under the chairmanship of Senator William P. Dillingham of Pennsylvania.

Although the Boas report was widely quoted and figured prominently in the immigration debates surrounding the Immigration Commission's work,[11] Boas's ideas were directly contradicted by the Dillingham Commission's own *Dictionary of Races or Peoples*, which was included in the report. Overall, the commission took a moderately restrictionist position on immigration, endorsing the literacy test that Henry Cabot Lodge had proposed years before. But, as John Higham says, the report cast its social and economic data in "the form of an invidious contrast between the northwestern and southeastern Europeans in the United States at the time."[12] The Dillingham Commission study was neither impartial not scientific, but instead was conducted by so-called "experts" who made little use of or completely ignored data available from state, federal, and private agencies. "In most cases the individual reports—on industry, crime, nationality, education, and literacy—did not contain materials for proper conclusions; the committee's conclusions for the most part sprang from its own prior assumptions."[13] The commission's underlying objective was to show that certain races were hereditarily incapable of Americanization because of immutable, biologically determined physical and cultural characteristics.[14] To that end, the report's *Dictionary of Races or Peoples* provided a taxonomy of racial differences among the immigrant groups.[15] Conceding that ethnography was still an imperfect science, the dictionary followed the then-popular classification system that divided the world's peoples into five broad categories: Caucasian, Ethiopian, Mongolian, Malay, and American—more familiarly known as the white, black, yellow, brown, and red races. The dictionary then generally used federal census data language and classifications to make finer distinctions among the five grand divisions. It paid particular attention to categories of races/peoples being used for statistical purposes by the Bureau of Immigration and Naturalization, as well as some of the ethnic or political terms commonly used to designate immigrants. Fundamentally a hierarchical scale of human development and worth, the dictionary grudgingly defines Caucasian as including "all races, which, although dark in color or aberrant in other directions, are, when considered from all points of view, felt to be more like the white race than like any of the other four races."[16]

In its section on Italians, the dictionary says that immigration from Italy is perhaps of most significance because it far outpaced that of other races and threatened to continue without relief. The dictionary, following the federal immigration bureau practice, makes an official distinction between "Italian, South" and "Italian, North." It is interesting that while the immigration bureau figures combined some smaller races and peoples into single categories, the Italians are the only ancient race that is divided not only geographically, but also physically and psychically as well. Italians, North and South, the dictionary claims, "differ from each other materially in language, physique, and character, as well as in geographical distribution." The north Italian is of a "very broad-headed ('Alpine') and tallish race," while south Italy is inhabited by a "long-headed, dark, 'Mediterranean' race of short stature." Speaking of south Italians, the dictionary cites an Italian ethnologist who traces their origins to the Hamitic stock of North Africa. However, the dictionary reminds its readers that the Hamites "are not true Negritic or true African, although there may be some traces of an infusion of African blood in this stock in certain communities of Sicily and Sardinia, as well as in northern Africa." Continuing to rely on Italian sources (in a bid for authority?), the dictionary cites an Italian sociologist who had pointed out that north Italians and south Italians also differ radically in their "psychic character." The south Italian is represented as "excitable, impulsive, highly imaginative, impracticable; as an individualist having little adaptability to highly organized society." The north Italian, conversely, is pictured as "cool, deliberate, patient, practical, and as capable of great progress in the political and social organization of modern civilization." In general, Italians, North and South, are "devoted to their families, are benevolent, religious, artistic, and industrious." But having said that, the dictionary cites an Italian statistician who "admits" that Italy still has the highest rate of crimes against the person among countries sending immigrants to America. Another Italian expert, the dictionary notes, had shown that all crimes, but especially violent offenses, are several times more numerous among south Italians than among north Italians. "The secret organizations of the Mafia . . . and Comorra, institutions of great influence among the people, which take the law into their own hands and which are responsible for much of the crime, flourish throughout southern Italy."[17]

The dictionary codified, or made official, representations of Italians that had been circulating for decades, both in the United States and in Italy. What is interesting is that forty years after Italian political unification had been achieved, the American government was dividing the country's people in two. Perhaps this racial bifurcation of Italy did indeed reflect some of the political, social, and cultural reality in Italy. However, as we have seen, this division was to a great extent a construct developed by northern Italian politicians and thinkers after unification, and given the stamp of "scientific" authority by Alfredo Niceforo's *L'Italia barbara contemporanea* (*Contemporary Barbarian Italy*) in 1898. Using positivist criteria to measure civilization and craniometric data to show racial differences, Niceforo gathered together existing stereotypes into an organized whole in which the South and its people were seen as lawless and barbarous, superstitious and corrupt, dirty and diseased.[18] At first, Americans had applied these same stereotypes to Italian immigrants in general, but over time these images were attached to southern Italian immigrants in particular. Just as Niceforo's *L'Italia barbara contemporanea* provided an authoritative *locus classicus* of prejudice toward southern Italians, so too did the *Dictionary of Races or People* institutionalize America's division of Italy into North and South. By dividing Italy in two and by making racial and cultural distinctions between northern and southern Italians, Americans could hold onto their image of an idealized Italy, while disparaging and rejecting the southern Italian immigrants. They could preserve their glorious, romantic, and cultured Italy, while at the same time finding in the picturesque Italians a degraded and menacing, yet sometimes alluring opposite. In broad terms, Nordic northern Italy and Italians furnished the romance, while Mediterranean southern Italy and Italians provided the racial "Other."

Six years after the Immigration Commission issued its voluminous reports and dictionary, and three years after Madison Grant published his polemic masquerading as a treatise, Congress passed a comprehensive immigration act over a presidential veto. Approved in 1917, in the midst of World War I, the act imposed a literacy requirement aimed at the so-called new immigrants, a move that historians now typically see as a thinly veiled act of discrimination against those groups. Four years later, America passed its first immigration quota law. When that failed to stem the flow of new immigrants, the Johnson Act of 1924 was passed, limiting annual immigration to 2 percent of each group's population according to 1890 census figures. This legislation effectively cut off immigration from southern and eastern Europe, while clearly favoring immigration from northern and western Europe. The law emerged from a report of the Eugenics Committee of the U.S. Committee on Selective Immigration, which was chaired by Madison Grant and included Congressman Albert Johnson of Washington, who was president of the Eugenic Research Association from 1923 to 1924. "The triumph of immigration restriction in the 1920s was in large measure a triumph of racism against new immigrants. Congress and the Ku Klux Klan, the media and popular opinion all reinforced the inbetween, and even non-white, racial status of Eastern and South Europeans."[19] However, even as Congress and a large segment of the American citizenry were consigning Italians and other new immigrants to in-between status, the American courts almost always defined them as white in naturalization cases.[20] Much like the Irish before them, Italian immigrants would assert their whiteness not only through "the powerful symbolic argument that the law declared them white and fit," but also through the power of the vote. For example, during Louisiana's constitutional convention to disenfranchise blacks in 1898, the bitter debate over Italian whiteness ended with a provision that gave new immigrants protections that were comparable, and even superior, to those that the "grandfather clause" gave to native-born white voters. The campaign for the plank was led by New Orleans' powerful Choctaw Club machine, which already had benefited from the Italian vote.[21]

As Matthew Frye Jacobson has shown, a number of factors helped to reverse the fracturing of whiteness into a hierarchy of "scientifically" determined whites races that had occurred during the period of mass European immigration. These included the new restrictive immigration laws, the emergence of American imperialism, and the intensifying struggles of American blacks for equality. The new restrictive immigration laws helped counteract what was seen as the dangerous over-inclusiveness of America's 1790 naturalization act, which offered citizenship to all "free white persons." American imperialist ventures, although pursued under the banner of "Anglo-Saxon" entitlement, was driven by the logic of pan-white supremacy. And as African Americans migrated to the North and West, black-versus-white civil rights politics tended to eclipse the lingering divisions among white races. These factors helped reforge a unified whiteness during the 1920s and after. Whiteness was reconsolidated, and the late nineteenth century's probationary white European immigrant groups were remade and reaffirmed as members of a unitary Caucasian race. These European races would remain white in part because of the bids for citizenship on the part of non-European groups such as the Chinese, the Indians, the Syrians, and the Filipinos.[22] As Lawrence Levine points out, every new wave of immigrants, from non-Anglo northern and western Europeans to southern and eastern Europeans to non-Europeans, has produced jeremiads about "barbarians" at the gates and predictions about the beginning of the end. "Hyperbole and anxiety have been basic components in American discussions of immigration throughout history."[23]

Today, hyperbole and anxiety over the Italian immigration of the late nineteenth and early twentieth centuries is but a distant memory. Italy itself retains some of the romance that Americans had attached to it over the years. It is still praised for its classical tradition, medieval and Renaissance art, opera, and picturesque beauty. Just as powerful, however—and perhaps just as "romantic"—are the images of Italian food, fashion, and *dolce far niente* that seem to play such important roles in today's construction of Italy and Italians. And judging from the slew of bestsellers over the past years, it seems as if everyone wants to buy and live in a villa in Tuscany. Complementing these "positive" images of Italians are less complimentary images, including those depictions of working-class and better-off Italian Americans as "philistines, tasteless boobs, Guidos, and Big Hair girls, the kind of people who would have mashed potatoes dyed blue to match their bridesmaids' dresses."[24] Versions of two Guidos, John Gotti, "the Teflon Don," and Joey Buttafuoco, the Latin Humbert Humbert of Long Island, too often have been the media's "representation" of contemporary Italian Americans. And judging from the popularity of the television series *The Sopranos*, the image of Italian Americans as *mafiosi* may never disappear from the American culture and consciousness. However, Italian Americans have come a long, long way. At least they are not being lynched anymore.

NOTES

Introduction

1. Richard Gambino, *Vendetta: The True Story of the Largest Lynching in U.S. History* (Toronto: Guernica, 1998), 4. Subsequent references are cited parenthetically.

2. George E. Cunningham, "The Italian, A Hindrance to White Solidarity in Louisiana 1890–98," *Journal of Negro History* 50 (Jan. 1965): 28. See generally Marco Rimanelli and Sheryl L. Postman, eds., *The 1891 New Orleans Lynching and U.S.-Italian Relations: A Look Back* (New York: Peter Lang, 1992).

3. John Higham, *Strangers in the Land: Patterns of American Nativism, 1860–1925* (New York: Atheneum, 1970), 66.

4. Thomas J. Archdeacon, *Becoming American: An Ethnic History* (New York: The Free Press, 1983), 141.

5. Rebecca Zurier, Robert W. Snyder, and Virginia M. Mecklenburg, eds., *Metropolitan Lives: The Ashcan Artists and Their New York* (New York: National Museum of American Art and W.W. Norton & Co., 1996), 29.

6. All immigration figures from Alan M. Kraut, *The Huddled Masses: The Immigrant in American Society, 1880–1921* (Arlington Heights, Ill.: Harlan Davidson Inc., 1982), 19–21. During the 1880s, nearly 270,000 Italian immigrants arrived, composing some 5 percent of the United States's total immigration that decade, a modest percentage compared to that of America's traditional immigrant sources in northwestern Europe. During the 1890s, the total number of Italian immigrants more than doubled to slightly more than 600,000, or 16.3 percent of total immigration. Italy now had become the single largest supplier of American immigrants. Italian immigration to the United States nearly tripled during the first decade of the twentieth century. More than 1.9 million Italians arrived, second only to the two million who came from Austria-Hungary. Together, Italy and Austria-Hungary provided one out of every two immigrants who landed in America during the first decade of the twentieth century. That decade, Italy's percentage

of the total immigration easily exceeded the combined percentages for those northern and western European countries, which, two decades earlier, had accounted for more than 70 percent of America's immigrants.

7. Edward Said, *Orientalism* (New York: Pantheon Books, 1978), 5, 38.

8. Italians were among the first Europeans to arrive in what would become the United States. The names of Christopher Columbus, Amerigo Vespucci, Giovanni Verrazano, and John Cabot have long been familiar to generations of American students. Filipo Mazzei has achieved a more limited celebrity, with his influence on the thinking of his good friend Thomas Jefferson acknowledged in some quarters. Others remain obscure and uncelebrated. They include: Enrico de Tonti, a soldier of fortune and fur trader who explored the Mississippi Valley with LaSalle; Francesco Vigo, a wealthy fur trader who provided intelligence to General George Rogers Clark during the Revolution and later reportedly became the first Italian American citizen; and Father Eusebio Francesco Chino, a scholar/cartographer/missionary who helped to explore and develop Spanish lands in the Southwest. Other early Italians in America included the four Venetian glassmakers who were brought to Jamestown in the 1620s; the Italian immigrants who accepted an offer of land from the proprietary colony of Maryland; and the nearly two hundred Protestant Italian Waldensians who escaped persecution by establishing a colony in New Amsterdam in 1657.

9. Humbert Nelli, *From Immigrants to Ethnics: The Italian Americans* (New York: Oxford University Press, 1983), 7.

10. Paul R. Baker, *The Fortunate Pilgrims: Americans in Italy, 1800–1860* (Cambridge, Mass.: Harvard University Press, 1964), 19. More generally, see Nathalia Wright, *American Novelists in Italy: The Discoverers: Allston to James* (Philadelphia: University of Pennsylvania Press, 1965); William Vance, *America's Rome* (New Haven, Conn.: Yale University Press, 1989); William Stowe, *Going Abroad: European Travel in Nineteenth-Century American Culture* (Princeton, N.J.: Princeton University Press, 1994); Van Wyck Brooks, *The Dream of Arcadia: American Writers and Artists in Italy, 1760–1915* (New York: W.P. Dutton & Co., 1958); Theodore E. Stebbins, Jr., *The Lure of Italy: American Artists and the Italian Experience, 1760–1910* (Boston and New York: Museum of Fine Arts and Harry N. Abrams, 1992); Erik Amfitheatrof, *The Enchanted Ground: Americans in Italy, 1760–1980* (Boston: Little, Brown and Co., 1980); Joy S. Kasson, *Artistic Voyagers: Europe and the American Imagination in the Works of Irving, Allston, Cole, Cooper, and Hawthorne* (Westport, Conn.: Greenwood Press, 1982); Beth Lynn Lueck, *American Writers and the Picturesque Tour: The Search for National Identity, 1790–1860* (New York: Garland Publishers, 1997); John Paul Russo, "The Harvard Italophiles: Longfellow, Lowell, Norton," in Joseph Cheyne and Lilla Maria Crisafulli Jones, eds., *L'esilio romantico: forme di un conflitto* (Bari, Italy: Adriatica Editrice, 1991); and John Paul Russo, "From Italophilia to Italophobia: Representations of Italian Americans in the Early Gilded Age," *Differentia* 6/7 (Spring/Autumn 1994): 45–75.

11. Between 1820 and 1860, approximately fourteen thousand Italians would arrive in the United States, nearly three-quarters of them during the 1850s (Nelli, *Immigrants to Ethnics*, 40). By 1850, nearly one thousand Italians were living in Louisiana [Jean Ann Scarpaci, "Immigrants in the New South: Italians in Louisiana's Sugar Parishes, 1880–1910," in Francesco Cordasco, ed., *Studies in Italian American Social History* (Totowa, N.J.: Roman and Littlefield, 1975), 137]. A part of the French

Quarter was known as Little Palermo. By the 1890s, prior to the lynching of the eleven Italians, this "Piccola Palermo" would also be known less affectionately as "Dago Street" and "Vendetta Alley" (Gambino 50). American newspapers acclaimed Garibaldi as "the distinguished champion of liberty" on his arrival in 1849, following the fall of the Roman republic. Less celebrated, but no less important in America's gallery of Italian types, were the organ-grinders who appeared in, among other places, Concord, Massachusetts. Henry David Thoreau, writing in his journals in 1851, described their music as "sounding as if a cheeta had skulked howling through the streets of the village with knotted tail." A few days later, in a less prickly mood, Thoreau praised the Italian boy who comes with his organ and serves him better than the musicians of "All Vienna" [Henry David Thoreau, *A Year in Thoreau's Journal: 1851* (New York: Penguin Books, 1993), 147, 150].

12. Baker, *Fortunate Pilgrims*, 20.

13. The major exceptions were Walt Whitman, Henry David Thoreau, and Emily Dickinson. Those who made cultural pilgrimages to Italy include Washington Irving, James Fenimore Cooper, Washington Allston, Ralph Waldo Emerson, James Russell Lowell, Nathaniel Hawthorne, Hiram Powers, William Wetmore Story, Thomas and Horatio Greenough, Thomas Crawford, Harriet Hosmer, Herman Melville, Margaret Fuller, Samuel Clemens, William Dean Howells, Henry James, Edith Wharton, Jane Addams, and Constance Fenimore Woolson.

14. Ann Douglas, *The Feminization of American Culture* (New York: Alfred A. Knopf, 1977), 284.

15. William Stowe, *Going Abroad: European Travel in Nineteenth-Century American Culture* (Princeton, N.J.: Princeton University Press, 1994), ix.

16. In 1853, George Stillman Hillard published *Six Months in Italy*, which went through twenty-one editions during the rest of the century and was probably the most popular book about Italy by an American. Additionally, magazines and newspapers "followed and further stimulated public interest with countless articles on Italian literature, art, society, and customs" (Baker 1).

17. George Templeton Strong, the New York diarist, commenting on a Bellini opera at Castle Garden in 1851, wrote, "The people are *Sonnambula*-mad." [Qtd. in Lawrence Levine, *Highbrow/Lowbrow: The Emergence of Cultural Hierarchy in America* (Cambridge, Mass.: Harvard University Press, 1988) 85]. The song sheets of Bellini, Rossini, and Donizetti sold alongside of those of Stephen Foster (Levine 96). *Rigoletto* was played at Abraham Lincoln's 1861 inauguration. And the writer and editor Nathaniel Parker Willis underscored the American attraction to Italian opera by noting "the quiet ease with which the luxury of the exclusives—Italian music—has passed into the hands of the people.... Now it is as much theirs as anyone's! ... Opera music has ... become a popular taste." Qtd. in Levine 97.

18. Qtd. in Baker, *Fortunate Pilgrims*, 26.

19. Levine, *Highbrow/Lowbrow*, 94. Audiences in New Orleans, which had America's first permanent opera company, demanded that "Yankee Doodle" and "Hail Columbia" complement the performances of Italian operas (Levine 95).

20. Qtd. in Levine, *Highbrow/Lowbrow*, 220. One year earlier, the *Atlantic* claimed that Italian opera, promoted by a group of "musical Jew-brokers," was not an art but "merely a few singers lifted up on the cheapest platform of an opera."

21. Van Wyck Brooks, *The Dream of Arcadia: American Writers and Artists in Italy, 1760–1915* (New York: W.P. Dutton & Co., 1958), 51.

22. Douglas, *The Feminization*, 283.

23. David A. J. Richards, *Italian American: The Racializing of an Ethnic Identity* (New York: New York University Press, 1999), 117.

24. This link is dramatized in an early chapter of Jane Addams's *Twenty Years at Hull-House*, when she recalls how, as a twelve year old, she walked into her father's room and found him solemnly holding a newspaper, overcome by the news that "Joseph Mazzini was dead." Young Jane had never heard of the Italian nationalist Giuseppe Mazzini (interesting that Addams's father anglicized the first name), so her father teaches her a lesson. He tells her that differences in nationality, language, and creed are less important than shared hopes and desires, and that the differences "count for absolutely nothing between groups of men who are trying to abolish slavery in America or to throw off Hapsburg oppression in Italy" [Jane Addams, *Twenty Years at Hull-House* (1910; New York: Signet Classic/Penguin, 1961), 21–32]. See generally Howard R. Marraro, *American Opinion on the Unification of Italy, 1846–1861* (New York: AMS Press, 1969).

25. James Russell Lowell spoke for many when, during a trip to Italy in 1851, he said that Americans found themselves at home in Rome as logical heirs of the old Roman Empire. "Our art, our literature, are, as theirs, in some sort exotics; but our genius for politics, for law, and, above all, for colonization, our instinct for aggrandizement and for trade, are all Roman," he wrote to his friend John Holmes on March 5, 1852. [Qtd. in Horace Elisha Scudder, *James Russell Lowell: A Biography*. 2 vols. (Boston: Houghton, Mifflin and Company, 1901), 1: 342].

26. Paul Baker says, "Few Americans took a knowledgeable interest in the political events, and only a limited number became personally concerned" (Baker 188). The few notable exceptions included Margaret Fuller, Horace Greeley, and the sculptors Horatio Greenough and Thomas Crawford. Fuller, as we know, took a passionate, active interest in the Italian revolution that culminated in the short-lived Roman republic of 1849, and promoted the cause in her dispatches to Horace Greeley's New York newspaper. Greeley also helped organize a series of public rallies held in New York in support of the Italian nationalists. At least two other Americans, the sculptors Horatio Greenough and Thomas Crawford, participated extensively in Italian society and later joined the republican Civic Guard in Florence.

27. Brooks, *The Dream*, 26.

28. All these themes, tropes, and images had been established earlier by traditional English accounts of Italy. Irving, the most influential of the American "discoverers," mines and develops them in his Italian travel journals and in his collection, *Tales of a Traveller* (1824).

29. Baker, *Fortunate Pilgrims*, 80, 83. Most American travelers had little contact with ordinary Italians. Like Henry James, they dealt mostly with the lower orders (carriage drivers, servants, self-appointed guides) who were doubly foreign in their class and culture.

30. Bayard Taylor, *View's A-Foot or Europe Seen with Knapsack and Staff* (New York: G.P. Putnam's Sons, 1879), 298, 305. Taylor writes: "This dark shadow in the

moral atmosphere of Italy hangs like a curse on her beautiful soil, weakening the sympathies of citizens of freer lands with her fallen condition. No people can ever become truly great or free, who are not virtuous" (305–306). Taylor was typical of many travelers to Italy from both America and northern Europe. As Luigi Barzini says, "They were thrilled by one of the pleasurable sensations Italy always gives visitors from the north, that of feeling morally superior to the natives." Furthermore, the Italians' "misfortunes seemed to be the natural result of their lack of virtue and their lack of virtue, in turn, the inevitable consequence of the misfortunes" [Luigi Barzini, *The Italians* (New York: Atheneum, 1981), 16, 38].

31. Baker, *Fortunate Pilgrims*, 86–88, 92, 104. Baker says, "The lower classes in particular were excoriated for cunning and avarice, a demeaning servility, and an insincerity of behavior" (92).

32. Jerre Mangione and Ben Morreale, *La Storia: Five Centuries of the Italian American Experience* (New York: HarperCollins Publishers, 1992), 26–27.

33. John Paul Russo, "From Italophilia to Italophobia: Representations of Italian Americans in the Early Gilded Age," *Differentia* 6/7 (Spring/Autumn 1994): 45–46.

34. Donna Gabaccia, *Italy's Many Diasporas* (Seattle: University of Washington Press, 2000), 39, 36.

35. Richards, *Italian American*, 99, 101.

36. Donna Gabaccia, *Militants and Migrants: Rural Sicilians Become American Workers* (New Brunswick, N.J.: Rutgers University Press, 1988), 19–20; Joseph Lopreato, *Italian Americans* (New York: Random House, 1970), 33; Patrick J. Gallo, *Old Bread, New Wine* (Chicago: Nelson-Hall, 1981), 31.

37. Richards, *Italian American*, 105.

38. John Dickie, "Imagined Italies," in David Forgacs and Robert Lumley, eds., *Italian Cultural Studies: An Introduction* (New York: Oxford University Press, 1996), 28–29.

39. John Dickie, "Stereotypes of the Italian South, 1860–1900," in Robert Lumley and Jonathan Morris, eds., *The New History of the Italian South: The Mezzogiorno Revisited* (Exeter, England: University of Exeter Press, 1997), 122; Dickie, "Imagined Italies," 28. See also Gabriella Gribaudi, "Images of the South: The Mezzogiorno as Seen by Insiders and Outsiders," in Lumley and Morris, *The New History*.

40. Mangione, *La Storia*, 60, 73.

41. Gabaccia, *Diasporas*, 57.

42. Jane Schneider, "Introduction: The Dynamics of Neo-orientalism in Italy (1848–1995)," in Jane Schneider, ed., *Italy's "Southern Question": Orientalism in One Country* (New York: Berg, 1998), 3, 19.

43. Dickie, "Stereotypes," 118–119.

44. James W. Ceaser, *Reconstructing America: The Symbol of America in Modern Thought* (New Haven, Conn.: Yale University Press, 1997), 112.

45. By the early nineteenth century in Great Britain and the Continent, ideas about the biological basis of racial inequality stimulated a mania for the kind of racial classifications found in Cuvier's *Le regne animal*, Gobineau's *Essai sur l'inegalité des races humaines*, and Robert Knox's *The Races of Man*.

46. Ceaser, *Reconstructing America*, 115.

47. Dana D. Nelson, *National Manhood: Capitalist Citizenship and the Imagined Fraternity of White Men* (Durham, N.C.: Duke University Press, 1998), 117. Morton's "racial rank-ordering and arguments about 'natural repugnance' transpose smoothly into late-century Darwinism, lent themselves as readily to eugenics, and offered 'scientific' evidence to popular theories that fostered racial and ethnic prejudice" (Nelson 117).

48. Russo, "From Italophilia," 51.

49. Higham, *Strangers*, 90.

50. Gabaccia, *Diasporas*, 124.

51. Again, American attitudes toward Italian opera are instructive. Toward the end of the nineteenth century, Italian opera was being criticized as lowbrow and compared unfavorably to German/Wagnerian opera, just as Italian immigrants were being disparaged in comparison to Germanic immigrants. Writing on America's Italophobia in 1879, William Francis Allen spoke for his class when he said that Italians "have by no manner of means reached so high a degree of development in their art of musical composition as the Germans have," and that the Germans "appeal to the feelings in a far higher way than the Italians." In 1884, *Harper's New Monthly Magazine* announced the appearance of "another audience of the highest cultivation and of another taste," which harbored "a significant disposition to regard Italian opera itself as a kind of Mother Goose melodies, good enough for a childish musical taste, but ludicrous for the developed and trained taste of to-day." That same year, the *New York Daily Tribune* dismissed Italian opera as "the sweetmeats of the hurdy-gurdy repertory" (Levine, *Highbrow/Lowbrow*, 220, 102).

52. Despite the country's material success, there were signs of moral panic. Before the Civil War Americans tended to see technology and mechanization—factories, railroads, telegraph wires—as instruments and engines of democracy, republicanism, and material wealth. But, as Alan Trachtenberg has shown, by the late nineteenth century these same instruments were being blamed for poverty, slums, and wretched industrial conditions [Alan Trachtenberg, *The Incorporation of America: Culture & Society in the Gilded Age* (New York: Hill and Wang, 1982), 38].

53. Trachtenberg, *The Incorporation*, 79.

54. Gail Bederman, *Manliness & Civilization: A Cultural History of Gender and Race in the United States, 1880–1917* (Chicago: The University of Chicago Press, 1995), 4, 78. Bederman says that by the end of the century, middle-class identity was being shaped by, and itself shaping, a discourse of manliness that stressed self-mastery and restraint (12). This discourse of manliness intersected with discourses on race and civilization: "Manliness was the achievement of a perfect man, just as civilization was the achievement of a perfect race" (27).

55. Qtd. in Gambino, *Vendetta*, 97.

56. Matthew Frye Jacobson, *Whiteness of a Different Color: European Immigrants and the Alchemy of Race* (Cambridge, Mass.: Harvard University Press, 1998), 33; Thomas F. Gossett, *Race: The History of an Idea in America* (Dallas: Southern Methodist University Press, 1963), 287.

57. Kathie Friedman-Kasaba, *Memories of Migration: Gender, Ethnicity, and Work in the Lives of Jewish and Italian Women in New York, 1870–1924* (Albany: State University of New York Press, 1996), 98.

58. Qtd. in Ronald M. Pavalko, "Racism and the New Immigration: A Reinterpretation of the Assimilation of White Ethnics in American Society," *Sociology and Social Research* 65 (Oct. 1980): 58. Hall argued that inbreeding "with the native American stock of the earlier and better immigrants who came over before 1880" would "dilute the Yankee gumption" and "pollute the Yankee blood." Qtd. in Pavalko 58.

59. Henry Cabot Lodge, "The Restriction of Immigration," *North American Review* 152 (Jan. 1891): 30, 45. Lodge quotes the American consul in Rome as saying that emigrants from northern and central Italy were generally industrious, trustworthy, strong, capable, and moral, all of which could not be said of the illiterate southern Italian emigrants who came from a land of endemic brigandage (31).

60. Francis A. Walker, "Immigration and Degradation," *Forum* 11 (Aug. 1891): 643–644. Walker argued that native-born Americans were breeding less because they did not want their sons to socialize or compete economically with the aliens who were willing to work for less. Walker theorized that ease of travel in the late nineteenth century tended to attract not "the more alert and enterprising" immigrants of the past, "but rather the unlucky, the thriftless, the worthless." The patrician assault on the new immigrants continued with a May 1893 piece by Harvard geologist Nathaniel S. Shaler in *The Atlantic Monthly*. Writing of "European Peasants as Immigrants," Shaler argued that the new non-Aryan, non-Germanic peasant peoples of Europe, pauperized by their armies and the (Catholic) Church, were wholly different from Americans in motives and aspirations, and represented a hardened social caste that was nearly innately impossible to Americanize on the civic front [N.S. Shaler, "European Peasants as Immigrants," *Atlantic* 71 (May 1893): 646–655].

61. Higham, *Strangers*, 101. Henry Cabot Lodge soon came to champion the literacy test as "chiefly a means of discriminating against 'alien races' rather than of elevating American working-men" (101).

62. Henry Cabot Lodge, "Lynch Law and Unrestricted Immigration," *North American Review* 152 (May 1891): 612.

63. Qtd. in Higham, *Strangers*, 143.

64. Henry Cabot Lodge, "A Million Immigrants a Year, I. Efforts to Restrict Undesirable Immigration," *Century* 67 (Jan. 1904): 467.

65. Qtd. in Gambino, *Vendetta*, 120. In a companion piece to Lodge's article, "Efforts to Restrict Undesirable Immigration," federal immigration commissioner Frank P. Sargent added this postscript: "We do not need aliens who have no regard for morality and for law and order, who in secret plan the murder of their own kindred, and whose mere presence is a menace to society" [*Century* 67 (Jan. 1904): 471].

66. Gambino, *Vendetta*, 135; Luciano J. Iorizzo, "The Padrone and Immigrant Distribution," in Silvano M. Tomasi and Madeline H. Engel, eds., *The Italian Experience in the United States* (Staten Island, N.Y.: Center for Migration Studies of New York, 1970), 50.

67. Nathaniel Shaler, "European Peasants as Immigrants," 649.

68. Michael La Sorte, *La Merica: Images of the Italian Greenhorn Experience* (Philadelphia: Temple University Press, 1985), 130.

69. Robert F. Harney, "The Padrone and the Immigrant," *The Canadian Review of American Studies* 5 (Fall 1974): 110.

70. Iorizzo, "The Padrone," 74.

71. Gunther Peck, *Reinventing Free Labor: Padrones and Immigrant Workers in the North American West, 1880–1930* (New York: Cambridge University Press, 2000), 17–18; Harney, "The Padrone," 101. See also Rudolph J. Vecoli, "Italian American Workers, 1880–1920: Padrone Slaves or Primitive Rebels?" in Silvano M. Tomasi, ed., *Perspectives in Italian Immigration and Ethnicity* (New York: Center for Migration Studies, 1977).

72. Qtd. in Harney, "The Padrone," 102.

73. S. Merlino, "Italian Immigrants and their Enslavement," *Forum* 15 (April 1893): 187.

74. La Sorte, *La Merica*, 74, 80–82. See also Peck, *Reinventing Fee Labor*, and Vecoli, "Italian American Workers."

75. Gambino, *Vendetta*, 56–57.

76. Qtd. in Cunningham, "The Italian, A Hindrance," 34.

77. Higham, *Strangers*, 169.

78. James R. Barrett and David Roediger, "Inbetween Peoples: Race, Nationality and the 'New Immigrant' Working Class," *Journal of American Ethnic History* 16 (Spring 1997): 6–7; David R. Roediger, *The Wages of Whiteness: Race and the Making of the American Working Class*, revised edition (New York: Verso, 1999), 146.

79. Jacobson, *Whiteness*, 7; Peck, *Reinventing*, 166; Jacobson, *Whiteness*, 5, 12. See generally Noel Ignatiev, *How the Irish Became White* (New York: Routledge, 1995); Karen Brodkin, *How Jews Became White Folks and What That Says about Race in America* (New Brunswick, N.J.: Rutgers University Press, 1998).

80. Said, *Orientalism*, 20–24.

81. Christopher Mulvey, *Transatlantic Manners: Social Patterns in Nineteenth-Century Anglo-American Travel Literature* (New York: Cambridge University Press, 1990), 8.

82. I am indebted to Edward Said here. See *Orientalism*, 23–24, 27.

Chapter 1

1. Jacob Riis, *How the Other Half Lives: Studies Among the Tenements of New York* (1890. New York: Dover Publications, 1971), 43.

2. John Paul Russo, "From Italophilia to Italophobia: Representations of Italian Americans in the Early Gilded Age," *Differentia* 6–7 (Spring/Autumn 1994): 45.

3. Qtd. in Russo, "Italophilia," 59.

4. Sally Stein, "Making Connections with the Camera: Photography and Social Mobility in the Career of Jacob Riis," *Afterimage* 10 (May 1983): 10.

5. Qtd. in James B. Lane, *Jacob A. Riis and the American City* (Port Washington, N.Y.: Kennikat Press, 1974), 10. According to Lane, "The very things he loved most, the rustic simplicity, unchanging traditions, and bucolic peacefulness, conflicted with his restless spirit and thus lured him to another country where he could satisfy his drive" (Lane 14).

6. Jacob Riis, *The Making of an American* (New York: The Macmillan Company, 1901), 35–36.

7. Bonnie Yochelson, *Jacob Riis* (New York: Phaidon Press, 2001), 7–8.

8. "Flashes from the Slums" appeared in the February 12, 1888, *Tribune*. The eighteen-page article for *Scribner's*, which appeared in December 1889, included nineteen illustrations based on the photographs.

9. Riis, *The Making*, 424.

10. Readers responded enthusiastically to the immigrant boy-makes-good saga and embraced the book's love interest: the story of how Riis first lost but later won the hand of his wife, Elizabeth. "Riis wanted his autobiography to provide a lesson in how a poor immigrant could find a useful place in American society if he had a strong will, proper values, steadfast purpose, and an abundance of faith. Strong moral purpose could help the rootless newcomer conquer the certain failures which he would face" (Lane 155). Riis's autobiography was the prototype for numerous immigrant success stories "which turned the process of assimilation into a romantic quest" (Stein 10). To this rhetorical end, *The Making of an American* engages in mythmaking not unlike that found in Mary Antin's *The Promised Land* (1912) and *The Americanization of Edward Bok* (1920), by the longtime editor of the *Ladies' Home Journal*. These autobiographies, which can also include Edward Steiner's less well-known *From Alien to Citizen* (1914), all "read the hardness of American life as a vindication of American idealism, equality, and upward mobility," according to Lewis F. Fried, *Makers of the City* (Amherst: The University of Massachusetts Press, 1990), 19.

11. Lewis F. Fried, *Makers of the City* (Amherst: The University of Massachusetts Press, 1990), 23.

12. At the time of Riis's death in 1914, a reporter for the *Outlook* expressed the general sentiment in writing that "No man has ever more vitally and faithfully expressed and interpreted the American Spirit than Jacob A. Riis." Qtd. in Fried 23.

13. Lane, *Riis and the American City*, 27–28.

14. Stein, "Making Connections," 10.

15. Fried, *Makers of the City*, 13.

16. Peter B. Hales, *Silver Cities: The Photography of American Urbanization, 1839–1915* (Philadelphia: Temple University Press, 1984), 185. William A. Rogers, an artist for *Harper's*, was a leading exponent of the picturesqueness of poverty throughout the 1880s and 1890s, producing in 1879 his iconographic *Ragpickers' Court*. Before Riis turned his attention to the tenements and police lodging houses, *Harper's Weekly* and *Frank Leslie's* magazine had published articles on the tenement poor, using engravings of drawings made on site.

17. *Harper's Weekly*, October 18, 1890, 817–819.

18. Titles include George Foster's *New York by Gaslight* (circa 1850), Matthew Hale Smith's *Sunshine and Shadow in New York* (1869), Charles Loring Brace's *The Dangerous Classes of New York, and Twenty Years' Work among Them* (1872), Edward Crapsey's *The Nether Side of New York* (1872), James D. McCabe Jr.'s *Lights and Shadows of New York Life; or, the Sights and Sensations of the Great City* (1872), Josiah Strong's *Our Country: Its Possible Future and Present Crisis* (1886), and Samuel L. Loomis's *Modern Cities and Religious Problems* (1887).

19. Maren Stange, *Symbols of Ideal Life: Social Documentary Photography in America, 1890–1950* (New York: Cambridge University Press, 1992), 17.

20. Fried, *Makers of the City*, 31.

21. Riis, *Other Half*, 2. Subsequent references are cited parenthetically.

22. Fried, *Makers of the City*, 33.

23. Keith Gandal, *The Virtues of the Vicious: Jacob Riis, Stephen Crane, and the Spectacle of the Slum* (New York: Oxford University Press, 1997), 8.

24. Lane, *Riis and American City*, 35, 4.

25. Alexander Alland Sr., *Jacob Riis: Photographer & Citizen* (Millerton, N.Y.: Aperture, 1974), 34. Bonnie Yochelson, "What are the Photographs of Jacob Riis?" *Culturefront* 3 (Fall 1994): 29. Alland was instrumental in rescuing Riis's photographs in the 1940s.

26. Stein, "Making Connections," 13.

27. Brace writes: "Here, in large tenement-houses, were packed hundreds of poor Italians, mostly engaged in carrying through the city and country 'the everlasting hand-organ,' or selling statuettes. In the same room I would find monkeys, children, men and women, with organs and plaster-casts, all huddled together; but the women contriving still, in the crowded rooms, to roll their dirty macaroni, and all talking excitedly; a bedlam of sounds, and a combination of odors from garlic, monkeys and the most dirty human persons. They were, without exception, the dirtiest population I had met with." *The Dangerous Classes of New York, and Twenty Years' Work among Them* (New York: Wynkoop and Hallenbeck, 1872), 194.

28. Riis, *The Making*, 38–39.

29. Michael A. La Sorte, "Immigrant Occupations: A Comparison," in Richard N. Juliani and Philip V. Cannistraro, eds., *Italian Americans: The Search for a Usable Past* (Staten Island, N.Y.: The American Italian Historical Association, 1989), 85.

30. Michael La Sorte, *La Merica: Images of Italian Greenhorn Experience* (Philadelphia, Temple University Press, 1985), 62–63; Donna Gabaccia, *Militants and Migrants: Rural Sicilians Become American Workers* (New Brunswick, N.J.: Rutgers University Press, 1988), 83. Donna R. Gabaccia, *From Sicily to Elizabeth Street: Housing and Social Change Among Italian Immigrants, 1880–1930* (Albany: State University of New York Press, 1984), 61, 64.

31. Gabaccia, *Elizabeth Street*, 76, 66, xvi, 74.

32. Samuel L. Baily, *Immigrants in the Land of Promise: Italians in Buenos Aires and New York City, 1870–1914* (Ithaca, N.Y.: Cornell University Press, 1999), 153, 159–160.

33. Baily, *Land of Promise*, 107. Miriam Cohen, *Workshop to Office: Two Generations of Italian Women in New York City, 1900–1950* (Ithaca, N.Y.: Cornell University Press, 1992), 45, 47, 56–57.

34. Gabaccia, *Elizabeth Street*, 92–93.

35. Donna R. Gabaccia, *Italy's Many Diasporas* (Seattle: University of Washington Press, 2000), 125–126.

36. Luciano J. Iorizzo, "The Padrone and Immigrant Distribution," in Silvano M. Tomasi and Madeline H. Engel, eds., *The Italian Experience in the United States* (Staten Island, N.Y.: Center for Migration Studies of New York, 1970), 74.

37. Gunther Peck, *Reinventing Free Labor: Padrones and Immigrant Workers in the North American West, 1880–1930* (New York: Cambridge University Press, 2000), 17–18. Robert F. Harney, "The Padrone and the Immigrant," *The Canadian Review of American Studies* 5 (Fall 1974): 101.

38. Harney, "The Padrone and the Immigrant," 102.
39. New York *Evening Sun,* March 18, 1892.
40. Jacob Riis, *The Children of the Poor* (1892; New York: Charles Scribner's Sons, 1902), 10. Subsequent references are cited parenthetically.
41. Henry Cabot Lodge, "The Restriction of Immigration," *North American Review* 152 (January 1891): 27–35.
42. Lane, *Riis and American City,* 85.
43. Jacob Riis, "Paolo's Awakening," *Atlantic* 78 (November 1896): 706–707.
44. Riis had now authored seven books, some in several editions. His works were on school and library recommended reading lists; sociologists and reformers quoted his homespun philosophy.
45. Lane, *Riis and American City,* 129, 150.
46. Jacob Riis, *The Battle with the Slum* (New York: Macmillan, 1902), 433, 436, 438. Subsequent references are cited parenthetically.
47. Jerre Mangione and Ben Morreale, *La Storia: Five Centuries of the Italian American Experience* (New York: HarperCollins Publishers, 1992), 82, 84. See generally Gabaccia, *Militants and Migrants.*
48. John Higham, *Strangers in the Land: Patterns of American Nativism, 1860–1925* (New York: Atheneum, 1970), 160; John Dickie, "Stereotypes of the Italian South 1860–1900," in Robert Lumley and Jonathan Morris, eds., *The New History of the Italian South: The Mezzogiorno Revisited* (Exeter, England: University of Exeter Press, 1997), 118–119.
49. Gabaccia, *Italy's Many Diasporas,* 125–126.
50. Yochelson, *Jacob Riis,* 3.
51. Stein, "Making Connections," 14.
52. Yochelson, *Jacob Riis,* 11.
53. Stein, "Making Connections," 14–15; Gandal, *Virtues of the Vicious,* 64–65.
54. Susan Sontag, *On Photography* (New York: Farrar, Straus and Giroux, 1973), 3.
55. Yochelson, "Photographs of Jacob Riis," 29–31, 36–37.
56. Yochelson, *Jacob Riis,* 11–12, 14–15. Yochelson, former curator of prints and photographs for the Museum of the City of New York, supervised the cataloguing and printing of the museum's Riis collection. She is an invaluable source of information on Riis's photography.
57. Stein, "Making Connections," 9–16.
58. Hales, *Silver Cities,* 193.
59. Riis, *The Making,* 271. Riis recalls a midnight expedition with the sanitary police to a lodging house: "When the report was submitted to the Health Board the next day, it did not make much of an impression— these things rarely do, put in mere words—until my negatives, still dripping from the dark-room, came to reinforce them. From them there was no appeal" (273).
60. Hales, *Silver Cities,* 194, 197.
61. Qtd. in Stange, *Symbols of Ideal Life,* 16. A newspaper reporter in Iowa, having heard Riis in December 1900, gave insight into Riis's popularity and success. "There is in each human breast an insatiable desire to go slumming. The lecture was an opportunity to visit the holes in the great American city . . . and at the same time to be free from contamination." Qtd. in Lane, *Riis and American City,* 152–153.

62. Stein, "Making Connections," 10, 14; Stange, *Symbols of Ideal Life*, 23. Stange says, "The idea of photography as surveillance, the controlling gaze as a middle-class right and tool, is woven throughout Riis's lectures and writings. Not only did Riis make use of others' surveillance photography, and deploy the insiders' humor that affirmed its power, but he also, and quite consistently, valued his own images in similar terms."

63. Gandal, *Virtues of the Vicious*, 9, 79.

64. Sontag, *On Photography*, 156. Riis's photographs exhibit other powers mentioned by Sontag. They exhibit the camera's capacity for both subjectivizing and objectifying reality, and for defining reality as spectacle for the masses and as object of surveillance for the rulers. Riis's camera made exotic things near and intimate, and helped the audience take possession of space in which they were insecure.

65. For example: "In the home of an Italian rag-picker, Jersey Street" (45) appears to be a sympathetic portrait, while "Typical toughs (from the Rogue's Gallery) [burglar and thief]" (170) are little more than mug shots. The subjects in "Lodgers in a crowded Bayard Street tenement—'five cents a spot'" (58) are surprised at a distance, while the people in "Fighting tuberculosis on the roof" (127) appear welcoming. "Tenement-house yard" (33) bursts forth from its frame, while "Vegetable stand in 'the Bend'" is ordered and inviting (220). [All photos in *How the Other Half Lives: Studies Among the Tenements of New York* (1890. New York: Dover Publications, 1971).]

66. Sontag, *On Photography*, 106, 109, 23.

67. Unless otherwise noted, photo titles used are those provided by the Museum of the City of New York.

68. Yochelson, "Photographs of Jacob Riis," 32; Yochelson, *Jacob Riis*, 20.

69. Jacob Riis, "Feast Days in Little Italy," *Century* 58 (August 1899): 494. Subsequent references cited parenthetically.

70. Denise Mangieri DiCarlo, "The Role of the Italian *Festa* in the United States," in Harral E. Landry, ed., *To See the Past More Clearly: The Enrichment of the Italian Heritage, 1890–1990* (Staten Island, N.Y.: The American Italian Historical Association, 1994), 204, 198.

71. Mangione, *La Storia*, 327–328, 330; La Sorte, *La Merica*, 149; Patrick J. Gallo, *Old Bread, New Wine* (Chicago: Nelson-Hall, 1981), 182–183.

72. Yochelson, *Jacob Riis*, 40.

73. Priscilla Wald, *Constituting Americans: Cultural Anxiety and Narrative Form* (Durham, N.C.: Duke University Press, 1995), 247.

74. Jacob Riis, *The Peril and the Preservation of the Home* (Philadelphia: George W. Jacobs & Co., 1903), 13, 24.

75. Yochelson, *Jacob Riis*, 88–89.

76. Riis, *The Peril*, 110–111.

77. Riis, *The Making*, 307. Riis says he treasures two letters he received from Lowell, the first granting permission to use the poem, the second praising *How the Other Half Lives*. Lowell wrote: "I have read your book with deep & painful interest... I had but a vague idea of these horrors before you brought them so feelingly home to me. I cannot conceive how such a book shall fail of doing great good, if it move other people as it has moved me. I found it hard to get to sleep the night after I had been reading it" (308).

78. See Edward Wagenknecht, *James Russell Lowell: Portrait of a Many-Sided Man* (New York: Oxford University Press, 1971), 175–176; Martin Duberman, *James Russell Lowell* (Boston: Houghton Mifflin Company, 1966), 307–308.

79. James Russell Lowell, *Leaves from My Journal in Italy and Elsewhere*. Vol. 1. *The Writings of James Russell Lowell* (Boston: Houghton, Mifflin and Company, 1891. 10 vols), 124–125, 131, 139, 165–166, 170, 178, 206–207; Horace Elisha Scudder, *James Russell Lowell: A Biography*. 2 vols. (Boston: Houghton, Mifflin and Company, 1901), 1: 342. See also John Paul Russo, "The Harvard Italophiles: Longfellow, Lowell, and Norton," in Joseph Cheyne and Lilla Maria Crisafulli Jones, eds., *L'Esilio romantico: forme di un conflitto* (Bari, Italy: Adriatica Editrice, 1990).

80. Lane, *Riis and American City*, 57.

81. Fried, *Makers of the City*, 24–25.

82. Lane, *Riis and American City*, 156, 205, 66–67.

83. Fried, *Makers of the City*, 18.

84. Lane, *Riis and American City*, 35.

85. Stein, "Making Connections," 10.

Chapter 2

1. Edward Steiner, *On the Trail of the Immigrant* (New York: Fleming H. Revell Company, 1906), 292. Subsequent references are cited parenthetically.

2. John Higham, *Strangers in the Land: Patterns of American Nativism, 1860–1925* (New York: Atheneum, 1970), 87, 95. Higham says that by the 1890s, a period exacerbated by depression and labor strife, southern and eastern European immigrants were becoming significant targets of American nativism. Higham writes: "An initial distrust, compounded largely out of their culture and appearance, swelled into a pressing sense of menace, into hatred, and into violence." Economic shocks discharged general anti-foreign feelings against the new immigrants, "so that each of the southeastern European groups appeared as a particularly insidious representative of the whole foreign menace" (87).

3. Reginald Horsman, *Race and Manifest Destiny: The Origins of American Racial Anglo-Saxonism* (Cambridge, Mass.: Harvard University Press, 1981), 38, 4–5, 1.

4. Higham, *Strangers*, 132.

5. David R. Roediger, *The Wages of Whiteness: Race and the Making of the American Working Class* (New York: Verso, 1999), 133. See also James R. Barrett and David Roediger, "Inbetween Peoples: Race, Nationality and the 'New Immigrant' Working Class," *Journal of American Ethnic History* 16 (Spring 1997): 3–44; Matthew Frye Jacobson, *Whiteness of a Different Color: European Immigrants and the Alchemy of Race* (Cambridge, Mass.: Harvard University Press, 1998); Noel Ignatiev, *How the Irish Became White* (New York: Routledge, 1995); Karen Brodkin, *How Jews Became White Folks and What That Says about Race in America* (New Brunswick, N.J.: Rutgers University Press, 1998).

6. Jacobson, *Whiteness*, 41.

7. Roediger, *Wages of Whiteness*, 180.

8. Higham, *Strangers*, 160.

9. John Dickie, "Stereotypes of the Italian South 1860–1900," in Robert Lumley and Jonathan Morris, eds., *The New History of the Italian South: The Mezzogiorno Revisited* (Exeter, England: University of Exeter Press, 1997), 118–119.

10. Edward A. Steiner, *Against the Current: Simple Chapters from a Complex Life* (New York: Fleming H. Revell Company, 1910), 7, 31, 110, 53. Steiner recounts how until age five he played with Gentile friends, innocent of any differences between them, until he is beaten by his older brother for sharing the Gentiles' Sabbath cakes. He runs away, falls in with a group of Catholics making a pilgrimage, but on the return home a cart driver calls him a "little Jew" and throws him out of the cart. The next day he was made to begin studying the Hebrew alphabet (27–28). His race consciousness deepens when, at age seven or eight, he is chosen as the Jewish children's representative during a visit to the town by a Magyar prince. He is devastated when the prince responds to his greeting by turning to an attendant and saying, "Too bad, too bad that he is a Jew. He doesn't look or act like one" (82).

11. David W. Jordan, "Edward A. Steiner and the Struggle for Toleration During World War I," *Annals of Iowa* 46 (1983): 523–542.

12. Edward A. Steiner, *From Alien to Citizen: The Story of My Life in America* (New York: Fleming H. Revell Company, 1914), 50–51, 79, 141.

13. Steiner, *Against the Current*, 202–203.

14. Qtd. in Jordan, "Struggle for Toleration," 530.

15. Jordan, "Struggle for Toleration," 524.

16. Steiner, *Alien to Citizen*, 7–8, 277, 332. In the Midwest, Steiner found factory work with the father of the girl he had loved as a child in Slovakia. The family sent him back East to become a rabbi, but instead Steiner landed in a unnamed Midwest town, where he found a philanthropic Jewish patroness, began writing for a free-thinking Jewish newspaper and working with immigrants, started feeling the power of Christ's love, and eventually ended up at Oberlin.

17. *The National Cyclopaedia of American Biography* (Ann Arbor, Mich.: University Microfilms, 1967), 45: 169.

18. Steiner, *Against the Current*, 217.

19. Steiner, *Alien to Citizen*, 17.

20. Steiner, *Alien to Citizen*, 20.

21. Qtd. in Geraldine Wojno Kiefer, *Alfred Stieglitz: Scientist, Photographer, and Avatar of Modernism, 1880–1913* (New York: Garland Publishing, 1991), 321.

22. Kenneth Scambray, "Outside the Framework of Time: The Briganti of Southern Italy," in Harral E. Landry, ed., *To See the Past More Clearly: The Enrichment of the Italian Heritage, 1890–1990* (Staten Island, N.Y. The American Italian Historical Association, 1994), 96.

23. Dickie, "Stereotypes," 119, 121–122.

24. Patrick J. Gallo, *Old Bread, New Wine* (Chicago: Nelson-Hall, 1981), 24.

25. Rudolph J. Vecoli, "Prelates and Peasants: Italian Immigrants and the Catholic Church," *Journal of Social History* 2 (1969): 228–229.

26. Joseph Lopreato, *Italian Americans* (New York: Random House, 1970), 88.

27. Vecoli, "Prelates and Peasants," 222.

28. Donna R. Gabaccia, *From Sicily to Elizabeth Street: Housing and Social Change Among Italian Immigrants, 1880–1930* (Albany: State University of New York Press,

1984), 64–66; Donna R. Gabaccia, *Italy's Many Diasporas* (Seattle: University of Washington Press, 2000), 77.

29. Samuel L. Baily, *Immigrants in the Land of Promise: Italians in Buenos Aires and New York City, 1870–1914* (Ithaca, N.Y.: Cornell University Press, 1999), 100.

30. Gabaccia, *Elizabeth Street*, 74.

31. Baily, *Land of Promise*, 153, 159–160.

32. Baily, *Land of Promise*, 107; Gabaccia, *Elizabeth Street*, 92–93; Miriam Cohen, *Workshop to Office: Two Generations of Italian Women in New York City, 1900–1950* (Ithaca, N.Y.: Cornell University Press, 1992), 45, 47, 56–57.

33. Valentine J. Belfiglio, "Italians in Small Town and Rural America," in Rudolph J. Vecoli, ed., *Italian Immigrants in Rural and Small Town America* (Staten Island, N.Y.: The American Italian Historical Association, 1987), 32–33, 35–36.

34. Luciano J. Iorizzo, "The Padrone and Immigrant Distribution," in Silvano M. Tomasi and Madeline H. Engel, eds., *The Italian Experience in the United States* (Staten Island, N.Y.: Center for Migration Studies of New York, 1970), 66, 70; Humbert S. Nelli, "Italians in Urban America," in Silvano M. Tomasi and Madeline H. Engel, eds., *The Italian Experience in the United States* (Staten Island, N.Y.: Center for Migration Studies of New York, 1970), 82–83.

35. Gabaccia, *Diasporas*, 125–126.

36. Baily, *Land of Promise*, 110.

37. Gabaccia, *Diasporas*, 92, 102.

38. Baily, *Land of Promise*, 118.

39. Baily, *Land of Promise*, 110; Gabaccia, *Diasporas*, 102–103.

40. Sr. Mary Fabian Matthews, "The Role of the Public School in the Assimilation of the Italian Immigrant Child in New York City, 1900–1914," in Silvano M. Tomasi and Madeline H. Engel, eds., *The Italian Experience in the United States* (Staten Island, N.Y.: Center for Migration Studies of New York, 1970), 131, 138.

41. Cohen, *Workshop to Office*, 12, 114.

42. Gallo, *Old Bread*, 57–58, 61.

43. Matthews, "Role of the Public School," 140.

44. Gallo, *Old Bread*, 59.

45. Baily, *Land of Promise*, 59; Michael La Sorte, *La Merica: Images of Italian Greenhorn Experience* (Philadelphia, Temple University Press, 1985), 193.

46. Gallo, *Old Bread*, 83.

47. Edward A. Steiner, *Old Trails and New Borders* (New York: Fleming H. Revell Company, 1921), 34.

48. Jordan, "Struggle for Toleration," 542, and more generally the rest of the article.

Chapter 3

1. In addition to his book of sketches/essays, *Italian Hours,* James used Italian scenes and characters in his biographical *William Wetmore Story and His Friends* (1903) and in fictional works such as *Roderick Hudson* (1875), *Daisy Miller* (1878), *The Portrait of a Lady* (1881), *The Princess Casamassima* (1886), *The*

Aspern Papers (1888), *The Wings of the Dove* (1902), and *The Golden Bowl* (1904), among others.

2. Carl Maves, *Sensuous Pessimism: Italy in the Works of Henry James* (Bloomington: Indiana University Press, 1973), 4.

3. Henry James, *A Small Boy and Others* (New York: Charles Scribner's Sons, 1913), 114–115.

4. James, *Small Boy*, 271.

5. Henry James, *The Complete Tales of Henry James*, ed. Leon Edel. 8 vols. (London: Rupert Hart-Davis, and Philadelphia and New York: J.B. Lippincott Company, 1962–1963), 3: 391.

6. Henry James, *The Letters of Henry James*, ed. Percy Lubbock. 2 vols. (New York: Charles Scribner's Sons, 1920), 1: 24–25.

7. James, *Letters*, 1: 57.

8. James, *Letters*, 1: 126.

9. For many Americans in the nineteenth century, travel to Europe was both a pilgrimage and a spiritual, intellectual, and cultural homecoming, the place where the American went to define himself by reference to another, the European. Travel was a mark of social status and, for writers, a way to claim the respect of the American audience. It was a site for personal freedom and the fulfillment of a host of desires, sensual and aesthetic.

10. William Stowe, *Going Abroad: European Travel in Nineteenth-Century American Culture* (Princeton, N.J.: Princeton University Press, 1994), 169.

11. Alan Holder, *Three Voyagers in Search of Europe: A Study of Henry James, Ezra Pound, and T.S. Eliot* (Philadelphia: University of Pennsylvania Press, 1966), 269–270; Larzer Ziff, *Great American Travel Writing, 1780–1910* (New Haven, Conn.: Yale University Press, 2000), 252.

12. Henry James, *Italian Hours*, ed. John Auchard (1909; New York: Penguin Books, 1995), 17. Subsequent references are cited parenthetically.

13. Richard H. Brodhead, *Cultures of Letters: Scenes of Reading and Writing in Nineteenth-Century America* (Chicago: University of Chicago Press, 1993).

14. Stowe, *Going Abroad*, 173.

15. Stowe, *Going Abroad*, 179. See also Mary Louise Pratt, *Imperial Eyes: Travel Writing and Transculturation* (New York: Routledge, 1992), 52, 201–205.

16. Brigitte Bailey, "Travel Writing and the Metropolis: James, London, and *English Hours*," *American Literature* 67 (June 1995): 201–232.

17. Ziff, *Return Passages*, 235.

18. Van Wyck Brooks, *The Dream of Arcadia: American Writers and Artists in Italy, 1760–1915* (New York: W.P. Dutton & Co., 1958), 172.

19. Brooks, *The Dream*, 150.

20. Qtd. in Holder, *Three Voyagers*, 93.

21. Holder, *Three Voyagers*, 94, 96–97.

22. William Dean Howells, *Venetian Life* (1866; Marlboro, Vt.: The Marlboro Press, 1989), 260.

23. Sara Blair, *Henry James and the Writing of Race and Nation* (New York: Cambridge University Press, 1996), 47–50, 54, 58.

24. Susan Sontag, *On Photography* (New York: Farrar, Straus and Giroux, 1973), 55.

25. Christof Wegelin, *The Image of Europe in Henry James* (Dallas: Southern Methodist University Press, 1958), 27.

26. Maves, *Sensuous Pessimism*, 5–6.

27. James, *The Complete Tales*, 2:175. Subsequent references are cited parenthetically.

28. Jacob Riis, *How the Other Half Lives: Studies Among the Tenements of New York* (1890; New York: Dover Publications, 1971), 77.

Chapter 4

1. For discussions of *The Golden Bowl*, see, for example, Christof Wegelin, *The Image of Europe in Henry James* (Dallas: Southern Methodist University Press, 1958); Carl Maves, *Sensuous Pessimism: Italy in the Works of Henry James* (Bloomington: Indiana University Press, 1973); Thomas Galt Peyser, "James, Race, and the Imperial Museum," *American Literary History* 6 (Spring 1994): 48–70; Jonathan Freedman, "The Poetics of Cultural Decline: Degeneracy, Assimilation, and the Jew in James's *The Golden Bowl*," *American Literary History* 7 (Fall 1995); Roslyn Jolly, *Henry James: History, Narrative, Fiction* (New York: Oxford University Press, 1993); Mark Seltzer, *Henry James and the Art of Power* (Ithaca, N.Y.: Cornell University Press, 1984).

2. Maves, *Sensuous Pessimism*, 125, 138.

3. Peyser, "James, Race," 51.

4. Freedman, "The Poetics," 477.

5. Henry James, *The Golden Bowl* (1904; Baltimore: Penguin Books, 1966), 30. Subsequent references are cited parenthetically.

6. Of course, the image of the plotting Italian assassin had a history dating as far back as the early seventeenth century. In 1606, for example, the Englishman Thomas Palmer warned his countrymen not to go to Italy unless they wanted to learn arts such as stiletto stabbing, poisoning, intriguing, and treason. See Luigi Barzini, *The Italians* (1964. New York: Atheneum, 1981), 27. As Barzini says, "The number of Italian traitors, cheats, pimps, spies, and murderers in nordic literature becomes practically endless from that time on." This parade of crafty and cowardly Italian killers begins in Elizabethan drama, proceeds through Gothic novels and nineteenth-century historical romances, and continues to this day with Sicilian gangsters.

7. Freedman, "The Poetics," 481.

8. Jolly, *Henry James*, 171

9. Maves, *Sensuous Pessimism*, 132.

10. Peter Conn, *The Divided Mind: Ideology and Imagination in America, 1898–1917* (Cambridge: Cambridge University Press, 1983), 27–29.

11. Henry James, *Italian Hours*, ed. John Auchard (1909; New York: Penguin Books, 1995), 19.

12. Peyser, "James, Race," 50–51, 60–61.

13. Peyser, "James, Race," 60.

14. Peyser, "James, Race," 55.

15. Maves, *Sensuous Pessimism*, 146.

16. Wegelin, *Image of Europe*, 138.

17. Maves, *Sensuous Pessimism*, 140.
18. Wegelin, *Image of Europe*, 139–140.
19. Jolly, *Henry James*, 193–194.
20. Seltzer, *James and Art of Power*, 71.
21. Peyser, "James, Race," 57.
22. Wegelin, *Image of Europe*, 140.
23. Maves, *Sensuous Pessimism*, 149.
24. Freedman, "The Poetics," 482–484, 494.
25. John F. Sears, Introduction to Henry James, *The American Scene* (1907; New York: Penguin Books, 1994), ix.
26. Conn, *Divided Mind*, 31.
27. Sears, Introduction, xi–xii.
28. Qtd. in Sears, Introduction, xxi.
29. Ross Posnock, *The Trial of Curiosity: Henry James, William James, and the Challenge of Modernity* (New York: Oxford University Press, 1991), vii.
30. Qtd. in Posnock, *Trial of Curiosity*, vii.
31. Sears, Introduction, xxii.
32. Conn, *Divided Mind*, 1, 15, 6. Some twelve million immigrants had arrived during James's long absence from the United States, this in a country whose total population was just seventy-five million in 1900. By the early 1900s, Americans were startled by the realization that upwards of three-fourths of the population of New York, Boston, Chicago and Cleveland consisted of first-generation immigrants and their children, many of them living in urban slums.
33. Conn, *Divided Mind*, 37.
34. Sara Blair, *Henry James and the Writing of Race and Nation* (New York: Cambridge University Press, 1996), 158–59.
35. See John Sears, Introduction; Conn, *Divided Mind*; Mark Seltzer, "Advertising America: *The American Scene*," in *Henry James and the Art of Power* (Ithaca, N.Y.: Cornell University Press, 1984); Kevin R. McNamara, "Building Culture: The Two New Yorks of Henry James's *The American Scene*," *Prospects* 18 (1993): 121–151; Posnock, *Trial of Curiosity*; and Blair, *Writing of Race*. Sears and Conn situate James in the nativist camp of his Boston Brahmin friend, Senator Henry Cabot Lodge, who advocated immigration restriction of alien races as a way to preserve America's Anglo-Saxon heritage and the democratic traditions that were believed to be rooted in Anglo-Saxon racial characteristics. Mark Seltzer extends the Sears/Conn critique, situating James within emergent professional discourses that sought to control the poor, the criminal, and the immigrant, which were often seen as one and the same (131, 139). Kevin R. McNamara sees a much more conflicted James. McNamara calls James a "paradoxical anti-assimilationist" who saw "the power of the margin—the homogenous, genteel Boston and New York of his youth as well as the immigrants' cultural consciousness—as alternatives to America's 'great gray wash'" (125). Ross Posnock and Sara Blair posit a James who stands alongside the contemporary social critic Randolph Bourne in rejecting Anglo-Saxon hegemony and racial anxiety. Posnock says James acknowledges that "the alien must be honored as alien, as other, unassimilable to one's own needs" (156). Blair sees James moving away from Anglo-Saxonism to a more problematic "internationalist" or "cosmopolitan" approach (9).

36. Henry James, *The American Scene* (1907; New York: Penguin Books, 1994), 66. Subsequent references are cited parenthetically.
37. Blair, *Writing of Race*, 164–165.
38. Posnock, *Trial of Curiosity*, 165.
39. Conn, *Divided Mind*, 42.
40. Conn, *Divided Mind*, 31.
41. McNamara, "Building Culture," 128–129.
42. Qtd. in Peyser, "James, Race," 50.
43. McNamara, "Building Culture," 137, 144.
44. Sears, Introduction, xiv.
45. Posnock, *Trial of Curiosity*, 153.
46. Blair, *Writing of Race*, 174.
47. Larzer Ziff, *Return Passages: Great American Travel Writing, 1780–1910* (New Haven, Conn.: Yale University Press, 2000), 268.
48. McNamara, "Building Culture," 137.

Chapter 5

1. Mark Twain, *Pudd'nhead Wilson and Those Extraordinary Twins*, ed. Sidney E. Berger (1894; New York: W.W. Norton & Company, 1980), 119, 122.
2. Robert A. Wiggins, *Mark Twain: A Jackleg Novelist* (Seattle: University of Washington Press, 1964); George Feinstein, "Vestigia in *Pudd'nhead Wilson*," *Twainian* (May 1942): 1–3; and Robert Rowlette, *Mark Twain's Pudd'nhead Wilson: The Development and Design* (Bowling Green, Ohio: Bowling Green University Popular Press, 1971) are among the critics who have seen the twins as undermining the unity of *Pudd'nhead Wilson*.
3. "Personal Habits of the Siamese Twins" (1875) was based on Chinese Siamese twins who were slave owners in North Carolina earlier in the century.
4. Another tempered and thoughtful English review said "the Twins altogether seem to have very little *raison d'etre* in the book." Both reviews quoted in Mark Twain, *Pudd'nhead Wilson and Those Extraordinary Twins*, Sidney E. Berger. ed. (1894; New York: W.W. Norton & Company, 1980), 290–291. Nearly seventy years later, critic Robert A. Wiggins repeated those charges, arguing that the twins are not only "irrelevant" but "distracting," with their "exotic personalities" representing a "jarring note on the landscape of Dawson's Landing" (Wiggins 109). More recent critics have seen the Italian twins as frauds who contribute to the work's irony [Murial B. Williams, "The Unmasking of Meaning: A Study of the Twins in *Pudd'nhead Wilson*," *Mississippi Quarterly* 33 (Winter 1979–1980): 40]; as Twain's burlesque characterization of contrary wills [Lawrence Howe, "Race, Genealogy, and Genre in Mark Twain's *Pudd'nhead Wilson*," *Nineteenth Century Literature* 46 (March 1992): 511]; as symbols of man's lack of brotherhood [Jo Ella Powell Exley, "Brothers under the Skin? The Use of Twins in *Pudd'nhead Wilson and Those Extraordinary Twins*," *Mark Twain Journal* 21 (Fall 1983): 10]; and as an emblem of both continuity and discontinuity, and identity and difference, hovering over Twain's text, foreclosing closure [Nancy Fredricks, "Twain's Indelible Twins," *Nineteenth-Century Literature* 43 (March 1989): 499]. Critics who have noticed the

Capello brothers' Italian antecedents have failed to explore their Italianness in any depth. For most critics, the twins' twinness is their salient feature, not their nationality or race, which is often overlooked, or, if noted, never explored in depth.

5. See Eric Sundquist, "Mark Twain and Homer Plessy," in Susan Gillman and Forrest G. Robinson, eds., *Mark Twain's Pudd'nhead Wilson: Race, Conflict, and Culture* (Durham, N.C.: Duke University Press, 1990). I am deeply indebted to Sundquist for inspiring my interest in (and much of my exploration of) *Pudd'nhead Wilson*.

6. The tour reportedly was one of the first, if not the first, organized transatlantic pleasure parties from American. Here was "a new American middle class trying out its wealth and leisure and about to put its homegrown culture to a kind of test among the monuments of the Old World" [Justin Kaplan, *Mr. Clemens and Mark Twain: A Biography* (New York: Simon and Schuster, 1966), 42].

7. The *Quaker City* pilgrims and Twain himself, as represented in his narrator, are a contradictory lot, both "innocents" and "vandals." They are parochial, chauvinistic, vulgar, acquisitive, and skeptical, but also gullible; they "responded docilely and with awe if not understanding to high European culture" (Kaplan 42).

8. Kaplan, *Mr. Clemens*, 48. As William W. Stowe has shown, Twain, like many other nineteenth-century writers, found in travel writing "an established, respectable, and relatively undemanding literary genre" that "offered aspiring authors a ready-made form, a surefire subject, and the opportunity to adopt one of several widely respected cultural roles." *Going Abroad: European Travel in Nineteenth-Century American Culture* (Princeton, N.J.: Princeton University Press, 1994), 11.

9. Mark Twain, *The Innocents Abroad or The New Pilgrims' Progress* (1869; Norwalk, Conn.: The Heritage Press, 1962), 188–189. Subsequent references are cited parenthetically.

10. Twain writes: "A mile away, a grove-plumed promontory juts far into the lake and glasses its palace in the blue depths; in midstream a boat is cutting the shining surface and leaving a long track behind, like a ray of light; the mountains beyond are veiled in a dreamy purple haze; far in the opposite direction a tumbled mass of domes and verdant slopes and valleys bars the lake, and here, indeed, does distance lend enchantment to the view—for on this broad canvas, sun and clouds and the richest of the atmospheres have blended a thousand tints together, and over its surface the filmy lights and shadows drift, hour after hour, and glorify it with a beauty that seems reflected out of Heaven itself. Beyond all question, this is the most voluptuous scene we have yet looked upon" (143).

11. Larzer Ziff, *Return Passages: Great American Travel Writing, 1780–1910* (New Haven, Conn.: Yale University Press, 2000), 187–188.

12. Mark Twain, *A Tramp Abroad* (1880; New York: Penguin Books, 1997), 99–100.

13. For example, in the late 1880s Twain on at least three occasions talks about buying the remains of Christopher Columbus and either burying them under the Statue of Liberty or the Capitol rotunda, or bringing them to the "fair of '02." *Mark Twain's Notebook*, ed. Albert Bigelow Paine (New York: Harper & Brothers Publishers, 1935), 190, 192, 209. In *Pudd'nhead Wilson*, he offers this classic maxim from Pudd'nhead's Calendar: "October 12, the Discovery. It was wonderful to find America, but it would have been more wonderful to miss it" (113).

14. Kaplan, *Mr. Clemens*, 33.

15. In a 1906 essay on Howells, Twain says, "I read his *Venetian Days* (sic) about forty years ago. I compare it with his paper on Machiavelli in a late number of *Harper's*, and I cannot find that his English has suffered any impairment." *The Complete Essays of Mark Twain*, ed. Charles Nieder (Garden City, N.Y.: Doubleday & Company, 1963), 400. Twain praised *A Hazard of New Fortunes* as "a great book" because of the "high art by which it is made to preach its great sermon." *Mark Twain–Howells Letters: The Correspondence of Samuel L. Clemens and William Dean Howells 1872–1910*, eds. Henry Nash Smith and William M. Gibson. 2 vols. (Cambridge, Mass.: The Belknap Press of Harvard University Press, 1960), 2:579.

16. The protagonist Basil March's sentimental and superficial reaction to the Italian immigrants in New York City stands in contrast to Howells's more penetrating treatment of Italians in his travel book, *Venetian Life*, which is one of the few accounts of the nineteenth century that puts Italian character and experience into a historical, political, and sociological context. Howells seems to be critiquing the tendency of Basil March and other Americans to aestheticize and sentimentalize the Italian in America.

17. *Mark Twain's Notebooks & Journals*, gen. ed. Frederick Anderson. 3 vols. (Berkeley: University of California Press, 1975–), 3:173; 3:405–406.

18. Twain, *Complete Essays*, 167.

19. Guy Cardwell, *The Man Who Was Mark Twain: Images and Ideologies* (New Haven, Conn.: Yale University Press, 1991), 188, 186.

20. *Twain–Howells Letters*, 1:241.

21. *Twain–Howells Letters*, 1:262.

22. Twain, *Complete Essays*, 8.

23. Twain, *Complete Essays*, 236.

24. Twain, *Complete Essays*, 248.

25. Shelley Fisher Fishkin, *Was Huck Black? Mark Twain and African-American Voices* (New York: Oxford University Press, 1993), 122–126.

26. Andrew Hoffman, *Inventing Mark Twain: The Lives of Samuel Langhorne Clemens* (New York: William Morrow and Company, 1997), 290, 340.

27. Ziff, *Return Passages*, 213–218.

28. His *A Connecticut Yankee in King Arthur's Court* had a mixed reception in England in 1889. The next year both his mother and his wife's mother died. There were the usual money problems, but now becoming graver, as Twain's heavy investments in both the Paige typesetter and in his publishing company were proving to be serious financial drains.

29. Two years before *Pudd'nhead Wilson* began serialization in *The Century*, the magazine published Henry Cabot Lodge's piece, "The Distribution of Ability in the United States," which purportedly showed "the enormous predominance" of the English racial strain in contributions to America's development, while suggesting the inferiority of all non-English groups. "[T]hereafter Lodge concentrated his fire on the new immigration, arguing that it presented a supreme danger transcending political or economic considerations: it threatened 'a great and perilous change in the very fabric of our race'" [John Higham, *Strangers in the Land: Patterns of American Nativism, 1860–1925* (New York: Atheneum, 1970), 141–42]. Also in 1891, Lodge wrote two

pieces for the *North American Review*: "The Restriction of Immigration" and "Lynch Law and Unrestricted Immigration."

30. See generally, among others: Matthew Frye Jacobson, *Whiteness of a Different Color: European Immigrants and the Alchemy of Race* (Cambridge, Mass.: Harvard University Press, 1998); James R. Barrett and David Roediger, "Inbetween Peoples: Race, Nationality and the 'New Immigrant' Working Class," *Journal of American Ethnic History* 16 (Spring 1997): 3–44; Gunther Peck, *Reinventing Free Labor: Padrones and Immigrant Workers in the North American West, 1880–1930* (New York: Cambridge University Press, 2000); John Higham, *Strangers in the Land: Patterns of American Nativism, 1860–1925* (New York: Atheneum, 1970); Michael La Sorte, *La Merica: Images of the Italian Greenhorn Experience* (Philadelphia: Temple University Press, 1985); Patrick J. Gallo, *Old Bread, New Wine* (Chicago: Nelson-Hall, 1981); Salvatore J. LaGumina, ed. and introduction, *WOP!—A Documentary History of Anti-Italian Discrimination in the United States* (New York: Straight Arrow Books, 1973).

31. Higham, *Strangers*, 66.

32. The slavery metaphor was not always exaggerated. In April 1893, *The Forum* ran a piece by an Italian researcher, titled "Italian Immigrants and Their Enslavement," that stated: "There have been cases where Italian laborers have suffered actual slavery, and in trying to escape have been fired upon by the guards and murdered, as happened not long ago in the Adirondacks." S. Merlino, "Italian Immigrants and their Enslavement," *Forum* 15 (April 1893): 187.

33. Higham, *Strangers*, 90.

34. During the decade, more than twenty-five Italians would be lynched or murdered by mobs in Colorado, West Virginia, Mississippi, and Louisiana, according to Luciano J. Iorizzo and Salvatore Mondello, *The Italian-Americans* (New York: Twayne Publishers, 1971), 223.

35. Henry Cabot Lodge, "Lynch Law and Unrestricted Immigration," *North American Review* 152 (Jan. 1891): 604. Lodge said the mob "acted on the belief that these men were guilty of the crime with which they were charged; that the crime was the work of a secret society known as the Mafia; and that the failure of the jury to convict was due either to terror of this secret organization or to bribery by its agents" (602).

36. One newspaper identified the suspects as "Sicilians, whose low, receding foreheads, repulsive countenances and slovenly attire, proclaimed their brutal natures." Jerre Mangione and Ben Morreale, *La Storia: Five Centuries of the Italian American Experience* (New York: HarperCollins Publishers, 1992), 205–206. The lynch mob hanged two Italians, and citizens either beat or took target practice with the swinging bodies. In one case the crowd roared out, "Kill the fuckin' Dago, kill him!" (209–210). *The New York Times*, then a respected newspaper, rationalized the killings in two editorials, saying that the Sicilians were "sneaking and cowardly . . . the descendants of bandits and assassins, who have transported to this country the lawless passions, the cut-throat practices and oath-bound societies of their native country, [who] are to us a pest without mitigation." Qtd. in Mangione 209–211. Also, see generally: Richard Gambino, *Vendetta: The True Story of the Largest Lynching in U.S. History* (Toronto: Guernica, 1998); Marco Rimanelli and Sheryl L. Postman, eds., *The 1891 New Orleans Lynching and U.S.–Italian Relations: A Look Back* (New York:

Peter Lang, 1992); Jacobson, *Whiteness of a Different Color*; Barrett and Roediger, "Inbetween Peoples."

37. Writing in *How the Other Half Lives*, Riis condemned the mingling of Italians, blacks, and tramps in the area of Thompson Street, saying there could be "no greater abomination." Jacob Riis, *How the Other Half Lives: Studies Among the Tenements of New York* (1890; New York: Dover Publications, 1971), 119. Riis does not elaborate on this theme, other than to equate this mingling with "common debauch" and to summarily conclude that it is immoral.

38. In 1890, Italians constituted nearly two-thirds of the nearly four thousand immigrants who arrived in New Orleans. The following year, nearly three thousand Italians arrived, all but thirty-five from Sicily, according to George E. Cunningham, "The Italian: A Hindrance to White Solidarity in Louisiana 1890–98," *Journal of Negro History* 50 (Jan. 1965): 23. See also: Donna Gabaccia, *Militants and Migrants: Rural Sicilians Become American Workers* (New Brunswick, N.J.: Rutgers University Press, 1988); Jean Ann Scarpaci, *Italian Immigrants in Louisiana's Sugar Parishes: Recruitment, Labor Conditions, and Community Relations, 1880–1910* (New York: Arno Press, 1980); Jean Ann Scarpaci, "Labor for Louisiana's Sugar Fields: An Experiment in Immigrant Recruitment," *Italian Americana* 7 (1981): 19–41; Barrett and Roediger, "Inbetween Peoples."

39. Arnold Shankman, "The Menacing Influx: Afro-Americans on Italian Immigration to the South, 1880–1915," *Mississippi Quarterly* 31 (1977–78): 68.

40. See Gabaccia, *Militants and Migrants*; Scarpaci, *Italian Immigrants in Louisiana's Sugar Parishes*; George E. Cunningham, "The Italian: A Hindrance to White Solidarity in Louisiana 1890–98," *Journal of Negro History* 50 (Jan. 1965): 22–36; Arnold Shankman, "The Menacing Influx," 67–88. Relations were cordial, if not warm. Some Italian businesses catered to blacks. There is disagreement on the nature and extent of Italian–black social relations, but initially, at least, Italians apparently showed little racial prejudice against the black.

41. Twain, *The Innocents Abroad*, 175.

42. Caricatures of the Italian immigrants began appearing in local newspapers. *The Mascot*, the same paper that would later describe the New Orleans lynching in delightful detail, drew the Italian as a dirty, bearded, hook-nosed man carrying a battered basket filled with bananas. Italian fruit peddlers were pictured with thick broad mouths and hooked noses, a caricature that seems to incorporate facial elements from caricatures of blacks and Jews. A series of cartoons, titled "The Italian Population," ran in October 1890. One panel, captioned "The Way to Dispose of Them," depicted a group of immigrants in a cage being lowered into the river (Mangione, *La Storia*, 201).

43. Mangione, *La Storia*, 203, 212.

44. Higham, *Strangers*, 169.

45. At least two communities reportedly lynched Italians for associating with blacks on terms of near equality. And although some blacks participated in the lynching of Italians accused of murdering a native-born white in Hahnville, Louisiana, in 1896, many black sympathizers attended the burial of the victims, prompting white fears of blacks helping Italians seeking revenge for the lynching. Cunningham, "The Italian: A Hindrance," 25–26, 32, 36; Mangione, *La Storia*, 212.

46. Alexander J. Karlin, "The Italo-American Incident of 1891 and the Road to Reunion," *Journal of Southern History* 8 (May 1942): 244.

47. In a short article in the Chicago *American* titled "What Makes the Color Line?," Cable attacked the idea that there was any natural, instinctive antagonism between the white and black races. Cable also attacked in speeches southern moves to disenfranchise the blacks, and eventually would speak out in favor of renewed Federal intervention in the post-Reconstruction South. Louis D. Rubin, Jr., *George Washington Cable: The Life and Times of a Southern Heretic* (New York: Pegasus, 1969), 204, 207, 210.

48. Arthur G. Pettit, *Mark Twain & the South* (Lexington: The University Press of Kentucky, 1974), 131. In early 1882, Cable hosted Twain and Joel Chandler Harris in his home city of New Orleans. In 1884, Cable visited Twain in Hartford. They talked for hours, much of the time discussing race relations, a "deep subject" on which Cable had developed a refined perspective, according to Twain. Andrew Hoffman, *Inventing Mark Twain: The Lives of Samuel Langhorne Clemens* (New York: William Morrow and Company, 1997), 308. From late November 1884 through February 1885, Twain and Cable shared a successful reading tour that took them to some seventy cities. In a letter to his wife, Twain wrote, "Cable is a great man" whose "greatness will be recognized" if he continued to fight for the Negro (Kaplan 265). Although Twain was less impressed with Cable's religiosity, Cable "did convert him to a faith in the fundamental equality of all people" (Hoffman 314).

49. Mark Twain, *Mark Twain's Notebooks & Journals*, gen. ed. Frederick Anderson. 3 vols. (Berkeley: University of California Press, 1975–), 3: 88.

50. Sherburn calls the lynchers' manhood into question, telling the mob, "If any real lynching's going to be done it will be done in the dark, Southern fashion; and when they come they'll bring their masks, and fetch a *man* along." Mark Twain, *Adventures of Huckleberry Finn* (1884; New York: W.W. Norton & Company, 1962), 116–118. As early as 1869, Twain satirized lynching in an article titled "Only a Nigger" for the *Buffalo Express*. As Twain's indignation grew in the 1880s and 1890s, he began collecting incidents for a book on lynching. Twain worked on two lynching-related projects. The first was an article, "The United States of Lyncherdom" (1901), intended for the *North American Review* but not published until after Twain's death. The second project was a proposed subscription-book historical anthology of lynching in America for which he would write the introduction. One has to wonder whether the New Orleans lynching, with eleven Italians dead, was not high on Twain's list. Twain eventually accepted his publisher's advice and set aside the project as dangerous to the sales of his other works in the South (Pettit, *Mark Twain & the South*, 135–136).

51. Sundquist, "Mark Twain and Homer Plessy," 47, 69. Sundquist appears to be the first critic to pay close attention to the twins' ethnicity, touching on their Italianness in his broader examination of racial themes in *Pudd'nhead Wilson*. Sundquist historicizes *Pudd'nhead Wilson* in the context of late nineteenth-century racial problems, particularly lynching, Jim Crow laws, and the Supreme Court's "separate-but-equal" ruling in *Plessy v. Ferguson* (1896). Arguing that it is not unimportant that the twins are Italian, Sundquist links the tale of these "immigrants" to the main story of the racial changelings, Tom Driscoll and Chambers. Obviously, I am greatly indebted to Sundquist's richly perceptive reading.

52. Williams, "The Unmasking of Meaning," 42–43.

53. Twain, *Pudd'nhead Wilson*, 28. Subsequent references are cited parenthetically.

54. In the late 1840s, Margaret Fuller's dispatches from Italy for Horace Greeley's *New-York Tribune* specifically link America's "horrible cancer of Slavery" and the foreign oppression of European peoples such as the Italians and Poles. *These Sad But Glorious Days: Dispatches from Europe, 1846–1850*, eds. Larry J. Reynolds and Susan Belasco Smith (New Haven, Conn.: Yale University Press, 1991), 165. In 1860, Karl Marx wrote in the *New-York Tribune* that "no country or no people have suffered such terrible slavery, conquest and foreign oppression and no people have struggled so strenuously for their emancipation as Sicily and Sicilians." Qtd. in Mangione, *La Storia*, 58. William Dean Howells wrote of the "slavery" of the Venetians in *Venetian Life*, a book Twain admired. William Dean Howells, *Venetian Life* (1866; Marlboro, Vt.: The Marlboro Press, 1989), 292. In 1893, just about the time Twain would be writing *Pudd'nhead Wilson*, *The Forum* ran an article titled "Italian Immigrants and Their Enslavement," which featured not only metaphorical but literal examples of Italian immigrants enslaved in America.

55. Barbara Ladd, *Nationalism and the Color Line in George W. Cable, Mark Twain, and William Faulkner* (Baton Rouge: Louisiana State University Press, 1996), 107–108. Ladd reads "the personal history of the twins in terms of the romance of the American Revolution," but says that the Puritan Angelo and Cavalier Luigi "function as tools for the anatomizing of U.S. pretensions toward a redemptive national unity."

56. See generally John Dickie, "Stereotypes of the Italian South 1860–1900," in Robert Lumley and Jonathan Morris, eds. *The New History of the Italian South: The Mezzogiorno Revisited* (Exeter, England: University of Exeter Press, 1997); Gabriella Gribaudi, "Images of the South: The *Mezzogiorno* as Seen by Insiders and Outsiders," in Lumley and Morris, *The New History of the Italian South*; David A. J. Richards, *Italian American: The Racializing of an Ethnic Identity* (New York: New York University Press, 1999).

57. Mangione, *La Storia*, 73, 147, 247–248.

58. See Henry Cabot Lodge, "The Restriction of Immigration," *North American Review* 152 (Jan. 1891): 31; Francis A. Walker, "Restriction of Immigration," *Atlantic Monthly* 77 (June 1896): 828–829; George J. Manson, "The 'Foreign Element' in New York City. V.—The Italians," *Harper's Weekly* 34 (Oct. 18, 1890): 818; Jacob A. Riis, *The Battle with the Slum* (New York: Macmillan, 1902), 176–177.

59. William P. Dillingham, *Reports of the Immigration Commission: Dictionary of Races or Peoples* (Washington, D.C.: Government Printing Office, 1911), 81–85.

60. Hoffman, *Inventing Mark Twain*, 255.

61. Paul R. Baker, *The Fortunate Pilgrims: Americans in Italy, 1800–1860* (Cambridge, Mass.: Harvard University Press, 1964), 1.

62. Qtd in Mangione, *La Storia*, 205–206.

63. Gregg Camfield, *Sentimental Twain: Samuel Clemens in the Maze of Moral Philosophy* (Philadelphia: University of Pennsylvania Press, 1994), 191.

64. Michael Kammen, *Mystic Chords of Memory: The Transformation of Tradition in American Culture* (New York: Alfred A. Knopf, 1991), 220–221. Kammen says many Americans, including the eminent Harvard geologist Nathaniel S. Shaler, really did believe in the biological implications of bloodlines and literally meant it when he said in 1888 that "a man is what his ancestral experience has made him."

65. Camfield, *Sentimental Twain*, 189.

66. Jacob A. Riis, *How the Other Half Lives: Studies Among the Tenements of New York* (1890; New York: Dover Publications, 1971), 44.

67. See Twain's essay "Dueling," in *The Writings of Mark Twain*, 37 vols. (New York: Gabriel Wells, 1922–1925), 29: 229.

68. Driscoll here sounds very much like the European duelists, satirized in Twain's essay "Dueling," who would disqualify from the field of honor any opponent suspected of dishonest behavior such as cheating at cards. Twain, *The Writings of Mark Twain*, 29: 227–228.

69. Qtd. in Richard Gambino, *Vendetta: The True Story of the Largest Lynching in U.S. History* (Toronto: Guernica, 1998), 97.

70. Camfield, *Sentimental Twain*, 187. Camfield says Twain "implies a parallel between the Twins—ostensibly freakish, natural outcasts who had traded notoriety for distinction—and Wilson."

71. In this essay, Twain says that although religious persecution of the Jews has ended, race prejudice against the group would continue. Addressing the Jews, Twain says, "You will always be by ways and habits and predilections substantially strangers—foreigners—wherever you are, and that will probably keep the race prejudice against you alive." Twain uses the term foreigner in the German sense to mean stranger. He applies both terms to the Italian twins. Here Twain is underscoring the intensity of the period's race thinking, even while acknowledging the cultural and social differences that were often being equated with racial differences. *The Complete Essays of Mark Twain*, ed. Charles Nieder (Garden City, N.Y.: Doubleday & Company, 1963), 248.

72. T. T. Munger, "Immigration by Passport," *Century* 35 (March 1888): 798.

Conclusion

1. Alberto Pecorini, "The Italians in the United States," *Forum* 44 (Jan. 1911): 21.

2. See John Higham, *Strangers in the Land: Patterns of American Nativism, 1860–1925* (New York: Atheneum, 1970), 183–184. In southern Illinois, after an Italian and two native-born Americans were killed in a street brawl, a surviving Italian was quickly lynched, with apparent collusion from the local mayor. A few months later, an Italian, arrested on faint suspicion of conspiring to assassinate a mine superintendent, was dragged from the jail and hanged.

3. Alan M. Kraut, *Silent Travelers: Germs, Genes, and the "Immigrant Menace"* (New York: Basic Books, 1994), 120–121.

4. Qtd. in Kraut, *Silent Travelers*, 109. Although mortality studies would later prove Ross wrong, many Americans of the period were willing to believe Ross and others who made sweeping statements about race, turning details into generalizations and generalizations into immutable laws.

5. Samuel L. Baily, *Immigrants in the Land of Promise: Italians in Buenos Aires and New York City, 1870–1914* (Ithaca, N.Y.: Cornell University Press, 1999), 87.

6. Donna Haraway, "Teddy Bear Patriarchy: Taxidermy in the Garden of Eden, New York City, 1908–1936," in Amy Kaplan and Donald E. Pease, eds., *Cultures of*

United States Imperialism (Durham, N.C.: Duke University Press, 1993), 282. Grant was a successful corporation lawyer, staunch conservationist, trustee of the American Museum of Natural History in New York, and powerful secretary of the New York Zoological Society.

7. Madison Grant, *The Passing of the Great Race or the Racial Basis of European History*. 4th ed. (New York: Charles Scribner's Sons, 1936), 27. Grant says the Nordics are "a race of soldiers, sailors, adventurers and explorers, but above all, of rulers, organizers and aristocrats . . . domineering, individualistic, self-reliant and jealous of their personal freedom both in political and religious systems and as a result they are usually Protestant" (228). Subsequent references cited parenthetically.

8. Lothrop Stoddard, *The Rising Tide of Color Against White World-Supremacy* (London: Chapman and Hall, Limited, 1922). In his introduction, Grant claims that the "great hope of the future here in America lies in the realization of the working class that competition of the Nordic with the alien is fatal, whether the latter be the lowly immigrants from southern or eastern Europe or whether he be the more obviously dangerous Oriental against whose standards of living the white man cannot compete" (xxx–xxxi).

9. John Paul Russo, "From Italophilia to Italophobia: Representations of Italian Americans in the Early Gilded Age," *Differentia* 6–7 (Spring/Autumn 1994): 51.

10. John Paul Russo, "The Harvard Italophiles: Longfellow, Lowell, and Norton," in Joseph Cheyne and Lilla Maria Crisafulli Jones, eds., *L'Esilio romantico: forme di un conflitto* (Bari, Italy: Adriatica Editrice, 1990), 323, 303–304.

11. Higham, *Strangers*, 125.

12. Higham, *Strangers*, 189.

13. Patrick J. Gallo, *Old Bread, New Wine* (Chicago: Nelson-Hall, 1981), 135–136.

14. Kathie Friedman-Kasaba, *Memories of Migration: Gender, Ethnicity, and Work in the Lives of Jewish and Italian Women in New York, 1870–1924* (Albany: State University of New York Press, 1996), 99.

15. William P. Dillingham, *Reports of the Immigration Commission: Dictionary of Races or Peoples* (Washington, D.C.: Government Printing Office, 1911), 1–8. The dictionary included "more than six hundred subjects," according to its writers/editors, "covering all the important and many of the obscure branches or divisions of the human family" then furnishing America's immigrants or likely to do so in the future.

16. Matthew Frye Jacobson, *Whiteness of a Different Color: European Immigrants and the Alchemy of Race* (Cambridge, Mass.: Harvard University Press, 1998), 79.

17. Dillingham, *Reports*, 81–84. The dictionary says that north Italians include those natives (and their descendants) of the Po River basin (Piedmontese, Lombards, Venetians, and Emelians) and the Italian districts of France, Switzerland, and Austria. All the people of the peninsula proper and the islands of Sicily and Sardinia are south Italians.

18. John Dickie, "Stereotypes of the Italian South 1860–1900," in Robert Lumley and Jonathan Morris, eds., *The New History of the Italian South: The Mezzogiorno Revisited* (Exeter, England: University of Exeter Press, 1997), 115–119.

19. James R. Barrett and David Roediger, "Inbetween Peoples: Race, Nationality and the 'New Immigrant' Working Class," *Journal of American Ethnic History* 16 (Spring 1997): 14.

20. Barrett and Roediger, "Inbetween Peoples," 10; Jacobson, *Whiteness*, 201.
21. Barrett and Roediger, "Inbetween Peoples," 11.
22. Jacobson, *Whiteness*, 7–8, 201, 225.
23. Lawrence Levine, *The Opening of the American Mind: Canons, Culture, and History* (Boston: Beacon Press, 1996), 124.
24. Micaela di Leonardo, *Exotics at Home: Anthropologies, Others, American Modernity* (Chicago: The University of Chicago Press, 1998), 109.

BIBLIOGRAPHY

Addams, Jane. *Twenty Years at Hull-House*. 1910. New York: Signet Classic/Penguin, 1961.

Agnew, Jean-Christophe. "The Consuming Vision of Henry James." In *The Culture of Consumption*, eds. Richard Wightman Fox and T. J. Jackson Lears. New York: Pantheon Books, 1983.

Alba, Richard D. *Italian Americans: Into the Twilight of Ethnicity*. Englewood Cliffs, N.J.: Prentice-Hall Inc., 1985.

Alland, Sr., Alexander. *Jacob Riis: Photographer & Citizen*. Millerton, N.Y.: Aperture, 1974.

Amfitheatrof, Erik. *The Children of Columbus: An Informal History of the Italians in the New World*. Boston: Little, Brown and Co., 1973.

Amfitheatrof, Erik. *The Enchanted Ground: Americans in Italy, 1760–1980*. Boston: Little, Brown and Co., 1980.

Anderson, Frederick. Introduction to *Pudd'nhead Wilson/Those Extraordinary Twins*, by Mark Twain. 1894. San Francisco: Chandler, 1968.

Appel, John J. "American Negro and Immigrant Experiences. Similarities and Differences." *American Quarterly* 18 (Spring 1966): 95–103.

Appel, John J. *The New Immigration*. New York: Pitman Publishing Corp., 1971.

Archdeacon, Thomas J. *Becoming American: An Ethnic History*. New York: The Free Press, 1983.

Arthur, John. *The Best Years of the Century: Richard Watson Gilder*, Scribner's Monthly *and* Century Magazine, *1870–1909*. Urbana: University of Illinois Press, 1981.

Bacigalupo, Fr. Leonard. "Some Religious Aspects Involving the Interaction of the Italians and the Irish." In *Italians and Irish in America*, ed. Francis X. Femminella. Staten Island, N.Y.: The American Italian Historical Association, 1985.

Bailey, Brigitte. "Travel Writing and the Metropolis: James, London, and *English Hours*." *American Literature* 67 (June 1995): 201–232.

Baily, Samuel L. *Immigrants in the Land of Promise: Italians in Buenos Aires and New York City, 1870–1914*. Ithaca, N.Y.: Cornell University Press, 1999.

Baker, Paul R. *The Fortunate Pilgrims: Americans in Italy, 1800–1860*. Cambridge, Mass.: Harvard University Press, 1964.

Barolini, Helen. *Images: A Pictorial History of Italian Americans*. Staten Island, N.Y.: Center for Migration Studies, 1981.

Barrett, James R., and David Roediger. "Inbetween Peoples: Race, Nationality and the 'New Immigrant' Working Class." *Journal of American Ethnic History* 16 (Spring 1997): 3–44.

Barzini, Luigi. *The Italians*. 1964. New York: Atheneum, 1981.

Bederman, Gail. *Manliness & Civilization: A Cultural History of Gender and Race in the United States, 1880–1917*. Chicago: The University of Chicago Press, 1995.

Belfiglio, Valentine J. "Italians in Small Town and Rural Texas." In *Italian Immigrants in Rural and Small Town America*, ed. Rudolph J. Vecoli. Staten Island, N.Y.: The American Italian Historical Association, 1987.

Blair, Sara. *Henry James and the Writing of Race and Nation*. New York: Cambridge University Press, 1996.

Boas, Franz. *The Mind of Primitive Man*. 1911. Revised edition. New York: The Macmillan Company, 1938.

Bodnar, John. *The Transplanted: A History of Immigrants in Urban America*. Bloomington: Indiana University Press, 1985.

Botein, Barbara. "The Hennessy Case: An Episode in Anti-Italian Nativism." *Louisiana History* 20 (1979): 261–279.

Boyer, Paul. *Urban Masses and Moral Order in America, 1820–1920*. Cambridge, Mass.: Harvard University Press, 1978.

Brace, Charles Loring. *The Dangerous Classes of New York, and Twenty Years' Work among Them*. New York: Wynkoop and Hallenbeck, 1872.

Bradbury, Malcolm. *Dangerous Pilgrimages: Transatlantic Mythologies and the Novel*. New York: Viking Press, 1996.

Brand, John M. "The Other Half: A Study of *Pudd'nhead Wilson*." *Mark Twain Journal* 21 (Spring 1983): 14–16.

Brodhead, Richard H. *Cultures of Letters: Scenes of Reading and Writing in Nineteenth-Century America*. Chicago: University of Chicago Press, 1993.

Brodkin, Karen. *How Jews Became White Folks and What That Says about Race in America*. New Brunswick, N.J.: Rutgers University Press, 1998.

Brooks, Van Wyck. *The Confident Years, 1885–1915*. New York: W.P. Dutton & Co., 1952.

Brooks, Van Wyck. *The Dream of Arcadia: American Writers and Artists in Italy, 1760–1915*. New York: W.P. Dutton & Co., 1958.

Brooks, Van Wyck. *The Pilgrimage of Henry James*. New York: Octagon Books, 1972.

Budd, Louis J. *Mark Twain: Social Philosopher*. Bloomington: Indiana University Press, 1962.

Buonomo, Leonardo. *Backward Glances: Exploring Italy, Reinterpreting America, 1831–1866*. Rutherford, N.J.: Fairleigh Dickinson University Press, 1995.

Camfield, Gregg. *Sentimental Twain: Samuel Clemens in the Maze of Moral Philosophy*. Philadelphia: University of Pennsylvania Press, 1994.

Campbell, Helen, Thomas W. Knox, and Thomas Byrnes. *Darkness and Daylight; or Lights and Shadows of New York Life*. Hartford, Conn.: The Hartford Publishing Company, 1896.

Campbell, Neil, and Alasdair Kean, eds. *American Cultural Studies: An Introduction to American Culture*. London and New York: Routledge, 1997.

Candeloro, Dominic. "Italian-Americans." In *Multiculturalism in the United States: A Comparative Guide to Acculturation and Ethnicity*, eds. John D. Buenker and Lorman A. Ratner. New York: Greenwood Press, 1992.

Cardwell, Guy. *The Man Who Was Mark Twain: Images and Ideologies*. New Haven, Conn.: Yale University Press, 1991.

Ceaser, James W. *Reconstructing America: The Symbol of America in Modern Thought*. New Haven, Conn.: Yale University Press, 1997.

Cerase, Francesco. "Nostalgia or Disenchantment: Considerations on Return Migration." In *The Italian Experience in the United States*, eds. Silvano M. Tomasi and Medeline H. Engel. New York: Center for Migration Studies, 1971.

Cheyne, Joseph, and Lilla Maria Crisafulli Jones, eds. *L'Esilio romantico: forme di un conflitto*. Bari, Italy: Adriatica Editrice, 1990.

Cleman, John. *George Washington Cable Revisited*. New York: Twayne Publishers, 1996.

Clifford, James. "Travelling Cultures." In *Cultural Studies*, eds. Lawrence Grossberg et al. New York: Routledge, 1992.

Clifford, James. "Notes on Theory and Travel." *Inscriptions* 5 (1989): 177–185.

Coffey, John W. *Twilight of Arcadia: American Landscape Painters in Rome, 1830–1880*. Brunswick, Maine: Bowdoin College Museum of Art, 1987.

Cohen, Miriam. *Workshop to Office: Two Generations of Italian Women in New York City, 1900–1950*. Ithaca, N.Y.: Cornell University Press, 1992.

Colajanni, Napoleon. "Homicide and the Italians." *Forum* 31 (March 1901): 62–68.

Conn, Peter. *The Divided Mind: Ideology and Imagination in America, 1898–1917*. Cambridge: Cambridge University Press, 1983.

Cook, Ann et al., eds. *City Life, 1865–1900: Views of Urban America*. New York: Praeger, 1973.

Cordasco, Francesco, ed. *The Italian American Experience: An Annotated and Classified Bibliographic Guide*. New York: B. Franklin, 1974.

Cordasco, Francesco, ed. *Italian Americans: A Guide to Information Services*. Detroit: Gale Publishing, 1978.

Cordasco, Francesco, ed. *Jacob Riis Revisited: Poverty and the Slum in Another Era*. Garden City, N.J.: Doubleday & Company, 1968.

Cordasco, Francesco, ed. *Studies in Italian American Social History*. Totowa, N.J.: Roman and Littlefield, 1975.

Cordasco, Francesco, and Salvatore LaGumina, eds. *Italians in the United States: A Bibliography of Reports, Texts, Critical Studies*. New York: Oriole, 1972.

Cordasco, Francesco, and Eugene Bucchioni, eds. *The Italians: Social Backgrounds of an American Group*. Clifton, N.J.: A.M. Kelley, 1974.

Coxe, John E. "The New Orleans Mafia Incident." *The Louisiana Historical Review* 20 (October 1937): 1066–1100.

Cunningham, George E. "The Italian, A Hindrance to White Solidarity in Louisiana 1890–98." *Journal of Negro History* 50 (January 1965): 22–36.

Curtis, George Ticknor. "The Law and the Lynchers." *North American Review* 152 (June 1891): 691–695.

D'Amato, Gaetano. "The Black Hand Myth." *North American Review* 187 (April 1908): 643–649.

DeConde, Alexander. "Endearment or Antipathy?: Nineteenth-Century American Attitudes toward Italians." *Ethnic Groups* 4 (1982): 131–148.

DeConde, Alexander. *Half Bitter, Half Sweet: An Excursion into Italian-American History*. New York: Scribner, 1971.

Deiss, Joseph Jay. *The Roman Years of Margaret Fuller*. New York: Thomas Y. Crowell Co., 1969.

Di Carlo, Denise Mangieri. "The Role of the Italian *Festa* in the United States." In *To See the Past More Clearly: The Enrichment of the Italian Heritage, 1890–1990*, ed. Harral E. Landry. Staten Island, N.Y.: The American Italian Historical Association, 1994.

Dickie, John. "Imagined Italies." In *Italian Cultural Studies: An Introduction*, eds. David Forgacs and Robert Lumley. New York: Oxford University Press, 1996.

Dickie, John. "Stereotypes of the Italian South 1860–1900." In *The New History of the Italian South: The Mezzogiorno Revisited*, eds. Robert Lumley and Jonathan Morris. Exeter, England: University of Exeter Press, 1997.

Dillingham, William P. *Reports of the Immigration Commission: Dictionary of Races or Peoples*. Washington, D.C.: Government Printing Office, 1911.

di Leonardo, Micaela. *Exotics at Home: Anthropologies, Others, American Modernity*. Chicago: The University of Chicago Press, 1998.

Dore, Grazia. "Some Social and Historical Aspects of Italian Emigration to America." *Journal of Social History* 2 (Winter 1968): 95–122.

Douglas, Ann. *The Feminization of American Culture*. New York: Alfred A. Knopf, 1977.

Duberman, Martin. *James Russell Lowell*. Boston: Houghton Mifflin Company, 1966.

Duggan, Christopher. *A Concise History of Italy*. Cambridge: Cambridge University Press, 1994.

Eble, Kenneth E. *Old Clemens and W.D.H.: The Story of a Remarkable Friendship*. Baton Rouge: Louisiana State University Press, 1985.

Edel, Leon. *Henry James: A Life*. New York: Harper & Row, Publishers, 1985.

Exley, Jo Ella Powell. "Brothers under the Skin? The Use of Twins in *Pudd'nhead Wilson* and Those Extraordinary Twins." *Mark Twain Journal* 21 (Fall 1983): 10–11.

Fasel, George. *Europe in Upheaval: The Revolutions of 1848*. Chicago: Rand McNally, 1970.

Feinstein, George. "Vestigia in *Pudd'nhead Wilson*." *Twainian* (May 1942): 1–3.

Femminella, Francis X., ed. *Italians and Irish in America*. Staten Island, N.Y.: The American Italian Historical Association, 1985.

Fiedler, Leslie. "As Free as Any Cretur . . ." *New Republic* 133 (August 15 and 22, 1955): 130–139.

Fine, David M. "Attitudes Toward Acculturation in the English Fiction of the Jewish Immigrant, 1900–1917." *American Jewish Historical Quarterly* 63 (September 1973): 45–56.

Fishkin, Shelley Fisher. "Race and Culture at the Century's End: A Social Context for *Pudd'nhead Wilson*." *Essays in Arts and Sciences* 19 (May 1990): 1–27.

Fishkin, Shelley Fisher. *Was Huck Black? Mark Twain and African-American Voices.* New York: Oxford University Press, 1993.

Foerster, Robert. *The Italian Emigration of Our Times.* New York: Russell & Russell, 1968.

Forgacs, David, and Robert Lumley, eds. *Italian Cultural Studies: An Introduction.* New York: Oxford University Press, 1996.

Foster, George. *New York by Gaslight.* New York: M.J. Ivers, circa 1850.

Franchot, Jenny. *Roads to Rome: The Antebellum Protestant Encounter with Catholicism.* Berkeley: University of California Press, 1994.

Fredricks, Nancy. "Twain's Indelible Twins." *Nineteenth-Century Literature* 43 (March 1989): 484–499.

Freedman, Jonathan. "The Poetics of Cultural Decline: Degeneracy, Assimilation, and the Jew in James's *The Golden Bowl.*" *American Literary History* 7 (Fall 1995): 477-499.

Fried, Lewis F. *Makers of the City.* Amherst: The University of Massachusetts Press, 1990.

Fried, Lewis F., and John Fierst, eds. *Jacob A. Riis: A Reference Guide.* Boston: G.K. Hall, 1977.

Friedman-Kasaba, Kathie. *Memories of Migration: Gender, Ethnicity, and Work in the Lives of Jewish and Italian Women in New York, 1870–1924.* Albany: State University of New York Press, 1996.

Fuller, Margaret. *These Sad But Glorious Days: Dispatches from Europe, 1846–1850*, eds. Larry J. Reynolds and Susan Belasco Smith. New Haven, Conn.: Yale University Press, 1991.

Gabaccia, Donna R. *From Sicily to Elizabeth Street: Housing and Social Change among Italian Immigrants, 1880–1930.* Albany: State University of New York Press, 1984.

Gabaccia, Donna R. *Italy's Many Diasporas.* Seattle: University of Washington Press, 2000.

Gabaccia, Donna R. *Militants and Migrants: Rural Sicilians Become American Workers.* New Brunswick, N.J.: Rutgers University Press, 1988.

Gallo, Patrick J. *Ethnic Alienation: The Italian Americans.* Rutherford, N.J.: Fairleigh Dickinson University Press, 1974.

Gallo, Patrick J. *Old Bread, New Wine.* Chicago: Nelson-Hall, 1981.

Gambino, Richard. *Vendetta: The True Story of the Largest Lynching in U.S. History.* Toronto: Guernica, 1998.

Gandal, Keith. *The Virtues of the Vicious: Jacob Riis, Stephen Crane, and the Spectacle of the Slum*. New York: Oxford University Press, 1997.

Gans, Herbert J. et al., eds. *On the Making of Americans: Essays in Honor of David Riesman*. Philadelphia: University of Pennsylvania Press, 1979.

Gans, Herbert J. *Urban Villagers: Group and Class in the Life of Italian-Americans*. New York: Free Press, 1962.

Gillman, Susan. *Dark Twins: Imposture and Identity in Mark Twain's America*. Chicago: The University of Chicago Press, 1989.

Gillman, Susan, and Forrest G. Robinson, eds. *Mark Twain's Pudd'nhead Wilson: Race, Conflict, and Culture*. Durham, N.C.: Duke University Press, 1990.

Gillman, Susan, and Robert L. Patten. "Dickens:Doubles::Twain:Twins." *Nineteenth-Century Fiction* 39 (March 1985): 441–458.

Gossett, Thomas F. *Race: The History of an Idea in America*. Dallas: Southern Methodist University Press, 1963.

Grant, Madison. *The Passing of the Great Race or the Racial Basis of European History*. 4th ed. New York: Charles Scribner's Sons, 1936.

Greenleaf, Barbara Kay. *American Fever: The Story of American Immigration*. New York: Four Winds Press, 1970.

Gribaudi, Gabriella. "Images of the South: The Mezzogiorno as Seen by Insiders and Outsiders." In *The New History of the Italian South: The Mezzogiorno Revisited*, eds. Robert Lumley and Jonathan Morris. Exeter, England: University of Exeter Press, 1997.

Hahamovitch, Cindy. *The Fruits of Their Labor: Atlantic Coast Farmworkers and the Making of Migrant Poverty, 1870–1945*. Chapel Hill: The University of North Carolina Press, 1997.

Hales, Peter B. *Silver Cities: The Photography of American Urbanization, 1839–1915*. Philadelphia: Temple University Press, 1984.

Handlin, Oscar. *The Uprooted*. 2nd enlarged edition. Boston: Little, Brown and Company, 1973.

Haraway, Donna. "Teddy Bear Patriarchy: Taxidermy in the Garden of Eden, New York City, 1908–1936." In *Cultures of United States Imperialism*, eds. Amy Kaplan and Donald E. Pease. Durham, N.C.: Duke University Press, 1993.

Harney, Robert F. "The Padrone and the Immigrant." *The Canadian Review of American Studies* 5 (Fall 1974): 101–118.

Higham, John. "The Re-orientation of American Culture in the 1890s." In *The Origins of Modern Consciousness*, ed. John Weiss. Detroit: Wayne State University Press, 1965.

Higham, John. *Strangers in the Land: Patterns of American Nativism, 1860–1925*. New York: Atheneum, 1970.

Hoffman, Andrew. *Inventing Mark Twain: The Lives of Samuel Langhorne Clemens*. New York: William Morrow and Company, 1997.

Holder, Alan. *Three Voyagers in Search of Europe: A Study of Henry James, Ezra Pound, and T.S. Eliot*. Philadelphia: University of Pennsylvania Press, 1966.

Holt, Edgar. *Risorgimento: The Making of Italy, 1815–1870*. London: Macmillan, 1970.

Horsman, Reginald. *Race and Manifest Destiny: The Origins of American Racial Anglo-Saxonism*. Cambridge, Mass.: Harvard University Press, 1981.

Howe, Lawrence. "Race, Genealogy, and Genre in Mark Twain's *Pudd'nhead Wilson*." *Nineteenth-Century Literature* 46 (March 1992): 495–516.

Howells, William Dean. *A Hazard of New Fortunes*. 1890. New York: Penguin Books, 1994.

Howells, William Dean. *Selected Letters*, eds. George Arms, Richard H. Ballinger, Christoph K. Lohmann. Boston: Twayne Publishers, 1980.

Howells, William Dean. *Venetian Life*. 1866. Marlboro, Vt.: The Marlboro Press, 1989.

Hoy, Suellen. *Chasing Dirt: The American Pursuit of Cleanliness*. New York: Oxford University Press, 1995.

Hughes, H. Stuart. *The United States and Italy*. Cambridge, Mass.: Harvard University Press, 1965.

Ignatiev, Noel. *How the Irish Became White*. New York: Routledge, 1995.

Iorizzo, Luciano J. "The Padrone and Immigrant Distribution." In *The Italian Experience in the United States*, eds. Silvano M. Tomasi and Medeline H. Engel. New York: Center for Migration Studies, 1971.

Iorizzo, Luciano J., and Salvatore Mondello. *The Italian-Americans*. New York: Twayne Publishers, 1971.

"Italian Life in New York." *Harper's New Monthly Magazine* 62 (April 1881): 676–684.

Jacobson, Matthew Frye. *Whiteness of a Different Color: European Immigrants and the Alchemy of Race*. Cambridge, Mass.: Harvard University Press, 1998.

James, Henry. *The American Scene*. 1907. Ed. John F. Sears. New York: Penguin Books, 1994.

James, Henry. *The Complete Notebooks of Henry James*. Eds. Leon Edel and Lyall H. Powers. New York: Oxford University Press, 1987.

James, Henry. *The Complete Tales of Henry James*. Ed. Leon Edel. 8 vols. London: Rupert Hart-Davis, and Philadelphia and New York: J.B. Lippincott Company, 1962–1963.

James, Henry. *The Golden Bowl*. 1904. Baltimore: Penguin Books, 1966.

James, Henry. *Italian Hours*. 1909. Ed. John Auchard. New York: Penguin, 1995.

James, Henry. *The Letters of Henry James*. Ed. Percy Lubbock. 2 vols. New York: Charles Scribner's Sons, 1920.

James, Henry. *A Small Boy and Others*. New York: Charles Scribner's Sons, 1913.

James, Henry. *Transatlantic Sketches*. Boston and New York, Houghton Mifflin and Company, 1882.

James, Henry. *William Wetmore Story and His Friends*. London: Thames & Hudson, 1903..

Jehlen, Myra. "The Ties that Bind: Race and Sex in *Pudd'nhead Wilson*." *American Literary History* 2 (Spring 1990): 39–55.

Jolly, Roslyn. *Henry James: History, Narrative, Fiction*. New York: Oxford University Press, 1993.

Jordan, David W. "Edward A. Steiner and the Struggle for Toleration During World War I." *Annals of Iowa* 46 (1983): 523–542.

Joslin, Katharine, and Alan Price, eds. *Wretched Exotic: Essays on Edith Wharton in Europe*. New York: Peter Lang Publishing, 1996.

Juliani, Richard N. "The Interactions of Irish and Italians from Conflict to Integration." In *Italians and Irish in America*, ed. Francis X. Femminella. Staten Island, N.Y.: The American Italian Historical Association, 1985.

Juliani, Richard N., and Philip V. Cannistraro, eds. *Italian Americans: The Search for a Usable Past*. Staten Island, N.Y.: The American Italian Historical Association, 1989.

Kallen, Horace M. "Democracy Versus the Melting Pot." *The Nation* 100 (February 18 and 25, 1915): 190–94, 217–220.

Kammen, Michael. *Mystic Chords of Memory: The Transformation of Tradition in American Culture*. New York: Alfred A. Knopf, 1991.

Kaplan, Amy, and Donald E. Pease, eds. *Cultures of United States Imperialism*. Durham, N.C.: Duke University Press, 1993.

Kaplan, Caren. *Questions of Travel: Postmodern Discourses of Displacement*. Durham, N.C.: Duke University Press, 1996.

Kaplan, Fred. *Henry James: The Imagination of Genius*. New York: William Morrow and Company, 1992.

Kaplan, Justin. *Mr. Clemens and Mark Twain: A Biography*. New York: Simon and Schuster, 1966.

Karlin, J. Alexander. "The Italo-American Incident of 1891 and the Road to Reunion." *Journal of Southern History* 8 (May 1942): 242–246.

Karlin, J. Alexander. "New Orleans Lynchings of 1891 and the American Press." *Louisiana Historical Quarterly* 24 (January 1941): 187–203.

Kasson, Joy S. *Artistic Voyagers: Europe and the American Imagination in the Works of Irving, Allston, Cole, Cooper, and Hawthorne.* Westport, Conn.: Greenwood Press, 1982.

Kessner, Thomas. *The Golden Door: Italian and Jewish Immigrant Mobility in New York City, 1880–1915.* New York: Oxford University Press, 1977.

Kiefer, Geraldine Wojno. *Alfred Stieglitz: Scientist, Photographer, and Avatar of Modernism, 1880–1913.* New York: Garland Publishing, 1991.

Krase, Jerome, and Judith N. DeSena, eds. *Italian Americans in a Multicultural Society.* Stony Brook, N.Y.: Forum Italicum, 1993.

Kraut, Alan M. *The Huddled Masses: The Immigrant in American Society, 1880–1921.* Arlington Heights, Ill.: Harlan Davidson Inc., 1982.

Kraut, Alan M. *Silent Killers: Germs, Genes, and the "Immigrant Menace."* New York: Basic Books, 1994.

Ladd, Barbara. *Nationalism and the Color Line in George W. Cable, Mark Twain, and William Faulkner.* Baton Rouge: Louisiana State University Press, 1996.

LaGumina, Salvatore, ed. and Introduction. *"WOP"!: A Documentary History of Anti-Italian Discrimination in the United States.* San Francisco: Straight Arrow Books, 1973.

Landry, Harral E., ed. *To See the Past More Clearly: The Enrichment of the Italian Heritage, 1890–1990.* Staten Island, N.Y.: The American Italian Historical Association, 1994.

Lane, James B. *Jacob A. Riis and the American City.* Port Washington, N.Y.: Kennikat Press, 1974.

La Sorte, Michael A. "Immigrant Occupations: A Comparison." In *Italian Americans: The Search for a Usable Past*, eds. Richard N. Juliani and Philip V. Cannistraro. Staten Island, N.Y.: The American Italian Historical Association, 1989.

La Sorte, Michael, ed. and Introduction. *La Merica: Images of Italian Greenhorn Experience.* Philadelphia: Temple University Press, 1985.

Lears, T. J. Jackson. *No Place for Grace: Antimodernism and the Transformation of American Culture, 1880–1920.* New York: Pantheon, 1981.

Leavis, F. R. "Mark Twain's Neglected Classic: The Moral Astringency of *Pudd'nhead Wilson.*" *Commentary* 21 (February 1956): 128–136.

Leviatin, David. "Framing the Poor." Introduction to *How the Other Half Lives*, by Jacob A. Riis. Boston: Bedford Books, 1996.

Levine, Lawrence. *Highbrow/Lowbrow: The Emergence of Cultural Hierarchy in America.* Cambridge, Mass.: Harvard University Press, 1988.

Levine, Lawrence. *The Opening of the American Mind: Canons, Culture, and History*. Boston: Beacon Press, 1996.

Lodge, Henry Cabot. "The Distribution of Ability in the United States." *Century* 42 (September 1891): 687–694.

Lodge, Henry Cabot. "Efforts to Restrict Undesirable Immigration." *Century* 67 (January 1904): 466–469.

Lodge, Henry Cabot. "Lynch Law and Unrestricted Migration." *North American Review* 152 (May 1891): 602–612.

Lodge, Henry Cabot. "The Restriction of Immigration." *North American Review* 152 (January 1891): 27–35.

Lombardo, Agostino, and James W. Tuttleton, eds. *The Sweetest Impression of Life: The James Family and Italy*. New York: Oxford University Press, 1990.

Lopreato, Joseph. *Italian Americans*. New York: Random House, 1970.

Lott, Eric. "White Like Me: Racial Cross-Dressing and the Construction of American Whiteness." In *Cultures of United States Imperialism*, eds. Amy Kaplan and Donald E. Pease. Durham, N.C.: Duke University Press, 1993.

Lowell, James Russell. *Leaves from My Journal in Italy and Elsewhere*. Vol. 1. *The Writings of James Russell Lowell*. Boston: Houghton, Mifflin and Company, 1891. 10 vols.

Lowell, James Russell. *Literary and Political Addresses*. Vol. 6. *The Works of James Russell Lowell*. Boston: Houghton, Mifflin and Company, 1890–92. 11 vols.

Lowell, James Russell. *The Poetical Works of James Russell Lowell*. Boston: Houghton Mifflin Company, 1978.

Lowry, Richard S. *"Littery Man": Mark Twain and Modern Authorship*. New York: Oxford University Press, 1996.

Lubove, Roy. Introduction to *The Making of an American*, by Jacob A. Riis. New York: Harper & Row, 1966.

Lueck, Beth Lynn. *American Writers and the Picturesque Tour: The Search for National Identity, 1790–1860*. New York: Garland Publishers, 1997.

Lumley, Robert, and Jonathan Morris, eds. *The New History of the Italian South: The Mezzogiorno Revisited*. Exeter, England: University of Exeter Press, 1997.

McCabe, James D. Jr. *Lights and Shadows of New York Life; or, the Sights and Sensations of the Great City*. circa 1872. New York: Farrar, Straus and Giroux, 1970.

MacCannell, Dean. *The Tourist: A New Theory of the Leisure Class*. New York: Shocken, 1989.

McGlinchee, Claire. *James Russell Lowell*. New York: Twayne Publishers, 1967.

McNamara, Kevin R. "Building Culture: The Two New Yorks of Henry James's *The American Scene*." *Prospects* 18 (1993): 121–151.

Madison, Charles A. Preface to *How the Other Half Lives*, by Jacob A. Riis. New York: Dover Publications, 1971.

"The Mafia, and What Led to the Lynching." *Harper's Weekly* 35 (March 28, 1891): 226–227.

Mangione, Jerre, and Ben Morreale. *La Storia: Five Centuries of the Italian American Experience*. New York: HarperCollins Publishers, 1992.

Manson, George J. "The 'Foreign Element' in New York City. V.—The Italians." *Harper's Weekly* 34 (October 18, 1890): 817–819.

Margavio, Anthony V. "The Reaction of the Press to the Italian-American in New Orleans, 1880–1920." *Italian Americana* 4 (1978): 72–83.

Marraro, Howard R. *American Opinion on the Unification of Italy, 1846–1861*. New York: AMS Press, 1969.

Marraro, Howard R. "Italians in New York in the Eighteen Fifties." *New York History* (April, July 1949): 181–203; 276–303.

Matthews, Sr. Mary Fabian. "The Role of the Public School in the Assimilation of the Italian Immigrant Child in New York City, 1900–1914." In *The Italian Experience in the United States*, eds. Silvano M. Tomasi and Medeline H. Engel. New York: Center for Migration Studies, 1971.

Maves, Carl. *Sensuous Pessimism: Italy in the Works of Henry James*. Bloomington: Indiana University Press, 1973.

Melton, Jeffrey Alan. *Mark Twain, Travel Books, and Tourism: The Tide of a Great Popular Movement*. Tuscaloosa: The University of Alabama Press, 2002.

Merlino, S. "Italian Immigrants and their Enslavement." *Forum* 15 (April 1893): 183–190.

Michaels, Walter Benn. *Our America: Nativism, Modernism, and Pluralism*. Durham, N.C.: Duke University Press, 1995.

Michelson, Bruce. "Mark Twain the Tourist: The Form of *The Innocents Abroad*." *American Literature* 49 (November 1977): 385–398.

Mondello, Salvatore. "Italian Migration to the U.S. as Reported in American Magazines, 1880–1920." *Social Science* 39 (June 1964): 131–142.

Mulvey, Christopher. *Transatlantic Manners: Social Patterns in Nineteenth-Century Anglo-American Travel Literature*. New York: Cambridge University Press, 1990.

Mumford, Lewis. *The City in History*. New York: Harcourt, Brace & World, 1961.

Munger, T. T. "Immigration by Passport." *Century* 35 (March 1888): 791–799.

Murray, William. *Italy: The Fatal Gift*. New York: Dodd, Mead, 1982.

The National Cyclopaedia of American Biography. Ann Arbor, Mich.: University Microfilms, 1967.

Nelli, Humbert S. *From Immigrants to Ethnics: The Italian Americans.* New York: Oxford University Press, 1983.

Nelli, Humbert S. "Italians in Urban America." In *The Italian Experience in the United States*, eds. Silvano M. Tomasi and Medeline H. Engel. New York: Center for Migration Studies, 1971.

Nelson, Dana D. *National Manhood: Capitalist Citizenship and the Imagined Fraternity of White Men.* Durham, N.C.: Duke University Press, 1998.

Norman, Dorothy. *Alfred Stieglitz: An American Seer.* New York: Random House, 1973.

Pavalko, Ronald M. "Racism and the New Immigration: A Reinterpretation of the Assimilation of White Ethnics in American Society." *Sociology and Social Research* 65 (October 1980): 56–77.

Peck, Gunther. *Reinventing Free Labor: Padrones and Immigrant Workers in the North American West, 1880–1930.* New York: Cambridge University Press, 2000.

Pecorini, Alberto. "The Italians in the United States." *Forum* 44 (January 1911): 15–29.

Pettit, Arthur G. *Mark Twain & the South.* Lexington: The University Press of Kentucky, 1974.

Peyser, Thomas Galt. "James, Race, and the Imperial Museum." *American Literary History* 6 (Spring 1994): 48–70.

Pinto Surdi, Alessandro. *Americans in Rome, 1764–1870: A Descriptive Catalogue of the Exhibition Held in the Palazzo Antici Mattei.* Rome: Centro Studi Americani, 1984.

Porter, Dennis. *Haunted Journeys: Desire and Transgression in European Travel Writing.* Princeton, N.J.: Princeton University Press, 1991.

Posnock, Ross. *The Trial of Curiosity: Henry James, William James, and the Challenge of Modernity.* New York: Oxford University Press, 1991.

Pozzetta, George E. "Immigrants and Ethnics: The State of Italian-American Historiography." *Journal of American Ethnic History* 9 (Fall 1989): 67–95.

Pratt, Mary Louise. *Imperial Eyes: Travel Writing and Transculturation.* London: Routledge, 1992.

Reynolds, Larry. *European Revolutions and the American Literary Renaissance.* New Haven, Conn.: Yale University Press, 1988.

Riall, Lucy. *The Italian Risorgimento: State, Society and National Unification.* London and New York: Routledge, 1994.

Richards, David A.J. *Italian American: The Racializing of an Ethnic Identity.* New York: New York University Press, 1999.

Richardson, Edgar P., and Otto Wittmann. *Travelers in Arcadia: American Artists in Italy, 1830–1875.* Detroit: Detroit Institute of Art, 1951.

Riis, Jacob A. *The Battle with the Slum*. New York: Macmillan, 1902.

Riis, Jacob A. *The Children of the Poor*. 1892. New York: Charles Scribner's Sons, 1902.

Riis, Jacob A. "Feast Days in Little Italy." *Century* 58 (August 1899): 491–499.

Riis, Jacob A. *How the Other Half Lives: Studies Among the Tenements of New York*. 1890. New York: Dover Publications, 1971.

Riis, Jacob A. *The Making of an American*. New York: The Macmillan Company, 1901.

Riis, Jacob A. *Out of Mulberry Street, Stories of Tenement Life in New York City*. New York: Century, 1898.

Riis, Jacob A. "Paolo's Awakening." *Atlantic* 78 (November 1896): 702–707.

Riis, Jacob A. *The Peril and the Preservation of the Home*. Philadelphia: George W. Jacobs & Co., 1903.

Riis, Jacob A. "Real Wharf Rats, Human Rodents that Live on Garbage under the Wharves," New York *Evening Sun*, 18 March 1892.

Rimanelli, Marco, and Sheryl L. Postman, eds. *The 1891 New Orleans Lynching and U.S.-Italian Relations: A Look Back*. New York: Peter Lang, 1992.

Robertson, Priscilla. *Revolutions of 1848: A Social History*. Princeton, N.J.: Princeton University Press, 1952.

Robinson, Forrest G. "Patterns of Consciousness in *The Innocents Abroad*." *American Literature* 58 (March 1986): 46–63.

Roediger, David R. *The Wages of Whiteness: Race and the Making of the American Working Class*. New York: Verso, 1999.

Roseboro, Viola. "The Italians in New York." *Cosmopolitan* 4 (January 1888): 396–406.

Rowlette, Robert. *Mark Twain's Pudd'nhead Wilson: The Development and Design*. Bowling Green, Ohio: Bowling Green University Popular Press, 1971.

Rubin Jr., Louis D. *George Washington Cable: The Life and Times of a Southern Heretic*. New York: Pegasus, 1969.

Rubin-Dorsky, Jeffrey. *Adrift in the Old World: The Psychological Pilgrimage of Washington Irving*. Chicago: The University of Chicago Press, 1988.

Russo, John Paul. "From Italophilia to Italophobia: Representations of Italian Americans in the Early Gilded Age." *Differentia* 6–7 (Spring/Autumn 1994): 45–75.

Russo, John Paul. "The Harvard Italophiles: Longfellow, Lowell, and Norton." In *L'Esilio romantico: forme di un conflitto*, eds. Joseph Cheyne and Lilla Maria Crisafulli Jones. Bari, Italy: Adriatica Editrice, 1990.

Rydell, Robert W. *All the World's a Fair: Visions of Empire at American International Expositions, 1876–1916*. Chicago: The University of Chicago Press, 1984.

Said, Edward W. *Orientalism*. New York: Pantheon Books, 1978.

Salamone, A. William. "The Nineteenth-Century Discovery of Italy." *American Historical Review* 173 (1968): 1360–1362.

Sanford, Charles L. *The Quest for Paradise: Europe and the American Imagination*. Urbana: University of Illinois Press, 1961.

Scambray, Kenneth. "Outside the Framework of Time: The Briganti of Southern Italy." In *To See the Past More Clearly: The Enrichment of the Italian Heritage, 1890–1990*, ed. Harral E. Landry. Staten Island, N.Y. The American Italian Historical Association, 1994.

Scarpaci, Jean Ann. "Immigrants in the New South: Italians in Louisiana's Sugar Parishes, 1880–1910." In *Studies in Italian American Social History*, ed. Francesco Cordasco. Totowa, N.J.: Roman and Littlefield, 1975.

Scarpaci, Jean Ann. *Italian Immigrants in Louisiana's Sugar Parishes: Recruitment, Labor Conditions, and Community Relations, 1880–1910*. New York: Arno Press, 1980.

Scarpaci, J. Vincenza. "Labor for Louisiana's Sugar Fields: An Experiment in Immigrant Recruitment." *Italian Americana* 7 (1981): 19–41.

Schneider, Jane. "Introduction: The Dynamics of Neo-orientalism in Italy (1848–1995)." In *Italy's "Southern Question": Orientalism in One County*, ed. Jane Schneider. New York: Berg, 1998.

Schneider, Jane, ed. *Italy's "Southern Question": Orientalism in One County*. New York: Berg, 1998.

Scudder, Horace Elisha. *James Russell Lowell: A Biography*. 2 vols. Boston: Houghton Mifflin and Company, 1901.

Sears, John F. Introduction to *The American Scene*, by Henry James. New York: Penguin Books, 1994.

Seltzer, Mark. "Advertising America: *The American Scene*." In *Henry James and the Art of Power*, Mark Seltzer. Ithaca, N.Y.: Cornell University Press, 1984.

Senner, Joseph H. "Immigration from Italy." *North American Review* 162 (June 1896): 649–657.

Shaler, N.S. "European Peasants as Immigrants." *Atlantic* 71 (May 1893): 646–655.

Shankman, Arnold. "The Image of the Italian in the Afro-American Press, 1886–1915." *Italian Americana* 1978 4 (1): 30–49.

Shankman, Arnold. "The Menacing Influx: Afro-Americans on Italian Immigration to the South, 1880–1915." *Mississippi Quarterly* 31 (1977–78): 67–88.

Shell, Marc. "Those Extraordinary Twins." *Arizona Quarterly* 47 (Summer 1991): 29–73.

Shiavo, Giovanni E. *Four Centuries of Italian-American History*. New York: Vigo Press, 1952.

Shiavo, Giovanni E. *The Italians in America Before the Civil War*. New York: Vigo Press, 1934.

Smith, Dennis Mack. *Italy: A Modern History*. Ann Arbor: University of Michigan Press, 1969.

Sollors, Werner. *Beyond Ethnicity: Consent and Descent in American Culture*. New York: Oxford University Press, 1987.

Sollors, Werner, ed. *The Invention of Ethnicity*. New York: Oxford University Press, 1989.

Sontag, Susan. *On Photography*. New York: Farrar, Straus and Giroux, 1973.

Sowell, Thomas. *Ethnic America*. New York: Basic Books, 1981.

Stange, Maren. *Symbols of Ideal Life: Social Documentary Photography in America, 1890–1950*. New York: Cambridge University Press, 1992.

Stebbins, Jr., Theodore E. "American Painters and the Lure of Italy." In *The Lure of Italy: American Artists and the Italian Experience, 1760–1914*, ed. Theodore E. Stebbins, Jr. Boston: Museum of Fine Arts and New York: Harry N. Abrams, 1992.

Stebbins, Jr., Theodore E., ed. *The Lure of Italy: American Artists and the Italian Experience, 1760–1914*. Boston: Museum of Fine Arts and New York: Harry N. Abrams, 1992.

Stein, Sally. "Making Connections with the Camera: Photography and Social Mobility in the Career of Jacob Riis." *Afterimage* 10 (May 1983): 9–16.

Steinbrink, Jeffrey. "Why the Innocents Went Abroad: Mark Twain and American Tourism in the Late Nineteenth Century." *American Literary Realism* 16 (Autumn 1983): 278–286.

Steiner, Edward A. *Against the Current: Simple Chapters from a Complex Life*. New York: Fleming H. Revell Company, 1910.

Steiner, Edward A. *The Broken Wall: Stories of the Mingling Folk*. New York: Fleming H. Revell Company, 1911.

Steiner, Edward A. *From Alien to Citizen: The Story of My Life in America*. New York: Fleming H. Revell Company, 1914.

Steiner, Edward A. *Introducing the American Spirit*. New York: Fleming H. Revell Company, 1915.

Steiner, Edward A. *Old Trails and New Borders*. New York: Fleming H. Revell Company, 1921.

Steiner, Edward A. *On the Trail of the Immigrant*. New York: Fleming H. Revell Company, 1906.

Steiner, Edward A. "What to Do for the Immigrant." In *Conservation of National Ideals*, D. B. Wells et al. New York: Fleming H. Revell Company, 1911.

Stoddard, Lothrop. *The Rising Tide of Color Against White World-Supremacy*. London: Chapman and Hall, Limited, 1922.

Stout, Janis P. *The Journey Narrative in American Literature: Patterns and Departures*. Westport, Conn.: Greenwood Press, 1983.

Stowe, William. *Going Abroad: European Travel in Nineteenth-Century American Culture*. Princeton, N.J.: Princeton University Press, 1994.

Strong, Josiah. *Our Country*. 1886. Ed. Jurgen Herbst. Cambridge, Mass.: The Belknap Press of Harvard University Press, 1963.

Sullivan, James W. *Tenement Tales of New York*. New York: Holt, 1895.

Sundquist, Eric. "Mark Twain and Homer Plessy." In *Mark Twain's* Pudd'nhead Wilson: *Race, Conflict, and Culture*, eds. Susan Gillman and Forrest G. Robinson. Durham, N.C.: Duke University Press, 1990.

Talmon, J. L. *Romanticism and Revolt: Europe 1815–1848*. New York: Harcourt, Brace, 1967.

Taylor, Bayard. *Views A-Foot or Europe Seen with Knapsack and Staff*. New York: G.P. Putnam's Sons, 1879.

Thomas, Brook. "Tragedies of Race, Training, Birth, and Communities of Competent Pudd'nheads." *American Literary History* 1 (Winter 1989): 754–785.

Thoreau, Henry David. *A Year in Thoreau's Journal: 1851*. New York: Penguin Books, 1993.

Tolnay, Stewart Emory. *A Festival of Violence: An Analysis of Southern Lynchings, 1882–1930*. Urbana: University of Illinois Press, 1995.

Tomasi, Silvano M. "The Ethnic Church and the Integration of the Italian Immigrant in the United States." In *The Italian Experience in the United States*, eds. Silvano M. Tomasi and Medeline H. Engel. New York: Center for Migration Studies, 1971.

Tomasi, Silvano M., ed. *Italian Americans: New Perspectives in Italian Immigration and Ethnicity*. New York: Center for Migration Studies, 1985.

Tomasi, Silvano M., ed. *Perspectives in Italian Immigration and Ethnicity*. New York: Center for Migration Studies, 1977.

Tomasi, Silvano, and Medeline H. Engel, eds. *The Italian Experience in the United States*. New York: Center for Migration Studies, 1971.

Tomes, Nancy. *The Gospel of Germs: Men, Women, and the Microbe in American Life*. Cambridge, Mass.: Harvard University Press, 1998.

Torrielli, Andrew J. *Italian Opinion on America as Revealed by Italian Travelers, 1850–1900*. Cambridge, Mass.: Harvard University Press, 1941.

Trachtenberg, Alan. *The Incorporation of America: Culture & Society in the Gilded Age.* New York: Hill and Wang, 1982.

Trachtenberg, Alan et al. *The City: American Experience.* New York: Oxford University Press, 1971.

Turner, Arlin. "Mark Twain and the South: An Affair of Love and Anger." *Southern Review* 4 (April 1968): 493–519.

Twain, Mark. *Adventures of Huckleberry Finn.* 1884. eds. Scully Bradley, Richmond Croom Beatty, E. Hudson Long. New York: W.W. Norton & Company, 1962.

Twain, Mark. *The Autobiography of Mark Twain.* Ed. Charles Neider. New York: Harper & Row, 1990.

Twain, Mark. *The Complete Essays of Mark Twain.* Ed. Charles Neider. Garden City, N.Y.: Doubleday & Company, 1963.

Twain, Mark. *The Innocents Abroad or The New Pilgrims' Progress.* 1869. Norwalk, Conn.: The Heritage Press, 1962.

Twain, Mark. *Mark Twain-Howells Letters: The Correspondence of Samuel L. Clemens and William Dean Howells 1872–1910.* Eds. Henry Nash Smith and William M. Gibson. 2 vols. Cambridge, Mass.: The Belknap Press of Harvard University Press, 1960.

Twain, Mark. *Mark Twain's Letters.* Ed. Albert Bigelow Paine. 2 vols. New York: Harper & Brothers Publishers, 1917.

Twain, Mark. *Mark Twain's Notebook.* Ed. Albert Bigelow Paine. New York: Harper & Brothers Publishers, 1935.

Twain, Mark. *Mark Twain's Notebooks & Journals.* Gen. Ed. Frederick Anderson. 3 vols. Berkeley: University of California Press, 1975– .

Twain, Mark. *Mark Twain Speaking.* Ed. Paul Fatout. Iowa City: University of Iowa Press, 1976.

Twain, Mark. *Pudd'nhead Wilson and Those Extraordinary Twins.* 1894. Ed. Sidney E. Berger. New York: W.W. Norton & Company, 1980.

Twain, Mark. *A Tramp Abroad.* 1880. New York: Penguin Books, 1997.

Twain, Mark. *The Writings of Mark Twain.* 37 vols. New York: Gabriel Wells, 1922–25.

Vance, William. *America's Rome.* 2 vols. New Haven, Conn.: Yale University Press, 1989.

Vance, William. "Seeing Italy: The Realistic Rediscovery by Twain, Howells, and James." In *The Lure of Italy: American Artists and the Italian Experience, 1760–1914*, ed. Theodore E. Stebbins, Jr. Boston: Museum of Fine Arts and New York: Harry N. Abrams, 1992.

Vecoli, Rudolph J. "Italian American Workers, 1880–1920: Padrone Slaves or Primitive Rebels?" In *Perspectives in Italian Immigration and Ethnicity*, ed. Silvano M. Tomasi. New York: Center for Migration Studies, 1977.

Vecoli, Rudolph J. "Italian Immigrants and Working-Class Movements in the United States: A Personal Reflection on Class and Ethnicity." *Journal of the Canadian Historical Association* 4 (1933): 293–305.

Vecoli, Rudolph J. "Prelates and Peasants: Italian Immigrants and the Catholic Church." *Journal of Social History* 2 (1969): 217–268.

Vecoli, Rudolph J, ed. *Italian Immigrants in Rural and Small Town America*. Staten Island: N.Y. The American Italian Historical Association, 1987.

Wagenknecht, Edward. *James Russell Lowell: Portrait of a Many-Sided Man*. New York: Oxford University Press, 1971.

Wald, Priscilla. *Constituting Americans: Cultural Anxiety and Narrative Form*. Durham, N.C.: Duke University Press, 1995.

Walker, Francis A. "Immigration and Degradation." *Forum* 11 (August 1891): 634–644.

Walker, Francis A. "Restriction of Immigration." *Atlantic Monthly* 77 (June 1896): 822–829.

Wegelin, Christof. *The Image of Europe in Henry James*. Dallas: Southern Methodist University Press, 1958.

Wells, D. B. et al. *Conservation of National Ideals*. New York: Fleming H. Revell Company, 1911.

Wiggins, Robert A. *Mark Twain: Jackleg Novelist*. Seattle: University of Washington Press, 1964.

Williams, Murial B. "The Unmasking of Meaning: A Study of the Twins in *Pudd'nhead Wilson*." *Mississippi Quarterly* 33 (Winter 1979–1980): 39–53.

Williamson, Joel. *The Crucible of Race: Black-White Relations in the American South Since Emancipation*. New York: Oxford University Press, 1984.

Wood, Robert J. "Europe in American Historical Romances." *Midcontinent American Studies Journal* (Spring 1967): 90–97.

Woodress, James L. *Howells and Italy*. Chapel Hill: University of North Carolina Press, 1952.

Wright, Nathalia. *American Novelists in Italy: The Discoverers: Allston to James*. Philadelphia: University of Pennsylvania Press, 1965.

Yans-McLaughlin, Virginia. *Family and Community: Italian Immigrants in Buffalo, 1880–1930*. Ithaca, N.Y.: Cornell University Press, 1977.

Yochelson, Bonnie. *Jacob Riis*. New York: Phaidon Press, 2001.

Yochelson, Bonnie. "What Are the Photographs of Jacob Riis?" *Culturefront* 3 (Fall 1994): 28–38.

Ziff, Larzer. *The American 1890s: Life and Times of a Lost Generation.* New York: Viking Press, 1966.

Ziff, Larzer. *Return Passages: Great American Travel Writing, 1780–1910.* New Haven, Conn.: Yale University Press, 2000.

Zurier, Rebecca, and Robert W. Snyder and Virginia M. Mecklenburg, eds. *Metropolitan Lives: The Ashcan Artists and their New York.* New York: National Museum of American Art and W.W. Norton & Co., 1996.

Index

Alighieri, Dante, 8, 138, 160–61
Alland, Alexander, Sr., 27, 40–41
Alta California (San Francisco), 150
American Immigration Commission, 66, 85
American Whig Review, 1, 6
Anglo-Saxon. *See* race, Anglo-Saxon
Atlantic, 6, 13, 35, 96

Baker, Joshua G., 2
Beecher, Henry Ward, 145
Bemis, Edward W., 13
Black Hand Society. *See* mafia
Boas, Franz, 174
  The Mind of Primitive Man, 174
Boston Common, 137–38
Bourget, Paul, 151
Brace, Charles Loring, 26, 188n 27
  The Dangerous Classes of New York, 26, 28, 188n 27
Bronson, Mrs. Arthur (Katherine De Kay), 95
Bryan, Texas, 80–81
Buttafuoco, Joey, 178
Byron, Lord, 5
  Childe Harold's Pilgrimage, 5

Cable, George Washington, 153, 157, 202nn 47, 48

camorra. *See* mafia
campanilismo, 32, 47, 81
Carr, John Foster, 173
  Guide for the Italian Immigrants in the United States, 173
Castle Garden, 89
Catholic Church, Italian, 7, 77–78, 145–46, 148, 151
Central Park, 130–31, 134, 137
Century, 13–14, 45
Chang and Eng, 144
Clemens, Samuel Langhorne. *See* Twain, Mark
Cole, Thomas, 89
Como, Lake, 145
Cooper, James Fenimore, 6, 23–24, 65
Cosmopolitan, 22, 150
de Crèvecoeur, Hector St. John, 70
  Letters from an American Farmer, 70
Critic, 40, 42

Dante Alighieri, 8, 138, 160–61
Darwin, Charles, 11
Debs, Eugene V., 125
Des Moines Capital, 66, 85
Dictionary of Races or Peoples, 159, 171, 175–77, 205n 15
Dillingham Commission (U.S. Immigration Commission), 171, 174–75

Dillingham, William P., 175
DuBois, W.E.B., 125

Emerson, Ralph Waldo, 6
Ellis Island, 64, 67, 126–30, 133–34
Eugenic Research Association, 177
Eugenics Committee of the U.S. Committee on Selective Immigration, 177

Fasci Siciliani, 9–10, 37
Fava, Baron, 15, 33
Forum, 13, 15
Frustaci, Giuseppe, 172
Fuller, Margaret, 8, 11, 158, 203n 54

Galton, Francis, 11
Garibaldi, Giuseppe, 5, 7–9, 58
Glackens, William, 3
Gliddon, George, 10
   Types of Mankind, 10
Gobineau, Joseph Arthur Comte de, 10
   Essay on the Inequality of the Human Races, 10
Gotti, John, 178
Gramsci, Antonio, 172
   Prison Notebooks, 172
Grant, Madison, 173–74, 177, 205nn 7, 8
   The Passing of the Great Race, 173–74, 205n 7
Grinnell College, 66

Hall, Prescott Farnsworth, 13, 69–70, 185n 58
Harper's, 13, 22
Harper's Weekly, 25
Harrison, Benjamin, 2
Harvard Yard, 129
Hawthorne, Nathaniel, 6, 17–18, 105, 138
Hay, John, 124
Heffren, Harvey, 41
Hennessy, David C., 1–2, 156, 162, 165, 167
Hine, Louis, 41
House of the Seven Gables, 138–39

Howells, William Dean, 3, 8, 18, 23, 93–94, 98–99, 148, 158
   A Hazard of New Fortunes, 150–51, 199n 15
   Venetian Life, 93–94, 98–99, 150, 199nn 15, 16, 203n 54

Idler, 144
immigrants, Italian. *See also* immigration, Italian; James, Henry, *The American Scene*; Riis, Jacob A., *How the Other Half Lives*; Steiner, Edward A., *On the Trail of the Immigrant*
   and African Americans, 14–16, 28, 30, 64, 137, 154–58, 162–63, 170, 201nn 37, 40, 45
   crime, 26–28, 30, 38, 64, 73, 76, 80–81
   domestic economy, 30–33, 48–50, 52, 78–80, 82
   education, 29, 34, 37–38, 82–83
   farming, 80–81
   and Irish Americans, 4, 47, 77
   in New Orleans/Louisiana, 2–3, 155–56, 162, 177, 180–81n 11, 201nn 38, 42, 45
   occupations, 31–32, 43, 79–80, 149
   religion, 45–48, 77–78, 80
   return migration, 83–84
   southern, 8–9, 13–14, 25–26, 31–34, 69, 71–76, 159–60, 164, 172–77
immigration
   Italian, 3–5, 8–9, 23, 25–26, 34, 36, 160, 172, 175–77, 179–80n 6, 180n 11. *See also* immigrants, Italian
   "new," 3–4, 13, 16, 23, 25, 62–63, 67, 70–71, 88, 125, 153–54, 158, 170
immigration restriction, 14, 58, 85, 152, 154, 165, 175, 177–78, 185nn 61, 65
Immigration Restriction League, 13, 69–70
Irving, Washington, 7, 75
Italy, unification of, 7, 9, 76, 94, 96–97, 159

Index

James, Henry, 3, 6, 17–20, 61–62, 73, 75, 78, 83–84, 144–45, 148, 151, 160–62, 169, 173–74
  biographical, 6, 87–90, 124
  and race, 96, 98–104, 107, 110, 114–17, 119–20, 123, 125, 129–30, 134–37, 140–42
  and travel writing, 90–92, 162. *See also* works: *Italian Hours*, *Transatlantic Sketches*
  works: "Adina," 107–08, 114; *The American Scene*, 19, 61, 78, 84, 88–90, 96, 100, 113–15, 117, 119–20, 123–42, 151; "At Isella," 101, 104–06; "Benvolio," 90; *The Golden Bowl*, 88, 100, 106–08, 111, 113–24, 133; *Italian Hours*, 87, 89, 91–100, 114, 117, 123, 139; "The Jolly Corner," 127; "The Last of the Valerii," 100, 106–07, 122–23; "The Madonna of the Future," 105–06; "The Real Thing," 87–88, 108–11, 114; *Roderick Hudson*, 106; *A Small Boy and Others*, 89; "The Speech and Manners of American Women," 132–33; *Transatlantic Sketches*, 91; "Travelling Companions," 101–04
James, William, 90
Johnson, Albert, 177

Keats, John, 120
Koch, Robert, 12
Kossuth, Louis (Lajos), 58

Lange, Dorothea, 41
Lawrence, Richard Hoe, 24, 45
Lodge, Henry Cabot, 3, 34, 68, 119, 124, 154–56, 159, 185n 59, 199n 29
  and immigration restriction, 14, 58, 154, 175, 185n 61, 199n 29
  "Lynch Law and Unrestricted Immigration," 13–14, 154–55, 200n 35

Longfellow, Henry Wadsworth, 174
Lowell, James Russell, 56, 101, 116, 174, 190n 77
  "A Parable," 56–57
Luks, George, 3
lynching, 2–3, 14, 19, 125, 155–57, 166–67, 169, 173, 200n 34, 201n 45, 202nn 50, 51, 204n 2
  lynching, New Orleans, 2–3, 13–14, 19, 144, 154–57, 167, 200n 36

McKinley, William, 125
mafia (camorra, Black Hand Society), 2, 10–11, 14, 38, 76, 81, 173, 178
Marx, Karl, 158
Mayer, Grace, 40
Mazzei, Filipo, 78, 180n 8
Merlino, S., 15, 200n 32, 203n 54
  "Italian Immigrants and Their Enslavement," 200n 32, 203n 54
Morton, Samuel George, 11, 184n 47
Munger, Theodore, 168
Museum of the City of New York, 40–41

NAACP, 2
Nation, 124
nativism, 8, 12–16, 19, 59, 63–64, 72, 125, 152–55, 157–58, 166, 172–73, 191n 2. *See also* race, theory/thinking
new immigration. *See* immigration, "new"
New Orleans Times-Democrat, 2, 156
New York Evening Sun, 39, 43, 45, 50
New-York Historical Society, 41
New York Tribune, 24, 95
Niceforo, Alfredo, 10, 64, 176
  L'Italia barbara contemporanea, 10, 64, 176
North American Review, 13, 34, 124
Norton, Charles Eliot, 174
Norton, Grace, 90
Nott, J.C., 10
  Types of Mankind, 10

O'Connor, William J., 2
opera, Italian, 6, 178, 181–82nn 17, 19, 20, 184n 51
Outlook, 61

padrone, 15–16, 29, 32–33, 35, 43, 58
Parkerson, William S., 2
Pasteur, Louis, 12
Patti, Adelina, 6, 89
Pecorini, Alberto, 172
    "The Italians in the United States," 172
Piffard, Henry G., 24, 45
Poe, Edgar Allan, 118

race. *See also* James, Henry, and race; nativism; Riis, Jacob A., and race; Steiner, Edward A., and race; Twain, Mark, and race
    Anglo-Saxon, 10–12, 14, 63–64, 68, 70, 98–104, 107–08, 114, 117, 119, 121, 129, 140, 154, 168, 174, 196n 35
        character, 27, 29, 34, 42, 59, 74–75, 98–103, 121, 123, 147, 154
    and manhood/nationhood, 12, 184n 54
    theory/thinking, 9–12, 13–14, 62–64, 68–70, 74–75, 86, 107, 116–17, 119–20, 152–53, 159, 164, 172–77, 184n 47, 203n 64. *See also* race, Anglo-Saxon
    "whiteness," 10, 16, 64, 136, 142, 154, 177–78. *See also* immigrants, Italian, and African Americans
Riis, Jacob A., 3, 17–20, 61–62, 64–66, 68, 71–73, 79–86, 94, 97–98, 101, 104, 121, 125–26, 130, 133, 144–45, 147, 150, 152, 155, 159, 161, 164, 169, 173
    biographical, 18, 23–25, 27, 58–59, 167, 186n 5, 187n 10, 189n 44
    photography, use of, 24, 39–43, 55, 189n 59, 190nn 62, 64. *See also* Riis, Jacob A., photographs

and race, 18, 25–30, 55–58
Riis Collection, 40
writings: *The Battle with the Slum*, 36–39, 59, 126; *The Children of the Poor*, 33–34, 41, 50–54; "Feast Days in Little Italy," 45–47; "Flashes from the Slums," 24; *How the Other Half Lives*, 21–22, 25–31, 33, 36, 39–43, 48–49, 53–54, 56–59, 80, 104, 150, 201n 37; *The Making of an American*, 18, 23–24, 36, 58, 64, 187n 10; "The Other Half—How It Lives and Dies in New York," 24; *Out of Mulberry Street: Stories of Tenement Life in New York*, 35; "Paolo's Awakening," 35–36, 83; *The Peril and the Preservation of the Home*, 21, 52–53; "Real Wharf Rats," 33, 50
photographs: "Bandit's Roost, 39 ½ Mulberry Street," 45–46, 54; "Feast of St. Rocco, Bandit's Roost, Mulberry Street," 45–48; "First Board of Election in the Beach Street Industrial School," 54–55; "In the Home of an Italian Rag-Picker, Jersey Street," 48–50; "An Italian Home Under a Dump," 50; "Mott Street Boys 'Keep Off the Grass,'" 53–54; "Pietro Learning to Write, Jersey Street," 50–53; "A Vegetable Stand in the Mulberry Bend," 43–45
Ripley, William Z., 174
Risorgimento, 7, 9, 76, 94, 96–97, 159
Ristori, Adelaide, 150
Rogers, William, 17, 25, 187n 16
Roosevelt, Theodore, 12, 24, 36, 47, 59, 124, 126, 167
Ross, Edward Alsworth, 171, 173
    The Old World in the New, 173

Scribner's, 33
Shakespeare, Joseph A., 2

Shaler, Nathaniel, 14–15, 203n 64
  "European Peasants as Immigrants," 14–15, 185n 60
Sinclair, Upton, 125
The Sopranos, 178
"Southern Question," 9–10
Spencer, Herbert, 11
de Staël, Madame Germaine, 5
  Corinne, 5
Steffens, Lincoln, 125
Steiner, Edward A., 18, 20, 23, 57, 101, 133, 144–45, 147, 159, 173–74
  biographical, 61–62, 64–67, 85, 192nn 10, 16
  and race, 18, 62, 65–72, 74–76, 79, 86, 192n 10
  works: *Against the Current: Simple Chapters from a Complex Life*, 18, 64–65, 68; *The Eternal Hunger*, 64; *From Alien to Citizen: The Story of My Life in America*, 18, 64, 66–68; *The Immigrant Tide*, 67; *Introducing the New American Spirit*, 67; *The Making of a Great Race*, 67; *Nationalizing America*, 67; *Old Trails and New Borders*, 67, 85; *On the Trail of the Immigrant*, 23, 61–62, 64, 67–84; *Sanctus Spiritus and Company*, 85
Stoddard, Lothrop, 174
  The Rising Tide of Color Against White World-Supremacy, 174

Tahoe, Lake, 145
Tarbell, Ida M., 125
Taylor, Bayard, 7
  Views A-Foot or Europe Seen with Knapsack and Staff, 7–8, 182n 30
Tocci Siamese twins, 144
Tolstoy, Leo, 65–66
travel, American in Italy/Europe, 5–6, 145, 162, 182n 25, 194n 9, 198n 6. See also Twain, Mark, *The Innocents Abroad*

travel writing, American about Italy, 5–8, 17, 22–23, 162, 181n 16, 194n 9, 198n 8. *See also* Howells, William Dean, *Venetian Life*; James, Henry, *Italian Hours*; Twain, Mark, *The Innocents Abroad*
Twain, Mark, 19–20, 75, 77, 92, 97, 124
  biographical, 149–50, 154, 157, 199n 28, 202n 48i and race, 144–45, 151–60, 162–64, 167–68, 170, 202n 48
  works: *Adventures of Huckleberry Finn*, 146, 153, 157, 202n 50; "Concerning the Jews," 152–53, 167, 204n 71; "Disgraceful Persecution of a Boy," 152; *Following the Equator*, 154; *The Innocents Abroad*, 19, 92, 145–49, 151, 156, 162; "The Quarrel in the Strong-Box," 153; *The Tragedy of Pudd'nhead Wilson and the Comedy of Those Extraordinary Twins*, 19, 143–45, 149–50, 153–55, 157–70; *A Tramp Abroad*, 149; "What Paul Bourget Thinks of Us," 151

Uncle Tom's Cabin, 65
U.S. Immigration Commission (Dillingham Commission), 171, 174–75

Vespucci, Amerigo, 114, 116

Walker, Francis A., 1, 13–14, 185n 60
  "Immigration and Degradation," 13–14, 185n 60
Washington Square, 128
Wharton, Edith, 18
Williams, William, 126
Wilson, Woodrow, 66, 85
Woolson, Constance Fenimore, 18

Yochelson, Bonnie, 41, 189n 56

Zangwill, Israel, 66